G000273053

...ONG ■ PLEASE STAND UP, PLEASE STAND UP ■ MA MAN TUPAC, NOTORIOUS B.I.G., SHUG, AND THE SNOOP ■ BIG BIOUNE
GAINST THE STATE ■ CLAMS CASINO ■ WINE EXPERT ■ GREAT PARTY ■ CHEERS ■ CIAO ■ OH BOY ■ KEEP DOIN' IT ■ AA
VISED—ME AND GIL ■ BIG EATER ■ THEEDS ■ THE BEATINGS WILL CONTINUE U   OUT
NDER CONTROL HERE? ■ RADICAL UNIT ■ EINE KLEINE FUFTEN HIER ■ MAUVAI   AK TO
HEIR TO THE [INSERT NAME OF CHOICE] FORTUNE ■ QUALITY WE HAVE COME 1   OY, KO
NGE, EVOLUTION NOT MUTATION, HELLO???? ■ PAL, AS IN HI OR OK ■ LIVING L   ≡ THAT
ERYWHERE ■ CELEBRITY MIKE'S POULTRY BARN ■ FULL METAL JACKET ■ GOOI   G EATE
CATION MAJORS HERE ■ WE'LL HAVE ONE OF EACH ■ WE'LL HAVE ONE OF EVE   GLISH M
ORE CHIVES ■ MORE GREEN ■ SHAD ROE ■ WHAT AM I, CHUMP CHANGE? ■ WI   AA . . . \
TERS ■ SUB . . . STANDARD ■ UN RACIÓN DE JAMÓN ■ IT'S CAVA TIME! ■ KEEP YOUR   XE ■ CO
DIS DANS L'OUEST ET MON NOM EST PERSONNE ■ IO SONO QUI OGGI PER VENDERE QUAL COSA QUE TUTTI DEVE AVERE E
E FUFTON HIER ABER NICHEN GESCHWINDIGKEITSBESCHRÄNKUNG (SPEED LIMIT) ■ YOU DISCO KIDS ■ THE NUMBERS DON
DO IT ■ MORE DUCK ■ HOW YA DOIN' ■ GOOD TO SEE YOU ■ THE KEY TO LIFE IS MOISTURE ■ I'M DA MAN YO DA MAN HE
THERE ■ WHAT A HOOT ■ WHAT A SCREAM ■ CHANGE IS GOOD ■ THE WORLD-FAMOUS MALIBU VINEYARD ■ YOU CAN DO
ORSE DEAD YET? ■ ALLARD VON PIPE ■ I'M BAACCCKKK, POLTERGEIST ■ CORNICHE GAME HEN, WIDER THAN A MILE ■ CA
BATHWATER ■ YOU SHOULD SEE THE OTHER GUY ■ DO YOU HAVE AN EXPERT BUSBOY DOWN THERE? (SM) ■ DO YOU HA
UR SOCKS OFF ■ BLOW YOUR SOCKS OFF ■ THE GGGGGGGG ■ THE CHASMAN ■ GOTTA GO TO THE JOHN ■ NO POINT IN C
ONCES ■ YOU CAN'T BEAT OUR MEAT ■ EAT OUT MORE OFTEN ■ WE CAN TAKE CARE OF ALL YOUR ENTERTAINING NEEDS
E PIKE ■ WHERE'S THE BEACH? ■ SAMPLER ■ WOULD YOU LIKE TO TRY A SAMPLER? ■ I THINK WE NEED TO TRY A SAMPI
NK YOU, NO, THANK YOU ■ FOUND SLAIN ■ WHAT'S YOUR EXCUSE? ■ THE DAANE SYSTEM ■ YOUR SORRY ASS! ■ FLEE NO
■ NOW OR NEVER ■ BANG IT OUT ■ BRING IT ON ■ FLAP THE GUMS ■ PIECE OF THE ACTION ■ WORK THE FLOOR ■ WOI
DOZ, GREAT MOVIE! ■ THE GOOD, THE BAD, AND THE UGLY ■ I'M DYIN, HERE! ■ LA GRANDE BOUFFE ■ CA GAZ? ■ ARE YC
GEONS QUI RECUL . . . LE, A TU BIEN FERMER LA CAGE A POUL . . . LE, A TU DONNER UN PEU D'HERBE AUX LAPINS . . . ? ■ C
IDNIGHT! ■ CODPIECE ■ THE PIECE ■ BEVERAGE OF CHOICE ■ SOIS POSITIF ET SE PLAINE PLUS ■ DOUBLE WIDE ■ WIDE
■ LAGGARDS ■ SUB, AS IN SUBLAGGARDS ■ LAGGARDESQUE ■ LIVING LARGE ■ THONG, TH, THONG, THONG, THONG ■ PI

elisms

THE WAY I READ IT ■ EAT THAT CHICKEN, THAD BE GIL SCOTT HERON ■ FREEWAY TRANSMISSION ■ CRIMES AGAINST THE
Y CUR ■ DON'T CALL ME SHIRLEY ■ GET THE POINT, POINT ■ MAY THE REVOLUTION BE TELEVISED—ME AND GIL ■ BIG EA
KSTER ■ THERE'S NO SUCH THING AS A FREE LUNCH ■ LIFE OF RILEY ■ IS EVERYTHING UNDER CONTROL HERE? ■ RADIC∤
ABAAABAAA CASHFLOW ■ IN THE REAR ■ HEIR TO THE BANQUE LAMBERT FORTUNE ■ HEIR TO THE [INSERT NAME OF CH
MBOWWA! ■ YOU GO, GIRL ■ I USED TO BE A NICE GUY ■ YOU'RE KILLING ME ■ LOVE CHANGE, EVOLUTION NOT MUTATIOI
LIVING LARGE ■ HIYA HIYA HIYA ■ YOU'VE GOT THE WHOLE TEAM HERE ■ VIPSSSSS ■ VIPS EVERYWHERE ■ CELEBRITY I
WN, MUSHY, AND SWEET ■ FLED WITH MILLIONS ■ THE DUDEMEISTER ■ WE'RE ALL COMMUNICATION MAJORS HERE ■ WI
WITH ONE OF MY BIG EATERS ■ MOISTURE IS THE KEY TO LIFE ■ RED FLAG ■ MORE ACID ■ MORE CHIVES ■ MORE GREE
NBELIEVABLE ■ SWAB THE DECKS ■ I SEE YOU ARE WITH ONE OF MY BIG EATERS ■ SUB . . . STANDARD ■ UN RACIÓN DE
MY NAME ■ EAT YOUR GREENS ■ THAT'S FOR SQUARES ■ IL ÉTAIT UNE FOIS DANS L'OUEST ET MON NOM EST PERSONNE
MPORTANTE DEL MUNDO ARTISTICO E CIENTÍFICO ■ YOU DISCO KIDS ■ THE NUMBERS DON'T LIE ■ DIE, DEVIL WENCH ■ L
' YA DOIN' ■ GOOD TO SEE YOU ■ THE KEY TO LIFE IS MOISTURE ■ I'M DA MAN YO DA MAN HE DA MAN ■ THE LIFE OF MI
WHAT A SCREAM ■ CHANGE IS GOOD ■ THE WORLD-FAMOUS MALIBU VINEYARD ■ YOU CAN DO IT ■ GO THE DISTANCE
D VON PIPE ■ I'M BAACCCKKK, POLTERGEIST ■ CORNICHE GAME HEN, WIDER THAN A MILE ■ CALIFORNIA COOUSINE FRE
ULD SEE THE OTHER GUY ■ DO YOU HAVE AN EXPERT BUSBOY DOWN THERE? (SM) ■ DO YOU HAVE AN EXPERT BUSBOY
R SOCKS OFF ■ BLOW YOUR SOCKS OFF ■ THE CHASMAN ■ GOTTA GO TO THE JOHN ■ NO POINT IN GETTING INTO A PISS
AN'T BEAT OUR MEAT ■ EAT OUT MORE OFTEN ■ WE CAN TAKE CARE OF ALL YOUR ENTERTAINING NEEDS ■ TWO FAT BA
S THE BEACH? ■ SAMPLER ■ WOULD YOU LIKE TO TRY A SAMPLER? ■ I THINK WE NEED TO TRY A SAMPLER ■ WOULD YO
OU ■ FOUND SLAIN ■ WHAT'S YOUR EXCUSE? ■ THE DAANE SYSTEM ■ YOUR SORRY ASS! ■ FLEE NOW! ■ DONC ■ ET AL
BANG IT OUT ■ BRING IT ON ■ FLAP THE GUMS ■ PIECE OF THE ACTION ■ WORK THE FLOOR ■ WORK THE CROWD ■ WC
GOOD, THE BAD, AND THE UGLY ■ I'M DYIN, HERE! ■ LA GRANDE BOUFFE ■ CA GAZ? ■ ARE YOU WITH THE PARTY IN THE
EN FERMER LA CAGE A POUL . . . LE, A TU DONNER UN PEU D'HERBE AUX LAPINS . . . ? ■ QUE TU ME DOIT DES MILLIO
ODPIECE ■ THE PIECE ■ BEVERAGE OF CHOICE ■ SOIS POSITIF ET SE PLAINE PLUS ■ DOUBLE WIDE ■ WIDE LOAD ■ LARG
UB, AS IN SUBLAGGARDS ■ LAGGARDESQUE ■ LIVING LARGE ■ THONG, TH, THONG, THONG, THONG ■ PLEASE STAND U

welcome to
MICHAEL'S

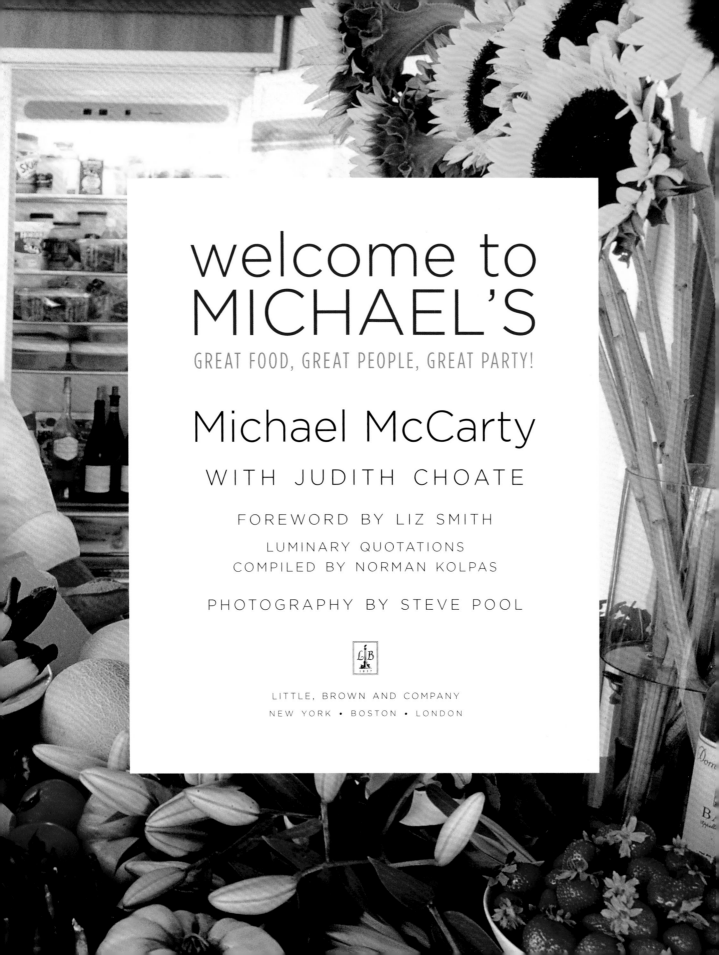

welcome to MICHAEL'S

GREAT FOOD, GREAT PEOPLE, GREAT PARTY!

Michael McCarty

WITH JUDITH CHOATE

FOREWORD BY LIZ SMITH

LUMINARY QUOTATIONS
COMPILED BY NORMAN KOLPAS

PHOTOGRAPHY BY STEVE POOL

LITTLE, BROWN AND COMPANY
NEW YORK · BOSTON · LONDON

Copyright © 2007 by Michael McCarty

Foreword copyright © 2007 by Liz Smith

All photographs copyright © 2007 by Stephen Pool, except
those on pages 5–7, 121 (left), and 218–219 (all but last), which are
courtesy of the author.

All rights reserved. Except as permitted under the U.S. Copyright
Act of 1976, no part of this book may be reproduced, distributed,
or transmitted in any form or by any means or stored in a data-
base or retrieval system, without the prior written permission of
the publisher.

Little, Brown and Company
Hachette Book Group USA
237 Park Avenue, New York, NY 10017
Visit our Web site at www.HachetteBookGroupUSA.com

First Edition: October 2007

Library of Congress Cataloging-in-Publication Data
McCarty, Michael.

Welcome to Michael's: great food, great people, great party!
/Michael McCarty with Judith Choate; foreword by Liz Smith.
p. cm.
Includes bibliographical references and index.
ISBN: 978-0-316-11815-6
1. Cookery, American — California style. 2. Michael's (Restaurant)
I. Choate, Judith. II. Title.

TX715.2.C34M338   2007
641.59794 — dc22   2006035163

10   9   8   7   6   5   4   3   2   1

Book and jacket design by Joel Avirom,
Jason Snyder, and Meghan Day Healey

Printed in China

For Kim, Clancy, Chas,
and Blanche . . .

. . . and, of course,
in memory of my father,
J. T. McCarty

contents

FOREWORD
by liz smith

Like a lot of basically true things in life, nobody really quite knows why Michael's became the hangout of choice for the media and the book business. Everybody just wanted to go there, and it was fun to see more people whom you knew there than at any other restaurant.

The rise of Michael's was fabulous because it was a sincere happening. It wasn't engineered by a press agent. I asked the media executive Joe Armstrong, who's from Fort Worth like me and eats lunch at Michael's so often that he has a cowboy-boot vase on his table and is called "The Mayor of Michael's," if he's on the cuff or owns part of it. And Joe just laughed, because he isn't and he doesn't.

I like and appreciate the fact that Michael's somehow created its own ambience. I'm sure a lot of hard work and planning went into it, and Michael himself and his general manager, Steve Millington, have great senses of humor. The wonderful thing about Michael's is that it's an authentic place to go to eat and see people. It reminds me of how people used to congregate at the Stork Club or at the Algonquin in the old days.

Let me give you an example, which I wrote about in my column in the *New York Post* on March 28, 2002:

Joe Armstrong had decided to invite an interesting group of people he liked to have lunch with him at Michael's. There was Robin Williams and his

*Michael working the floor in the garden room
of Michael's New York*

wife, Marsha, and former president Bill Clinton, and former Texas governor Ann Richards, and Billy Crystal and his wife, Janice, and the newswoman Diane Sawyer, and me. It was a grand get-together. I remember that while we were talking, a waiter went by with one of those big plates of French fries they serve at Michael's, and Bill Clinton said, "Hey, we'll have one of those." That was before Clinton had his heart surgery.

At some point, we all got up for a private group picture. A photographer happened to be out in front. Through the round window, she saw us all standing and ran in and snapped a picture. And that photo went around the world.

It's the sort of thing that just happens at Michael's. It was a real, true thing. And it rebounded to the restaurant's credit.

That's why I like to think of Michael's as the most exciting manifestation you'll find today of Manhattan as a small town.

FROM LEFT: *Janice Crystal, Billy Crystal, Ann Richards, Liz Smith, Joe Armstrong, Marsha Williams, Bill Clinton, Robin Williams, and Diane Sawyer*

Photo credit: Jimi Celeste/PMc

welcome to
MICHAEL'S

INTRODUCTION
it has been and still is a great party

For as long as I can remember, I have loved a party, and there is no better party than a great restaurant alive with conversation, clinking glasses, smooth service, and delicious food. You'll notice that I always emphasize the whole experience. That's because the most memorable meals are always complete and well-rounded: great food, great drinks, and great people in a great environment with impeccable service. I knew that I wanted to create just that kind of party atmosphere every night. Even at a very young age, I somehow also knew that I would have to build a strong foundation to allow myself the freedom to host a great party while also being confident that the food would be worthy.

It all started with my parents, John Thomas McCarty and Carol Holly McCarty Austell.

"Michael's world-in-a-salad aesthetic—bright colors, strong flavors, rare and diverse ingredients—became more or less the lingua franca of American cooking. Michael McCarty, at the age of twenty-five, was the most visionary restaurateur in the United States."

—JONATHAN GOLD, *LOS ANGELES*, 1997

Me and my man!

3

> **"Now, after two decades of rising decibels around the restaurant world, Michael's still soothes frazzled nerves as few establishments do. A meal with friends in the lush garden—amid tree ferns, orchids, and flowing streams—is Los Angeles at its most seductive."**
>
> —CAROLINE BATES, *GOURMET,* 1998

Throughout my childhood, they and their group of friends entertained. Whether the setting was along the Hudson River, where I grew up, or the beaches of Rhode Island, where we spent summers, or the mountains of Vermont, where we skied in winter, a party was always happening— and it was always appropriate to the place, the season, the people, the local ingredients, and the occasion.

The restaurant bug really bit me in September 1969, the night before I left to attend a high school junior-year-abroad program in Brittany. My parents and my father's best friend organized a send-off dinner for me at Laurent in midtown Manhattan. The place was designed to the nines, with spectacular beveled mirrors, mahogany woodwork, and perfect lighting. Everyone eating there looked like a million bucks: tan, fit, gorgeous, and beautifully dressed. The meal was sensational. But the highlight of the evening was when the owner, Laurent himself, entered the dining room. I could feel the buzz level soar. As he worked the floor, going from table to table, it hit me that something extraordinary was happening. Then the bill arrived. As I watched my father and his friend argue over who was going to pay, it all made sense. Every day of my life, I could throw the sort of parties my parents threw—and get paid for it.

The next morning, I sailed for France. The ship, the SS *Aurelia,* was staffed entirely with Italian waiters and cooks. Even though the ship had 1,500 American teenagers aboard, it still operated with a minimum of five meal periods a day, not to mention the after-midnight service. During the seven-day voyage, I literally absorbed the Italian passion for a life centered on food and beverages. (Yes, they served us sixteen-year-olds wine.) My memories of actually arriving at Le Havre are somewhat suspect.

My French home-stay hosts, the Brandilys, turned out to be wonderful. They were a huge extended family, numbering more than sixty, and like my parents they entertained constantly, whether on the beach at Quiberon, at their nine-hundred-year-old château, or at their urban digs

> **"McCarty opened Michael's restaurant in Santa Monica and fired one in a volley of shots heard 'round the gastronomic world. Almost overnight, Michael's became both a breeding ground for a new generation of chefs and a laboratory for what soon came to be called the New California (or New American) cuisine."**
>
> —DAVID SHAW, *LOS ANGELES TIMES,* 2004

ABOVE
Michael with Jonathan Waxman, Mark Peel, and Ken Frank, 1979.

TOP RIGHT
Michael in Santa Monica dining room, 1983.

RIGHT
The invitation for the Sixteenth Anniversary Party at Michael's in Santa Monica.

Kim and Michael McCarty
request the pleasure of your company at

A GREAT PARTY

Sunday, April 30, 1995, 3:00 to 7:00 PM

MICHAEL'S
1147 Third Street, Santa Monica

TO BENEFIT THE MUSEUM OF CONTEMPORARY ART; THE LOS ANGELES COUNTY MUSEUM OF ART; THE MUSIC CENTER OF LOS ANGELES COUNTY'S NEW DISNEY HALL; THE SANTA MONICA MUSEUM OF ART; AND TO CELEBRATE MICHAEL'S RESTAURANT'S SIXTEENTH ANNIVERSARY

Despite Los Angeles' recent difficult years and natural disasters, it is time we focus on our city's cultural landmarks once again. We need to rededicate ourselves to the preservation of someting truly important in all our lives.

Please join us in recognizing that support of our arts institutions is a necessary part of the reemergence of cultural Los Angeles in the mid nineties.

Good Eats, Good Drinks, and Good Times for All While We Reinforce Our Commitment to the Arts in Los Angeles.

A GREAT PARTY Celebrates Michael's Sixteenth Anniversary with sixteen of Michael's Great Chefs returning for this outstanding culinary and cultural event:

Ken Frank, *Fenix Restaurant, West Hollywood*
Jonathan Waxman, *Ark Restaurants, New York, NY*
Mark Peel, *Campanile, West Hollywood*
Nancy Silverton, *La Brea Bakery, West Hollywood*
Roy Yamaguchi, *Roy's, Hawaii*
Martin Garcia, *Il Presidente, Mexico*
Gordon Naccarato, *The Monkey Bar, West Hollywood*
Kazuto Matsusaka, *formerly Zenzero, Santa Monica*
James Brinkley, *Baker, Seattle, Washington*
Dennis Sharp, *formerly Adirondacks, D.C., and Michael's, New York, NY*
Sally Clarke, *Clarke's, London, England*
Eric Tanaka, *formerly Michael's, New York, NY*
Zach Bruel, *Z's, Cleveland, Ohio*
Billy Phlug, *The Nunnery, Boston, Massachusetts*
Rebecca Bolin, *Dessert Works, Seattle, Washington*
Buddy Trinidad, *Morton's, West Hollywood*
Catherine Dimanche, *Michael's, Santa Monica (current chef)*
Catalino Echeverria, *Michael's, Santa Monica (current chef)*
Dorte Lambert, *Michael's, Santa Monica (current pastry chef)*

in the wonderful city of Rennes. They were proud Bretons, and there was always a reason for a party, whether a marriage, a baptism, a birthday, a death, or all of the numerous French *and* Breton holidays. And of course I introduced them to my American holidays. After my experiences at Laurent and on the *Aurelia*, and with all the attention the Brandilys paid to food and beverage, at some point a member of my French family told me that one could study the restaurant business academically in the French school system. With that goal in mind, I returned to France as soon as I could, after my first year at the University of Colorado, Boulder.

My goal was to immerse myself in the restaurant world; I wanted to understand the back

70 Seaview • Montecito Shores • Santa Barbara, CA 93108
805 • 969-3662

Dear Michael and Kim:

What a splendid lunch chez vous. We thought it was very lively, good people, and, of course -- great food awd wine. I know of at least one pigeon cinched, and suspect there were more. You both are such generous sponsors of events -- where would be we be without you! It does seem as though AIWF things were marching along at last, and our different drummer is doing impressively well.

Have a wonderful trip in Europe -- would we could meet you there again. Happy Baby II, also, and much love from us goth.

P&J Child

AN AMERICAN CELEBRATION

Dinner Menu
4 May 1983
The Stanford Court
San Francisco

Reception
Cultured Olympia Oysters from Puget Sound, Washington
Belon Oysters from Tomales Bay, California
Portuguese Oysters from Vancouver Island, B.C.
Schramsberg Vineyards 1977 Reserve Napa Valley Champagne

❋

Terrine of 3 American Smoked Fish
with their Respective Caviars
LARRY FORGIONE, River Café, Brooklyn
Jordan Vineyard & Winery 1981 Estate Bottled Chardonnay

Red Pepper Pasta with Grilled Scallops
JONATHAN WAXMAN, Michael's, Santa Monica
Chalone Vineyard 1981 Chardonnay

Garden Salad
ALICE WATERS, Chez Panisse, Berkeley
Sanford Vineyards 1982 Vin Gris

Blackened Red Fish
PAUL PRUDHOMME, K-Paul's Louisiana Kitchen, New Orleans
Beringer Vineyards 1980 Private Reserve Chardonnay

Marinated Grilled Quail
with Poblano Chile, Cilantro & Lime Sauce
MARK MILLER, Fourth Street Grill, Berkeley
Iron Horse Vineyards 1982 Sauvignon Blanc

Roasted Rack of Lamb
Stuffed with Missouri Greens & Hazelnuts
Gratin of Wildroot Vegetables, Fiddlehead Ferns, & Cattail Sprouts
BRADLEY OGDEN, American Café, Kansas
JIMMY SCHMIDT, London Chop House, Detroit
Acacia Winery 1980 Pinot Noir St. Clair Vineyard

American Cheese Selections
Robert Mondavi Winery 1974 Private Reserve Cabernet Sauvignon

Pecan Pastry with Chocolate & Sabayon Sauce
JEREMIAH TOWER, Santa Fe Bar & Grill, Berkeley,
Balboa Café, San Francisco
Joseph Phelps Vineyards 1981 Scheurebe 'Late Harvest'

❋

After-Hours Party
Spago Pizza
WOLFGANG PUCK, Spago, Los Angeles
Domaine Chandon Blanc de Noir
Tripe Gumbo
BARBARA KAFKA, Star Spangled Foods, New York
Christian Brothers Private Reserve Centennial Sherry

The Greenwood Press

> **"The menu today reads like a textbook on what's come to be known as California cuisine. After all, along with Chez Panisse in Berkeley, Michael's pioneered this style of cooking. But while other restaurants took it to extremes, Michael's has kept a steady course."**
>
> —S. Irene Virbila, *Los Angeles Times Magazine*, 1995

of the house (the kitchen), the front of the house (the dining room), and all the business aspects of running a restaurant (the office). I lived in Paris and got my chops in French cooking, wines, and restaurant management at the Cordon Bleu, the Académie du Vin, and the Ecole Hôtelière de Paris. To be a successful restaurateur, I felt strongly that it was imperative for me to be an accomplished chef as well. And as any restaurateur knows, the time inevitably comes when some temperamental chef suddenly storms out of the kitchen in the middle of service, and I wanted to be able to jump behind the line at a moment's notice so my guests' dining experience never missed a beat. Little did I know that what I learned in those early years would have the biggest impact on Michael's when I opened it in Santa Monica five years later—that an American could decide to pursue a career as a chef, and that a chef could own a restaurant.

To me, the path seemed straightforward and clear: my vision was to take the foundations of classical French cuisine as codified by the great early-twentieth-century chef Auguste Escoffier; combine them with the simplicity and freshness of the nouvelle cuisine revolution that was sweeping through France while I lived there; and add a contemporary, youthful, open-minded California sensibility. We would use only the best fresh seasonal products to create a new American style of cooking, served in a totally modern American fine dining establishment. The food would be prepared by young, daring, American-born chefs (and one English woman) and

OPPOSITE TOP
Michael with Julia Child.

OPPOSITE CENTER
A note to Michael and Kim from Paul and Julia Child.

OPPOSITE BOTTOM
Michael with Danny Meyer and Drew Nieporent.

OPPOSITE RIGHT
An American Celebration menu signed by star-studded chefs.

ABOVE
Michael greets George H. W. and Barbara Bush in 1989.

served in a comfortable, beautiful setting by an informal yet highly trained and skilled American waitstaff. Throw in some great new American wines and original paintings, prints, and sculptures by some of the best contemporary artists, and the result was something that came to be called "a modern American restaurant" serving a new regional style of cooking: "California cuisine."

Today this idea does not seem so challenging or unusual, but in 1979 the critics used words like "exciting,"

> **"The food, called California cuisine by the press at first, became the working standard of what is now known as Modern American Cuisine. There are hints of Michael's cooking in restaurants all around the country."**
>
> **—LAURIE OCHOA,**
> *LOS ANGELES TIMES,* **1995**

"ambitious," "clever," "revelation," "elegance," "simplicity," and "wow." And it wasn't just the food and service. I replaced typical fancy-restaurant canned music with the Modern Jazz Quartet, Miles Davis, and Chet Baker. I 86'd the dress code: no tie and jacket required to dine, and no tuxedo required to serve (a then little-known Ralph Lauren designed our waiters' uniforms). It was a whole new ball game, where "eating out" was fun and every night was a party. It was "my joint," a very personal place that signaled a new era for food and dining in America.

From those heady early days, when a whole batch of young American chefs launched their star-studded careers in our kitchen, Michael's has not strayed far from my original intent. The restaurant now has two locations. The first one continues to rock in Santa Monica, California, and the East Coast version powers on in midtown Manhattan. I like to think of the two places as fraternal twins—same DNA, but slightly different personalities. Their design is similar, their atmosphere identical. The plates in both restaurants are big; the art eye-catching; the flowers stunning; the waitstaff cool and

> **"There is a crackling air of anticipation about a dinner at Michael's, like a Sugar Ray Leonard title defense, like Christmas morning. It's festive *and* serious, formal *and* relaxed. Most important, the restaurant is intensely personal."**
>
> **—JEFFREY FISKIN,** *CALIFORNIA,* **1985**

chic (now wearing Burberry); and the food decisively seasonal, fresh, simple, and knock-your-socks-off tasty.

Speaking of tasty, let me tell you about the recipes in this book. They're a collection of my favorites, the dishes I love to cook and serve at home when I'm entertaining friends and family. They feature my favorite ingredients, from soft-shell crabs to shad roe, leg of lamb to twenty-eight-day dry-aged New York strip steak, fiddlehead ferns to white truffles, huckleberries to white peaches.

Some of that stuff may at first sound hard to get. But a major change during the nearly

> "If there is a more pleasant dining place in greater Los Angeles than the backyard at Michael's—a converted house built in the thirties—I don't know about it."
>
> —MARK BITTMAN, *NEW YORK TIMES*, 2000

thirty years that have passed since I started in this business is that an amazing number of unique, high-quality ingredients are now available not just to top restaurant chefs, but also to home cooks everywhere, thanks to the World Wide Web. I know that people who love good food can now get anything and everything they need from anywhere to cook the recipes in this book. So go to www.welcometomichaels.com for great sources.

Whether I'm entertaining at home or welcoming guests in my restaurants, I always consider it my number one job to make everyone feel like a star at an awesome party. Scattered throughout this book you'll find quotations from my personal friends and restaurant guests, snippets of conversation you might overhear at one of my bashes.

Over the years, my exuberant cheer "Great party!" has become a sort of trademark.

I can honestly say that my years in the restaurant business have felt like one big party. When I think of the people I have met; the friends that I have made; the generosity I've experienced from people in the food and wine worlds; the superb chefs I have been privileged to know and work with; the meals I have cooked and eaten; the wines I've savored, both classic and new; and all the great parties, I feel overwhelmed by the fabulous journey it has been and continues to be. I am happy to invite you along, and I hope you have a helluva good time, filled with your own great food, great wine, great people, and great parties. Keep cookin', keep eatin', and . . . keep doin' it!

—Michael McCarty

> "Michael's is a new sort of thing: a fantasy of California as imagined by a dude who has spent an awful lot of time living the good life in Paris. The cellar is filled with Napa Valley wine; the patio is awash in Renoir-like stippled shade; the tables are set with Christofle silver. The art on the walls, Stellas and Rauschenbergs and Hockneys and such, is sufficient to endow a modest museum."
>
> —JONATHAN GOLD, *LA WEEKLY*, 2004

a good-looking plate of food—and a successful menu

Présentation! (When reading this opening, please do so with a French accent.)

When I studied cooking in Paris, one of the most important things I learned is that with food, as with so many things in life, first impressions count. The way you put food on a plate, and the plate you put it on, can add immeasurably to the pleasure your cooking delivers. Therefore, great presentation is a must!

I always like to think of a main course plate in terms of the basic protein-veg-carb-and-sauce combination. I start with my protein, and then work around it, creating what we call in restaurant jargon "the set." And there's always a sauce, which serves as the bridge between the dish and the wine that you choose to accompany it. This marriage between food and wine is why the food makes the wine taste better and why the wine makes the food taste better. Never forget the sauce, even if it's only olive oil or butter. As I always tell my cooks, "The key to life is moisture."

My mantra of "green, crunchy, and acidic" leads the way. I always think of it when putting plates together. The opposite, "brown, sweet, and mushy," is so old-school. I use lighter accents, usually based on wines, vinegars, or citrus juices (more acid!)—and always fresh herbs, incorporated into the sauce or vinaigrette just before serving and, more important, sprinkled as a garnish on the finished plate. Similar principles of harmony and balance apply to first courses, middle courses, and desserts.

I always keep the color, texture, temperature, shape, and volume of each component in mind as I arrange the art of the plate. Color, shape, and volume entice the eye; combinations of textures add the pleasures of our sense of touch; and proper temperatures ensure

> **"Some restaurants turn your plate into a work of art, and that puts me right off, that somebody's been breathing over it and designing it. Designed puts me right off. Give me a break! At Michael's, it just comes to you looking unaffected."**
>
> **—HARRY BENSON, PHOTOJOURNALIST**

Kim and Michael McCarty on the Malibu deck

Chas and Kim McCarty

maximum flavor. You'll find all of these factors in action in the recipes and photographs throughout this book.

Whether you are having only a couple of courses or a ton of courses, as I often do when entertaining at home, it is important that everything works together. Menu planning is a must. First think about what's in season. Then think about what wines you want to pour, and where those wines fit in a logical progression from light to big: sparkling wines and champagnes, light whites, big whites, light reds, big reds, and dessert wines. Finally, choose the recipes that will best showcase your wines and always use the same varietal for the acid in your sauce as the wine you're pouring.

"In 1979, when I first met Michael McCarty before he opened Michael's in Santa Monica, he really thought he was going to do something huge and new, and it never crossed his mind that he might fail. And Michael succeeded at doing everything he said he would.

"It was the food, however, that really set Michael's apart. Michael and his chefs took the light, fresh, ingredients-driven principles of the nouvelle cuisine movement so popular then in France and applied them to American products cooked by Americans. Today it all seems so obvious. But back then people still thought that you had to be French to be a great chef and that the ingredients in France were better than anything here.

"I think Michael has succeeded, first, because he is very, very smart about knowing his audience. Like his restaurants, he has also aged remarkably well. He has an enormous amount of personal charm, charisma, and graciousness. And he has an amazingly positive attitude about life."

—RUTH REICHL, EDITOR IN CHIEF, *GOURMET*

a few words on wine

Many, many people have great difficulty selecting a wine to pair with their meal. Often they resort to ordering one produced at an instantly recognized, highly esteemed vineyard or simply one that is extremely expensive (which they hope will assure great quality). Moving away from these quick decisions will often cause a panic attack. I have found that the easiest way to learn how to choose an appropriate wine is to be adventuresome in tasting and never to fear embarrassment. Forge ahead, and you will soon be able to identify the types of wines that appeal to your palate, pocketbook, and plate.

A few tips: Almost everything you need to know about a French wine can be found on the label (and, generally, the less information on the label, the lesser the wine). However, to understand the varietal makeup of the wine,

you have to know what grape is grown in what region. Austrian and German wine labels carry a wealth of information, perhaps even more than you need. American wine labels, on the other hand, carry the least amount of information but are the most informative, as they tell you, in typically direct American fashion, where the wine comes from, the varietal, and the vintage.

I particularly love American wines. They are, as a rule, larger than life, more vibrant than those from Old World vines. The food that I cook— simple, straightforward, and seasonal—marries perfectly with these newer wines on the block.

As you pair your selections with your meal, remember a couple of simple rules: (1) The food and wine should complement each other— delicately flavored dishes require elegant, almost ethereal wines; light food demands crisp, lively

wines; and robust meals cry out for full-bodied, rich wines. (2) Match the flavors of a dish to the basic characteristics of a wine; for instance, savor the spices or herbs in a recipe and then pair them with a wine in which those same flavors are found. And forget the old rule of thumb that says you must serve red wine with red meat and white wine with white meat and fish. Many light red wines go well with almost everything, and a big, buttery Chardonnay can bring out the best in a juicy, grilled pork or veal chop. Educate your palate and keep tasting— a few mistakes won't hurt, and you'll learn a lot about the wines that work for you. And, finally, whatever your wine-food pairing, use the same grape varietal in making the sauce, the bridge between the food and wine.

I'd like to add to this wine discussion the voices of two seminal sommeliers who worked with me at Michael's to set the style and tone of our wine list. First here's a sip of what Phil Reich, sommelier at Michael's Santa Monica from 1979 to 1996, had to say about matching wines and foods in my first cookbook back in 1989:

"Until the mid-to-late 1970s, if you talked at all about matching wines and foods, you were primarily talking about *French* wines and *French* cuisine. The French have had at least a 500-year jump on the rest of the world in the art of adapting their wines to the foods they cooked and ate, and adapting their foods to the wines they produced. But Michael McCarty was, to my mind, the first person to develop a California cuisine that specifically showed off the wines of California.

"American wines, as a rule, are bigger, bolder, and fresher-tasting than their European counterparts—a result of soil, climate, and winemaking methods. And Michael's cooking, with its emphasis on absolutely fresh, big-flavored American ingredients—quickly cooked to maintain and enhance their naturally intense flavors—is a natural match for such wines. The French wines that do work are the biggest, richest ones.

These happen to be the finest of the French wines, but they are also the most extravagantly priced of all wines."

Now some thoughts from David Rosoff, who was general manager and sommelier at Michael's Santa Monica from 1996 to 2001: "When I began my tour with Michael in 1996, I had not yet learned to appreciate how food and wine work together in his healthful, organic manner. Michael told me the food that he prepared was simply 'food that goes with wine,' a thought that seemed almost pedestrian to me then. But by the time I was ready to move on, I was a devout champion of his philosophy.

"Michael is large in every way, and he likes big, bold flavors. His palate is an extension of his persona . . . but he does not want his pristine ingredients to have their expression marred by competition. It's all about balance.

"As with his food, his wine preferences are those that are full-flavored and expressive. In this age of excess, where the consumer chases after opaquely colored trophy wines, you might assume that Mike is also drawn to these monsters of manipulation. But when you

cruise through his cellar, you will find early benchmark examples of his bold but balanced taste: Côte-Rôtie from Guigal and the late Gentaz-Dervieux, Hermitage from J. L. Chave; Châteauneuf du Pape from Beaucastel, Vosne-Romanée from Henri Jayer and DRC; old single-vineyard Pinots from Josh Jensen; early producers of classically styled California Cabernet such as Mayacamas, Joseph Phelps, and Heitz. You'll also find outstanding wines produced in other countries, such as big, bold Chardonnays from Italy; great Malbecs from Mendoza, Chile; and Tinto Nacional from Douro in Portugal.

"Not one of these wines could be considered reticent or austere, lacking in girth or complexity. But all are examples of wines whose ingredients are in perfect balance: acidity, alcohol, extract, tannin, oak, each in symbiotic harmony with the other, and all sitting exactly where they should in the 'bandwidths' of the wine. This is the key. As simple as it seems, it is a dying art. It was a concept never foreign to Mike and never lost on him throughout phases and fads that infiltrated the food and wine community."

shopping for
seasonal ingredients

At home and in the restaurants, my menus are driven by the seasons. The Santa Monica Farmers' Market is only steps away from Michael's Santa Monica, so we shop there before we place orders with our purveyors. In the east, the seasons are much more clearly defined and, although Manhattan's Union Square Greenmarket is open all year long, the winter months don't offer the variety that Southern California produces, so we have to adjust the New York menus accordingly, with a lot of help from FedEx. Overnight shipping also allows us to bring in seasonal ingredients from other parts of the world. But there is something very compelling about the beginnings and endings of seasons and the memory-fueled anticipation of ingredients that are available only once a year. Although you hear a lot of talk about locally grown, caught, or harvested ingredients, I love the world's bounty: Dutch white asparagus, French black truffles, Italian white truffles, English Dover sole, Spanish Serrano ham, and *rouget-barbet de roche* from the Mediterranean. And, hey, how about the French, Italian, Spanish, Portuguese, Australian, New Zealand, South African, Chilean, and Argentine wines? They all make my list! The key is always to use the best ingredients, in season, from wherever they may come.

With that goal in mind, on page 21 I list peak seasonal ingredients that I love to use, particularly those that appear in the recipes in this book. You'll see that the lists concentrate on vegetables, fruit, and seafood. That's because these are the ingredients that still, even in this day of airfreight and the Internet, have a strongly seasonal nature: you actually want to wait for them to come around. Poultry and meats, by contrast, are available and excellent year-round; even so-called spring lamb can be enjoyed at any time of year. So some of the items on my list are delicious at other times, but I have highlighted the season in which I find them to be at their most flavorful. I am lucky

"Michael is so much larger than life that when he goes shopping he comes back with enough food to feed a hundred people—but just for that day because it's all fresh food. Everyone should be as generous as Michael is."

—Kathryn Ireland,
INTERIOR AND FABRIC DESIGNER

because a bountiful spring starts early in California—we even get spring white corn—which makes it possible to enjoy such ingredients as strawberries, peas, morels, and asparagus long before they come to market in the east. And I can stretch the seasons, as I travel back and forth at least twice a month.

All this is to say that there is nothing that can take the place of pristine ingredients. If you begin with the best, you often have little to do at the stove to wow diners. I cook very simply—you won't find a recipe in this book that you can't finish in just a couple of hours—and I grill a lot, something that can be done all year in sunny Southern California and during the warmer months in the east (or on an indoor or stovetop grill in the middle of winter, although I personally have been known to barbecue on my New York terrace in the middle of a raging blizzard—with a warming beverage of choice, of course). I have easy routines and signature ingredients that have been part of my repertoire since I decided that I wanted to make a career in the culinary world: a quick sauté of first-rate vegetables, a light hand

with fats, lots of wild mushrooms and truffles and caviar (unbeatable extravagances that take an unpretentious dish to new heights), prepare-in-advance sauces and vinaigrettes that add just the right touch to a finished dish, and, always, fresh herbs. One of my secrets is that I cook a "taster" portion (the chef's prerogative), so that when I think something is done I can slice off a piece to make sure. It is a foolproof method to serve perfectly cooked meals.

I love to have my friends and family join me in the kitchen, at the grill, and on the deck or terrace. I've found that when I'm relaxed and enjoying myself, the food flies to the table. Right, you say, all you have to do is bring your prepped ingredients from the restaurants to put together dinner. This assumption is partly true, but I love shopping for myself and, if I haven't brought a stock or sauce home with me, I can throw together a simple wine sauce (see Syrah Sauce, page 131) or a flavorful vinaigrette in a couple of minutes, the flawless accent for a piece of grilled or roasted meat, poultry, or seafood. Remember: it all begins with the ingredients. Party on!

spring

vegetables: Asparagus (jumbo, white, and green) / Baby artichokes / Corn (early California white) / Fava beans / Fiddlehead ferns / Garlic (spring, green, wild) / Lettuces / Mushrooms (morels) / Parsley / Peas and pea shoots / Radishes / Ramps / Scallions / Spring onions (red and white) / Watercress (wild, upland, and cultivated)

fruit: Citrus (California) / Rhubarb / Strawberries (California)

seafood: Clams (littleneck) / Crabs (soft-shell, Dungeness) / Oysters / Salmon (wild, Copper River, sockeye) / Scallops (day boat or diver) / Shad roe

summer

vegetables: Beets / Corn (white) / Cucumbers / Eggplant / Fava beans / Haricots verts / Onions (Vidalia, Walla Walla) / Peppers (chili, sweet) / Squash (summer) / Squash blossoms / Tomatoes (beefsteak, heirloom)

fruit: Berries / Figs / Melon / Stone fruits

seafood: Clams (Ipswich soft-shell steamers, littleneck) / Crabs (Dungeness) / Crayfish / Lobsters (Maine) / Prawns (Santa Barbara spot) / Salmon (wild, Columbia River king) / Scallops (Baja diver, Long Island bay) / Striped bass (line-caught wild)

fall

vegetables: Mushrooms (porcini) / Onions (Vidalia) / Potatoes / Squash (winter) / Truffles (white)

fruit: Apples / Figs / Pears

seafood: Oysters (Atlantic Northeast, Pacific Northwest) / Prawns (Santa Barbara spot) / Scallops (Nantucket bay) / Stone crabs (Florida)

winter

vegetables: Potatoes / Truffles (black)

fruit: Citrus

seafood: Lobsters (West Coast spiny) / Scallops (Maine day boat) / Squid (West Coast) / Stone crabs (Florida)

year-round

meat: Beef / Lamb / Pork (including "party meats"—my name for charcuterie) / Veal

poultry: Chicken (and eggs, preferably fertile organic free-range) / Duck (including foie gras)

game birds: Quail / Squabs

OPPOSITE FROM TOP LEFT, CLOCKWISE

Michael and Kim shop at Santa Monica Farmers' Market; Michael with Josiah Citrin, chef-owner Mélisse, Santa Monica; Michael with Mark Peel, chef-owner Campanile, West Hollywood; Michael with Alex Weiser, owner Weiser Farm; Michael and Kim with Gerard Ferry, owner L'Orangerie, Hollywood; Michael with David West, wild mushroom dude; Michael with Randy Pudwill, berry farmer

greens and herbs

Everyone in my kitchens has heard me exclaim: "Green! Crunchy! Acidic!" And they've also heard me moan: "Brown. Mushy. Sweet." A great dish is alive with color and texture and bright in flavor, and the presence of greens and herbs makes it all happen. "More acid! Where's the green? More chives!"

about greens

Lettuces and other salad greens must be absolutely pristine—crisp and fresh, with great color. There should be no brown or yellow spots. Use them within a couple of days of purchase to maximize flavor, texture, and nutritional content. Always wash greens thoroughly, even those that are labeled "prewashed." To do so, first separate the leaves. Put them in a salad spinner, put the spinner in the sink, and fill it with cold water to cover. Then swish the water around to loosen any dirt. Toss the water and fill and swish again. Then drain and spin to dry the leaves thoroughly, pouring out any water left at the bottom of the spinner. Spin again, repeating until no water is left at the bottom.

Before we look at the individual greens, let's talk about mesclun, a French term for a mix of wild greens, other salad leaves, herbs, and even flowers. You'll find all kinds of great ready-to-use mixtures at almost all farmers' markets. Even supermarkets now stock relatively fine prepackaged mixed greens. And it is very easy to create your own mix from whatever variety of different salad leaves you happen to like.

Some of the better lettuces and salad greens that I use are:

arugula (aka rocket, roquette, or rucola): Slender, dark green leaves with a sharp, peppery flavor, frequently used in Italian salads. Farmers' markets may offer a couple of varieties, including wild rocket, which is sold with its yellow flowers. Then you have the jagged-edged, spicy variety and the milder-tasting flat, oblong type. All three are great together or individually.

belgian endive (aka witloof or French endive): Pointed, oval compact clusters of slightly bitter white leaves imported from Belgium. Now also available with red-tipped leaves.

bibb lettuce (aka Boston, butter, butterhead, California Bibb, Kentucky limestone, limestone, or Little Gem): Small, medium, and large heads of bright green, full-flavored, delicate leaves. Crisp in the center but soft and buttery at the edges.

cabbage Compact head of green, creamy, or red leaves. Not technically a salad green but often used in salads, particularly in the classic American coleslaw. When you've had it with "big eats," dine on bowls of steamed cabbage for a few days!

fennel Although not a traditional American salad green, fennel is now often found, raw, in Mediterranean-style salads. A rounded bulb with celery-like, creamy stalks and feathery, dill-like foliage. Licorice-flavored and crisply textured. Both the bulb and the foliage are used.

frisée (aka chicory, curly endive): Curly, flattened heads and slightly bitter, pale green leaves with a yellow-white center. Frisée is a delicately

flavored member of the chicory family that is used in a classic French salad with bacon lardons (see page 98).

iceberg lettuce Compact heads of pale green, crisp, almost watery leaves. I still think that there is nothing better to add some crunch to a great BLT, and I love to serve wedges of iceberg topped with Maytag blue cheese dressing.

leaf lettuce (aka loose-leaf, red leaf, butter leaf, green leaf, salad bowl, or oak leaf lettuce): Loose, slightly ruffled, open heads of bright or dark green or red-tipped leaves. Extremely mild in flavor.

mâche (aka corn salad, field salad, or lamb's lettuce): Slender, small, rounded, dark green, very soft leaves.

Originally found as a wild green growing in cornfields. Sweet flavor with terrific color and shape on the plate.

purslane A garden weed, now cultivated, having a thin, edible stem (when young), with small, oval, fleshy, padlike, green to yellowish green succulent leaves. Also foraged and known as wild purslane. Slightly acidic.

radicchio (aka radicchio di Verona, radicchio di Treviso, or Italian chicory): Small, compact, round or slightly oval heads of purple or white leaves that are slightly bitter. Radicchio's sibling, Treviso, is an elongated white and red head with a slightly sweeter flavor. Both are great on the grill!

romaine lettuce Large, compact head of oval, crisp, bright yellow to dark green leaves. Most prized are the smaller, pale yellow inner leaves, the ideal component for a great Caesar salad. Baby romaine leaves, in various shades of red and green, are perfect on their own or in your personal version of mesclun.

spinach For steaming purposes, I prefer the deep green, slightly crinkled, shiny variety. Baby spinach leaves are smaller, almost round, with a soft green color and a gentle fuzzy feel; they're great in salads.

watercress Small, vibrant green, peppery leaves attached to long, crisp stems. One of my favorite greens. I use three types, sometimes together, sometimes individually: cultivated, the kind you find in most supermarkets, which has medium-sized leaves and the classic peppery cress flavor; milder, broad-leafed, hydroponic watercress; and wild watercress, which has tiny leaves and a more delicate flavor.

about herbs

Fresh herbs add immeasurable seasoning and flavor to all types of dishes. Small bunches of fresh herbs are now available in most supermarkets. However, even a city gardener can keep small pots of herbs on the windowsill or terrace for that last-minute snip of fresh, cool flavor. I believe that every dish should contain at least one herb.

Fresh herbs are usually quite perishable and should be used as quickly as possible after picking. Never wash herbs before refrigerated storage, which will cause them to rapidly deteriorate. Wrap a bit of damp paper towel around the stems, place the whole bunch in a glass or plastic container, and cover tightly. Wash whatever you need as you go.

Although my recipes call for specific herbs, I suggest that you familiarize yourself with each herb so that you will instinctively know which one will give your dish the right personal touch. And try using two or more herbs at a time to develop your own flavor combinations.

My favorite herbs are:

basil Pungent, faintly sweet, with soft, pointed oval leaves on a rather hardy stem. Along with the now quite common green, Mediterranean variety, you can find special, delicately scented basils, such as Greek, opal, lemon, anise, clove, cinnamon, and purple-leaf in the market. However, I personally love the flavor purity of fresh green basil. The main ingredient of Italian pesto sauce, basil complements almost any vegetable, meat, or poultry and adds welcome flavor to soups and salads, especially tomatoes. It marries beautifully with mint and fennel.

chervil Fresh, clean, and mild, like parsley, with lacy leaves. A prominent component of the traditional French *fines herbes* mixture, chervil is an aromatic addition to a salad mix or a garnish for fish.

chives Mildly onion-flavored, slender grasslike stalks used as a garnish or flavoring agent or in a salad mix. The lavender or white blossoms are edible and can be used in salads or as a garnish. Chives add a clear, direct flavor to sauces and vinaigrettes. My staff knows that I can never get enough chives on the plate!

cilantro (aka green coriander): Spicy and biting, with round, notched leaves on a sprightly stem. Cilantro lends a distinctively pungent flavor to Southwestern, Mexican, East Indian, and Southeast Asian dishes. Great in salsas or in my California Bloody Bulls (page 209).

dill Subtle anise flavor with feathery foliage on tall, hollow stems. Dill is most often associated with seafood—as in my Gravlax (page 112)—and summer salads and, of course, is a major component of pickled vegetables.

mint Many flavors are available, with each having a definite leaf shape, aroma, and use. The two most common varieties are spearmint (with pale green, oval, slightly notched leaves and a warm, embracing flavor) and peppermint (smoother, deeper green leaves with a biting taste). Serve mint with melon and *un ración de jamón*.

oregano Strong, highly aromatic flavor with tiny triangular leaves. Often used in Mediterranean cooking or in combination with thyme.

parsley Fresh, clean taste with either bright green, tightly curled leaves (curly parsley) or flat, dark green, spiky leaves (Italian or flat-leaf parsley). The latter has a slightly stronger flavor.

rosemary Full-flavored, extremely aromatic evergreen with needlelike leaves on a woody branch. Rosemary is often used to flavor foods cooked on the grill. It's also great in marinades.

sage Soft, warm green, slightly fuzzy leaves often used in combination with rosemary and thyme. Used extensively in stuffing and as a flavoring agent for meats (especially pork), poultry, and vegetables.

tarragon Long, slender, dark green leaves with a very pronounced sweet yet mildly tart flavor. An essential component of *fines herbes* and a flavorful addition to salads and sauces. A perfect seasoning for poultry and fish.

thyme Tiny greenish leaves on small sprigs with a pungent, lemony aroma and taste. Especially good with grilled meats and poultry.

Michael cuts rosemary in his garden in Malibu.

kim's world-famous salad

Serves 4

This salad is my wife's favorite mix, served at all of our lunches and dinners. I call it world-famous because I make it for friends in France, Italy, Spain, and England, and none of them can believe how great it tastes. Spring, summer, fall, or winter, Kim has it at least once a day. The mix varies only with the season. In summer, she will add a touch of red with a few wedges of glorious, meaty, fresh-from-the-garden tomatoes. Otherwise, the salad is a symphony of greens and whites dabbed with just enough vinaigrette to moisten. One great big handful per person will make a perfect side salad, but nobody can eat just one.

1 head Bibb lettuce, leaves separated but left whole

1 to 3 small bunches watercress, different kinds (cultivated, hydroponic, or wild), tough stems removed

1 large or 2 small heads Belgian endive, leaves chopped

1 bunch arugula leaves, stemmed, leaves left whole

1 bulb fennel, with fronds, bulb thinly shaved with a mandoline, whole fronds separated from stalks

1 bunch scallions, both white and green parts, thinly sliced crosswise

1 sweet onion, shaved with a mandoline

1 hothouse cucumber, peeled, halved lengthwise, and cut into ¼-inch slices

4 large white button mushrooms, thinly sliced

White Wine–Dijon Vinaigrette (recipe follows)

¼ cup finely chopped fresh chives

Wash and dry all the salad leaves. Pile them into a large salad bowl. Add all the sliced and shaved vegetables and mushrooms. Just before serving, add enough of the vinaigrette to coat the leaves well and toss thoroughly. Place an equal portion on each of 4 salad plates. Sprinkle with those chives!

white wine–dijon vinaigrette

I'll often add a tablespoon of chives and a squeeze of lemon juice to this dressing, a favorite of my wife, Kim.

¼ cup dry white wine vinegar or champagne vinegar

1 tablespoon Dijon mustard

Sea salt and freshly ground black pepper

¾ cup extra-virgin olive oil

Combine the vinegar and mustard in a small mixing bowl. Add enough salt and pepper to dust the surface lightly and whisk to combine. Whisking constantly, add the oil in a thin stream, beating until well emulsified. Taste and adjust the seasonings with more salt and pepper if necessary.

salade verte

Serves 4

Salade Verte is my classic green side salad. Simple and direct—
no fussiness. Don't forget those chopped chives!

6 small bunches mâche, leaves separated

2 heads limestone lettuce, leaves separated but left whole

1 bunch arugula leaves, separated

Michael's Vinaigrette (recipe follows)

1 tablespoon chopped chives

In a large salad bowl, combine the mâche with the limestone and arugula, tossing to blend. Just before serving, add enough of the vinaigrette to coat the leaves well and toss thoroughly.

Place an equal portion on each of 4 salad plates. Sprinkle with chives.

michael's vinaigrette

This dressing is the classic light red-wine vinaigrette, with an added oomph of shallots.

¼ cup red wine vinegar

1 tablespoon minced shallot

Sea salt and freshly ground black pepper

¾ cup extra-virgin olive oil

Put the vinegar and shallot in a small mixing bowl. Add enough salt and pepper to coat the surface lightly and whisk. Whisking constantly, add the oil in a thin stream, beating until well emulsified. Taste and adjust the seasonings with more salt and pepper if necessary.

frisée aux lardons

Serves 4

Frisée aux Lardons is classically French. The lardons add a sweet smokiness to the slightly bitter green. I use only the pale inner yellowish leaves of the frisée, as I find the darker green leaves too bitter.

4 heads frisée, yellow-white interior leaves only, separated and trimmed

Four ¼-inch-thick slices fine-quality bacon, cut crosswise into ¼-inch pieces

3 tablespoons sherry wine vinegar

2 tablespoons Dijon mustard

¾ cup peanut oil

Sea salt and freshly ground black pepper

1 tablespoon chopped fresh chives

Put the frisée in a large salad bowl. Set aside.

Place the bacon in a frying pan over medium heat. Fry, stirring frequently, for about 5 minutes, or until crisp and golden brown. Using a slotted spoon, transfer the bacon to a double layer of paper towel to drain.

Leaving the frying pan on the heat, whisk the vinegar into the rendered bacon fat, stirring and scraping to deglaze the pan deposits. When the pan is deglazed, remove from the heat and whisk in the mustard, followed by the oil. Taste and season with salt if necessary along with pepper to taste.

Pour the warm dressing over the frisée and toss well. Place an equal portion on each of 4 salad plates. Garnish with the reserved bacon lardons and chives. Serve immediately.

NOTE: This salad makes a terrific brunch dish with the addition of 2 softly poached eggs (or an appetizer with only 1 egg) nestled into the top of the frisée. (Try to find fertile eggs, which have deep orange yolks and taste and look better.) You can also mix equal portions of Belgian endive and water-cress to use as the salad base (the famous *Cresson-Endive* Salad). Sauté a shallot or two in the bacon fat, then add the vinegar and proceed with the recipe.

> "Michael's never disappoints you. I've never walked in there and come away going, 'Yech!' It's a welcoming restaurant where they don't necessarily look at your latest ratings. They like you when you're up, and they like you when you're down."
>
> —JOAN RIVERS, COMEDIENNE

vegetables

When I first opened Michael's in Santa Monica, I flew in all of my produce from the markets of Rungis, near Paris. Bit by bit, I got local farmers in Southern California to plant those same varieties. Ten years later, when I opened in New York, I flew in produce daily from Los Angeles—and on my New York menu in those early years was my iconic salad of "San Fernando Valley Greens." Today anyone can find high-quality produce almost anywhere.

I know that I am spoiled by the proximity of Michael's Santa Monica to the farmers' market, where I can always find something in season that will be the prefect accent on any plate.

It is not necessarily as easy for people who don't live in Southern California to get farm-fresh vegetables all year long. But if you stick with the seasons and cook what flourishes during that period, you'll do just fine. It never ceases to surprise me how good supermarket produce sections are today, too.

"Michael understands that food needs to be connected with a cultural and an agricultural experience. When food is just out there, disconnected, it doesn't have a richness or beauty. Michael loves art, and he loves farmers, and he has made that love part of the dining experience."

—ALICE WATERS, EXECUTIVE CHEF AND OWNER, CHEZ PANISSE, BERKELEY, CALIFORNIA

artichokes

My preference is for the tiny, almost walnut-sized buds, what are commonly referred to as baby artichokes. I like them in a salad, thinly shaved, and eaten raw, preferably with some hard cheese or charcuterie (see page 143). But I also enjoy a beautifully steamed, large artichoke served with that ubiquitous melted sweet butter or Hollandaise Sauce (page 203).

baby artichokes with parmesan, meyer lemon, and extra-virgin olive oil

Serves 4

You need tiny, absolutely fresh baby artichokes to make this salad, which is Italian in feeling and Californian in execution. I use dark green cold-pressed, California olive oil. It is one of my favorites, simplicity in its most defined form.

8 pristine baby artichokes

5 tablespoons spicy green extra-virgin olive oil

Juice of 1 Meyer lemon

Sea salt and freshly ground black pepper

¼-pound chunk Parmesan cheese

Wash the artichokes under cold running water. Trim off any blemishes and prickly leaves. Using a sharp knife, trim the stem end and cut about ¼ inch from the top to make an even shape. Pat the artichokes dry.

With a very sharp knife, cut the artichokes lengthwise into almost thin slices. Place the slices in a shallow dish. Add 3 tablespoons of the oil along with the lemon juice and salt and pepper to taste.

Place an equal portion of the seasoned artichokes on each of 4 salad plates. Shave about 4 long strips of Parmesan over the artichokes on each plate. Sprinkle sea salt over the top and drizzle the remaining oil around the plates. Serve immediately.

> "Michael is all about the best possible ingredients being treated in a fundamentally elegant, simple way. That's something every home cook can learn to do— and get away from the complexity that, I think, has historically stultified cooking."
>
> —Tim Zagat, cofounder, cochair, and ceo, zagat survey

asparagus

I use four types of asparagus—European white, jumbo green, French wild, and American wild. I first experienced the white variety when I was a teenager in France. I was completely entranced and vowed to eat it every spring for the rest of my life, a vow that I'm glad to say I have kept. And it always appears on the spring restaurant menus at Michael's.

Although many have tried to (and do) grow white asparagus in the Americas, the finest still come from France, Germany, Austria, and Holland. When perfect, it has a magnificent taste, somewhat like an artichoke heart, mild, slightly sweet, but ultimately indefinable.

White asparagus is the same plant as green asparagus. However, it is grown underground in ridged rows covered by earth and black plastic sheeting or some other material that excludes light. The result is a pearly white spear available from mid-April through roughly the third week of June, the season ending on John the Baptist Day.

Like its white cousin, jumbo green asparagus will yield about eight stalks to a pound. It has much of the same nutty flavor of smaller green or purple spears, and it is simply gigantic. The spears are quite dramatic on the plate, and their crisp texture and sweet flavor need little more than a bit of saltiness or acid as an accent. These green jumbos can also be grilled, a cooking technique that I think heightens their rich flavor.

Wild American asparagus is available only in the spring, usually at farmers' markets. It is very thin and more distinctly flavored than the cultivated variety, but it can be cooked in the same manner (requiring less time) as the others. Wild French asparagus has a very thin stalk with a bulbous tip. The flavor is fabulous, heady and earthy.

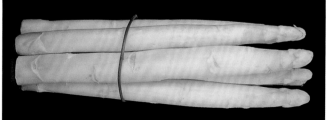

white and green asparagus with beurre blanc, serrano ham, and parmesan cheese

Serves 4

It's always a great moment when the white and jumbo green asparagus arrive to announce the beginning of spring. As is, this recipe is wonderful. But when they're in season, I can't resist adding sautéed fava beans and morels—or simply shaved black truffles with fresh asparagus alone.

8 spears white asparagus

8 spears green asparagus

½ cup dry white wine

½ cup champagne vinegar

1 tablespoon minced shallots

2 tablespoons heavy cream

1 cup (2 sticks) salted butter, chilled and cut into cubes

3 tablespoons fresh Meyer lemon juice

Sea salt and freshly ground black pepper

8 thin slices Serrano ham

Large chunk Parmesan cheese for grating

2 tablespoons minced fresh chives

Using a swivel vegetable peeler and starting just below the tip, carefully peel the outer skin from each asparagus spear. Peel a little more from the middle to the end to remove any toughness. There should be no evident peel. Cut about 1 inch (or more, as necessary to cut off the fibrous base) from the end of each spear. Because they are so expensive, you should work slowly and carefully, as you don't want to lose even one spear. Rinse each spear under cold, running water as you peel and place it on a double layer of paper towel to drain. Set aside.

To make the beurre blanc, combine the wine, vinegar, and shallot in a small saucepan over medium-high heat. Bring to a boil and boil for about 10 minutes or until all of the liquid has evaporated but the shallots remain moist, taking care that the pan does not burn. Add the cream and return to a simmer. Lower the heat to medium and, whisking constantly, begin adding the butter, a piece at a time. When all of the butter has been incorporated, whisk in 1 tablespoon of the lemon juice and season with salt and pepper to taste. Remove from the heat and keep warm.

Place a large shallow saucepan (a rondeau) of cold water over high heat. Add the remaining 2 tablespoons lemon juice and a good helping of salt and bring to a boil. Place the asparagus in the pan and cook for about 10 minutes or until the spears are tender and almost translucent. Check the degree of doneness constantly by poking the thickest part with the point of a small sharp knife. Do not overcook; a bit of crunchiness is good.

Remove from the heat and, using tongs, carefully transfer the asparagus to a double layer of paper towel to drain.

Place 2 spears of each type of asparagus down the center of each of 4 luncheon plates. Spoon an equal portion of beurre blanc over the asparagus. Lay 2 slices of ham over each pair of asparagus spears. Using a cheese grater, grate a generous helping of Parmesan cheese over the top. Garnish with chives. Serve immediately.

> "It's just really nice to have lunch in the shadow of a Diebenkorn."
>
> —JESSE KORNBLUTH, AUTHOR, EDITOR, AND CREATOR OF HEADBUTLER.COM

white asparagus with grilled treviso, mâche, and balsamic vinaigrette

Serves 4

Treviso is a slender, elongated, red-leafed radicchio. Grilling brings out its deeply rich and earthy flavor, a great complement to the sweet asparagus. The tender mâche and the robust balsamic vinaigrette complete the palette.

12 spears white asparagus

4 small heads Treviso

Approximately 3 tablespoons extra-virgin olive oil

Sea salt and freshly ground black pepper

4 bunches mâche

Balsamic Vinaigrette (recipe follows)

Large chunk Parmesan cheese for grating

2 tablespoons minced fresh chives

Using a swivel peeler and starting just below the tip, carefully peel the outer skin from each asparagus spear. Peel a little more from the middle to the end to remove any toughness. There should be no evident peel. Cut about 1 inch (or more, as necessary to cut off the fibrous base) from the end of each spear. Because they are so expensive, you should work slowly and carefully, as you don't want to lose even one spear. Rinse each spear under cold running water as you peel and place on a double layer of paper towel to drain.

Place salted water in a pan large enough to hold the asparagus easily. Place the pan over medium-high heat. Bring the water to a boil and add the asparagus. Boil for about 10 minutes or until the asparagus is crisp-tender. Immediately remove from the heat and, using tongs, carefully transfer the asparagus to a plate. Pat dry with paper towel.

Preheat and oil the grill.

Split each Treviso in half lengthwise. Rinse well under cold running water and place on a double layer of paper towel to drain. Pat dry.

Place the Treviso on a plate, drizzle with enough of the oil to moisten, and season with salt and pepper to taste. Place on the hot grill and cook, turning occasionally, for about 5 minutes or until nicely charred around the edges. Using tongs, transfer to a platter to cool slightly.

Place 3 spears of asparagus on each of 4 luncheon plates. Crisscross 2 pieces of Treviso across the asparagus. Make a small mound of mâche on top of the Treviso. Drizzle vinaigrette over the salad and around the plates. Sprinkle with grated Parmesan and chives. Serve immediately.

-----

balsamic vinaigrette

½ cup balsamic vinegar

½ cup extra-virgin olive oil

Sea salt and freshly ground black pepper

Place the vinegar in a small bowl. Whisking constantly, add the oil in a thin stream, beating until well emulsified. Season with salt and pepper to taste.

jumbo asparagus with a seven-minute egg and black truffles

Serves 4

This recipe makes a super breakfast or brunch treat. It's a terrific combination of flavors and textures—the slightly sweet asparagus, the familiarity of warm eggs, the crunch and bite of the raw shallots, and the elegance of the truffles.

12 spears jumbo green asparagus

Sea salt

4 extra-large eggs, at room temperature

2 shallots, minced

1 large fresh black truffle

2 tablespoons chopped fresh chives

Using a swivel vegetable peeler and starting just below the tip, carefully peel the outer skin from each asparagus spear. Peel a little more, from the middle to the end to remove any toughness. There should be no evident peel. Cut about 1 inch (or more, as necessary to cut off the fibrous base) from the end of each spear. Because they are so expensive, you should work slowly and carefully, as you don't want to lose even one spear. Rinse each spear under cold running water as you peel and place it on a double layer of paper towel to drain. Set aside.

Place salted water in a pan large enough to hold the asparagus easily. Place the pan over medium-high heat. Bring the water to a boil and add the asparagus. Boil for about 10 minutes or until the asparagus is crisp-tender. Immediately remove from the heat and, using tongs, carefully transfer the asparagus to a plate. Pat dry with paper towel.

While the asparagus is cooking, prepare the eggs.

Bring a medium saucepan of water to a boil over high heat. Add the eggs and bring to a soft boil. Set your kitchen timer and cook at a low boil for exactly 7 minutes. Remove from the heat and drain. You don't want to cook the eggs at a hard boil, which may crack the shells and toughen the eggs. Carefully peel and, using a sharp knife, cut the eggs crosswise into thin slices.

Place 3 spears of asparagus in the center of each of 4 salad plates. Sprinkle an equal portion of sliced egg and minced shallot across the center of the asparagus. Shave an equal portion of black truffle over the asparagus. Sprinkle each plate with chives and serve.

When I first opened Michael's, I kept asking local farmers for baby beets like the ones I had seen in France. It took a lot of persuasion, but once farmers saw that the interest and market were there, a whole new beet ball game began.

I used to hate beets—the canned, serrated, mostly red ones. Once in Bryce Canyon National Park, when I was a child, I refused to eat my beets. I was sent to the car, where I kept thinking, Those didn't taste like real beets . . . Years later in France, I found that I was right.

A major improvement on serrated slices of canned beets, Chioggias or candy stripes, albinos, skinny guys called Formanovas, glorious orange and yellow globes, and delectable baby reds are now commonplace. But there are also black, rosy pink, ivory, and brick-red beets grown in shapes ranging from great huge rounds to tiny orbs and cylindrical tapers.

I roast, steam, or boil beets. Their sweet, earthy flavor complements salty ingredients such as olives, tannic cheeses, pungent spices, bitter greens (just like those that come from beets themselves), or acidic fruit. They are really multipurpose.

Eat your beets!

goat cheese with beets and white wine–dijon vinaigrette
Serves 4

The American goat cheeses produced by Coach Farm or Laura Chenel, or a Montrachet-style fresh goat cheese, will make a fabulous version of this classic French salad. The salad is traditionally prepared with *cabécou de Rocamadour,* a small, artisanal or farmstead goat cheese carrying the *Appellation d'Origine Contrôlée*, which assures buyers that it is a product of high quality produced within a specific region (in this case Rocamadour) by an approved method. It has a thin rind with a creamy interior that offers a lingering taste of hazelnuts, a perfect complement to the sweet beets.

The number of beets required will vary greatly depending on their size. If you use larger Chioggas or golden beets, you may need only 1 per person, while you may need 2 to 3 smaller baby beets per person.

4 large beets or 8 to 12 small beets, in assorted colors

4 small heads mâche or 4 cups of other baby greens

Four 2-ounce rounds Rocamadour or other goat cheese

White Wine–Dijon Vinaigrette (page 28)

2 tablespoons minced fresh chives

Preheat the oven to 375°F. Trim off the greens and the root ends of the beets. Rinse the beets and wrap them securely in aluminum foil. Place in a baking pan in the oven and bake until tender when pierced with a skewer, 20 to 40 minutes, depending on size. Remove from the oven, let them cool to room temperature, and unwrap. Peel them with a paring knife and cut them crosswise, into ¼-inch slices. Cut any beet ends or small slices into julienne to be used as garnish on the finished plate. Set aside.

Fan an equal number of beet slices around the edge of each of 4 salad plates. Pile the mâche in the middle and place a piece of cheese in the center of the mâche. (If using baby greens, toss them with some of the vinaigrette. Place an equal portion of the greens on each of 4 plates. Place a cheese round in the center and fan an equal number of beet slices and julienne over the greens.) Drizzle with the vinaigrette and chives. Serve immediately.

bell peppers and chili peppers

I love the incredible variety of bell peppers and chili peppers I find in farmers' markets. To me, red, orange, and yellow bell peppers go beautifully together. I also use more than a dozen different kinds of chilies, both sweet and hot, in a wide range of colors, shapes, and sizes.

To prepare bell peppers or chili peppers for use in salads or as a side, I wash them well and then cut them in half lengthwise and seed them. Depending on their size, I cut each half into 3 or 4 pieces. I season the strips with a bit of olive oil, salt, and pepper and place them, skin side down, on a hot grill (you can also place them under a preheated broiler, skin up). I grill, without turning, for just a few minutes, as I like the skin side to be slightly charred and the flesh still a bit crisp.

grilled bell peppers
with other summer vegetables

Serves 4

Red, yellow, and orange bell peppers shine on the grill. Grill them along with other summer vegetables such as sweet onions, green asparagus, eggplant, corn, squash, squash blossoms (stuffed with goat cheese), radicchio and Treviso, or early potatoes, and you have a perfect side dish to serve with any main course.

Although I use the word "summer" here, I grill vegetables all year long. I think that this method brings out their richest, sweetest flavor. When combining vegetables on the grill, choose textures and flavors that complement one another as well as your main dish.

Cook whatever vegetables you like, seasoned with great olive oil and salt and pepper. I generally figure about 6 pieces per person.

Stone fruits such as peaches and nectarines are also excellent grilled, first lightly brushed with clarified butter (see Note, page 48). They make an easy dessert served with crème fraîche or a soft pungent cheese and some sparkling wine or dessert wine.

I have listed ingredients that I think are sufficient for 4 people, but feel free to improvise amounts and combinations. Just remember to use high-quality olive oil and fresh herbs.

Preheat the grill.

Place the vegetables on a platter and generously season with oil and salt and pepper to taste, tossing to coat.

Place the vegetables on the grill, without crowding, making sure the peppers are skin side down. Grill, turning everything but the peppers occasionally, until nicely charred, about 6 minutes total.

Using tongs, carefully transfer the vegetables to a platter. Drizzle with additional oil and sprinkle with herbs. Serve hot or at room temperature.

1 each red, yellow, and orange bell pepper, cored, seeded, and quartered

1 zucchini, sliced lengthwise

1 yellow summer squash, sliced lengthwise

16 cherry tomatoes

4 thin lengthwise slices Asian eggplant

4 large slices sweet onion, such as Walla Walla, Vidalia, Texas Sweet, or Maui

1 large head radicchio, quartered, or 2 small heads, halved

12 small new red potatoes or white peewee potatoes

Extra-virgin olive oil

Salt and freshly ground black pepper

3 tablespoons chopped fresh herbs

> "In a way, Michael is very much an artist. He's involved in making the restaurant and the food, the way it's served and presented, into something that hasn't been before. I appreciate his aesthetic a lot."
>
> —ROBERT GRAHAM, SCULPTOR

corn

What can I say about fresh corn—except that there is almost nothing better than an ear right from the stalk, thrown on the grill still in its husk, and eaten slathered with sweet butter and salt and pepper?

Now some specifics. I use two types, summer and California white spring corn. For the sweetest flavor, search for corn with the smallest kernels. Try to buy your corn from a farm stand or the farmers' market, where you'll get the freshest product.

grilled corn on the cob

Serves 4

In the summertime, I grill corn two ways, in or out of the husks. Both methods are fabulous.

8 ears white corn

Salted butter, at room temperature, *or* extra-virgin olive oil

Salt and freshly ground black pepper

Preheat the grill.

Meanwhile, place the unhusked ears of corn in a bucket or sink filled with cold water. Soak for 30 minutes.

Place the ears of corn in their husks directly on the hot grill.

Grill, turning frequently, until the husks are evenly browned, about 10 minutes.

Remove from the grill and carefully pull off the husks and silk. Serve immediately with lots of butter, salt, and pepper.

Alternatively, husk the raw corn without soaking, brush it generously with olive oil, season with salt and pepper, and grill, turning frequently, until the kernels are nicely browned on all sides, 5 to 6 minutes.

white corn blini with caviar

Serves 4

I am absolutely wild about these sweet, delicate corn cakes. They make a wonderful base for salty caviar, and chives add just the right hint of green. You can also use corn blini as an hors d'oeuvre base for smoked salmon. If I'm passing the hors d'oeuvres, as in this recipe, I make bite-size one-inch blini; for a sit-down first course, make the blini three inches in diameter.

3 ears fresh white corn, shucked

2 cups heavy cream

1 large egg

1½ tablespoons corn oil

¾ cup all-purpose flour, sifted

½ tablespoon baking soda

¼ cup chopped fresh chives, plus more for garnish

Sea salt and freshly ground black pepper

Approximately ¼ cup clarified butter (see Note)

Approximately 4 ounces caviar

Using a sharp knife, carefully cut the corn kernels from the cobs. Place the kernels in a medium saucepan and add the cream. Warm over medium heat, cover, and bring to a simmer. Lower the heat and cook for about 5 minutes or just until the kernels are tender. Remove from the heat.

Drain the kernels through a fine sieve, reserving the liquid. Place half of the kernels in a blender. Add the egg and begin processing. With the motor running, add the oil along with just enough of the cooking liquid to make a fairly thin purée.

Combine the flour and baking soda in a mixing bowl. Whisk in the corn purée, beating until the mixture has a pancake batter texture, adding additional cooking liquid if necessary. Fold in the chives and remaining corn and season with salt and pepper to taste.

Line a baking sheet with parchment paper. Set aside.

When ready to serve, heat a griddle (or nonstick frying pan) over medium heat. Brush generously with clarified butter. When very hot but not smoking, ladle a scant 1 tablespoon batter into the hot pan for each blin. You want the batter to form about a 1-inch circle. Cook for 30 seconds, then carefully flip and cook the remaining side for 30 seconds or until cooked through and lightly colored.

Place the cooked blini in a single layer on the parchment-lined sheet and keep warm until all of the blini are cooked.

Serve warm, garnished with a generous scoop of caviar and a sprinkle of chives.

NOTE: Clarified butter is salted butter that has been very slowly melted to separate out the milk solids and water. The clear bright yellow liquid that is left can be used to cook at high temperatures, as it will then have a much higher smoke point than solid butter.

> "If somebody said to Michael, 'You must give me a brief description of what you are trying to achieve,' I guess the answer for him would be 'Simply to produce good food.' "
>
> —GEORGE LANG, CULINARY CONSULTANT AND OWNER, CAFÉ DES ARTISTES, NEW YORK

fava bean, white corn, and wild mushroom succotash

Serves 4

This dish is one of my favorites for spring. Fortunately, in California, we get early spring corn and beautiful chanterelles and morels that make this combination possible. For those of you who aren't so lucky, make it in the summer, using any wild mushrooms or even cultivated shiitakes that are available.

1 pound fresh fava beans in the pod

3 tablespoons salted butter

½ pound morels or chanterelles, cleaned thoroughly and trimmed

Sea salt and freshly ground black pepper

¼ cup finely diced sweet onion, such as Walla Walla, Vidalia, Texas Sweet, or Maui

Kernels from 2 ears fresh white corn

1 tablespoon chopped fresh tarragon

Remove the fava beans from their pods. Set aside.

Bring a medium saucepan of water to a boil over high heat. Add the beans and blanch for no more than 1 minute for the largest beans. Remove from the heat and drain well. Rinse under cold running water and pat dry.

Working with one bean at a time and using your fingertips, pull a bit of the tough skin from the top of the bean and then push the bean out of the skin. It should come out whole. Set the beans aside.

Heat 1 tablespoon of the butter in a medium sauté pan over medium heat. Add the mushrooms and season with salt and pepper to taste. Sauté for about 4 minutes or just until softened. Using a slotted spoon, transfer the mushrooms to a plate.

Add another tablespoon of butter to the sauté pan. Add the onions and season with salt. Let the onions sweat their liquid for about 3 minutes or until soft but still colorless. Add the remaining butter along with the corn and sauté for 3 minutes. Stir in the fava beans and continue to sauté for another couple of minutes. Add the mushrooms and cook for another 2 minutes. Season with salt and pepper to taste. Stir in the tarragon and serve immediately or keep warm until ready to serve.

fava beans

I remember eating my first fava beans in Brittany. I was used to nasty canned lima beans, and I couldn't believe how *formidable* fresh *feves* were—*une merveille.*

Fava beans are labor-intensive to prepare. Most people run from "fava detail," but I've found that you can usually draft the same friends who enjoy shucking peas or plucking thyme leaves from their sprigs. And all that hard work is really worth it. Peel on, dude!

fiddlehead ferns

I have always been intrigued by fiddlehead ferns, which have a rather crunchy texture and a flavor that is reminiscent of very young asparagus and look almost prehistoric. When I was a boy, they were mostly a locally foraged, early springtime treat, but today you can find them in farmers' markets and the produce sections of good-sized food stores, as well as on the Internet.

spring vegetable sauté

Serves 4

Spring vegetables are extremely tender and sweet, as they have not had a chance to develop their mature texture and deepest flavor. It is for this reason that I generally give them a quick, simple sauté in butter with just a bit of salt and black pepper to pull out their full flavor.

I start with equal portions of a few vegetables such as fiddlehead ferns, peas and pea shoots, and fava beans and then accent them with ramps, red or white spring onions, morels, chanterelles, shiitakes, or other wild mushrooms. You will need about one pound of vegetables to serve four people.

You can, of course, sauté just one spring vegetable. Asparagus, endives, baby leeks, tiny fennel bulbs, and spring spinach all lend themselves to a simple sauté. Even ramps and spring onions are sweet enough to serve alone or accented by mushrooms and fresh herbs.

Some summer vegetables that also sauté beautifully are baby turnips, haricots verts, white corn, and cherry tomatoes.

I like the pure vegetable flavor. However, for something different, finish with a toss of fresh herbs.

Heat the butter in a large sauté pan over medium heat. Add the morels (if using) and sauté for about 4 minutes or until slightly crisp. Add the ramps, season with salt and pepper to taste, and sauté for about 4 minutes or just until beginning to soften. Add the fiddleheads. Allow to cook for 3 minutes. If using peas, toss in the pea shoots. Taste and, if necessary, add more salt and pepper.

Remove from the heat and toss in the herb(s). Serve immediately.

3 tablespoons salted butter

¼ pound very small morels, cleaned thoroughly and trimmed (optional)

4 ramps, cut crosswise into thin slices, or 3 spring onions, peeled and diced

Sea salt and freshly ground black pepper

1 pound fiddlehead ferns, cleaned (or 2 cups shelled English peas or peeled fava beans, see page 49, or a mixture of fiddleheads, peas, and favas)

Couple of handfuls pea shoots, if available (optional)

1 tablespoon chopped fresh mint, flat-leaf parsley, or tarragon (optional)

"With Michael, everything is always an adventure. The greatest gift a host can give his guests is to have a good time himself, which puts the guest at ease. You always feel that Michael is having as much fun as you are."

—D. CROSBY ROSS, FORMER EXECUTIVE DIRECTOR, AMERICAN INSTITUTE OF WINE & FOOD

haricots verts

Harry's Berries is a Santa Monica Farmers' Market institution and my source for haricots verts. Pristine produce and berries are its forte. Very elegant and thin, haricots verts or French beans are a type of green bean traditionally grown in France but now available almost everywhere. They are quite sweet, with an inviting crisp-tender texture. Although delicious simply steamed or sautéed, they also make a wonderful salad. In France, they are often garnished in springtime with the last of the black truffles and a slab o' foie gras, plus a tasty mustard vinaigrette.

steamed haricots verts
Serves 4

How much easier can a recipe get? Sweet, creamy butter is the perfect accent for tender-crisp French beans.

1 pound haricots verts, trimmed of stem ends

Melted unsalted butter

Salt and freshly ground black pepper

Bring about 2 inches water to boil in the bottom half of a steamer. Place the beans in a single layer in the top half. Cover and steam for about 5 minutes or until crisp-tender. Depending on the size of your steamer, you may have to work in batches, as it is imperative that the beans be in a single layer; otherwise the bottom layer will cook long before the top one. Place the beans on a serving plate and drizzle with butter. Season with salt and pepper, tossing to coat. Serve immediately.

"When you want to entertain like Michael at home, be organized so that you keep all the balls in the air—the music, the art, the mix of people, and the food—nice and balanced is what Michael does best."

—HARVEY FRIEND, GENERAL MANAGER, THE WILSHIRE RESTAURANT, LOS ANGELES, AND FORMER GENERAL MANAGER OF MICHAEL'S SANTA MONICA

sweet onions, ramps, scallions, and shallots

Sweet onions are much, much more than an aromatic addition to recipes; they, and their many cousins, are vegetables in their own right, pure and simple. I use an array of sweet onions in my kitchen, along with scallions, red and white spring onions, and ramps—not to mention shallots, my choice of aromatic for sauces.

Scallions are those ubiquitous thin, immature onions with long, edible greens and a small white root end that is an unformed bulb. They are also known as green onions in some parts of the country. Spring onion is the term generally ascribed to onions that have moved up the ladder of development so that they have a defined bulb. They get their name from the fact that they are harvested in the spring, before they have a chance to mature. They are quite tender, with a faint hint of heat, and are perfect for spring vegetable sautés or grilling whole.

Ramps, also known as wild leeks, are most commonly found along the eastern seaboard during the early spring. Their odor is almost overpowering, and if eaten raw their flavor is pungent. However, once cooked, ramps are very mild and quite sweet. Up until the mid-1980s, they were unknown in other parts of the country and never found on restaurant menus. They are now foraged and shipped overnight as they star on spring menus throughout the United States.

My favorite onions are large, crisp, sweet Mauis, Walla Wallas, or Vidalias. Besides these three, you might find Texas Sweets, Coachella Sweets (California), Grand Canyon Sweets, and so forth. As you might guess, their names come from their growing area. I find that they get even mellower when touched with heat, so I often grill or roast them for use as an accent with grilled meats, fish, or chicken. However, they are very mild, juicy, and tender, either raw or cooked. And because they tend to be large, sweet onions make great fried onion rings, as they pull apart into thick loops (see Crispy Maui Onions, page 107).

onion confit

Makes about 2 cups

I use this garnish constantly. The sweet onions melded into the rich butter create a perfect accent for meats, poultry, or game.

1 medium sweet onion, such as Maui or Vidalia, peeled, trimmed, and thinly sliced

1 cup (2 sticks) unsalted butter, cut into 1-inch pieces

2 tablespoons water

Fresh lemon juice to taste

Coarse salt and freshly ground black pepper

Combine the onion with one piece of the butter and the water in a small heavy-bottomed saucepan over low heat. Cover and cook, stirring occasionally, for about 15 minutes or until the onion is lightly browned but not falling apart.

Remove the pan from the heat and carefully pour off all the liquid.

Return the pan to low heat and begin adding the remaining butter, a few pieces at a time, beating in with a wooden spoon. Do not put in additional butter until the previous bit has been completely incorporated.

Taste and add a touch of lemon juice to brighten the flavor. Add salt and pepper to taste.

Remove from the heat and serve warm.

"Above all, in the two restaurants, Michael has created and maintained a scene. You feel comfortable when you walk in there. You know what to expect. It's a total experience. Michael is a restaurateur, a front man, one of the few in the great tradition, and there are very few of them left, and we desperately need them. He's a man who controls his dominion. And you know you're going to be treated like a lady or a gentleman. I have never ever heard or read where someone was shuffled off to Siberia at Michael's."

—James Villas,
AUTHOR AND FORMER FOOD AND WINE EDITOR
TOWN & COUNTRY

grilled vidalia
or red or white spring onions

Serves 4

The grill always intensifies the sweetness of onions, especially already sweet varieties such as Vidalias or the very fresh-tasting, tender early onions of spring.

3 large Vidalia or other sweet onions, trimmed, *or* 12 red or white spring onions, halved lengthwise

Approximately ¼ cup extra-virgin olive oil

Sea salt and freshly ground black pepper

Preheat the grill or a stovetop ridged grill pan.

Using a sharp knife, cut the onions crosswise into ⅓-inch-thick slices.

Generously coat the onions with oil and season with salt and pepper to taste.

Place on the hot grill and cook, turning occasionally, for about 5 minutes or until nicely charred and tender. Remove from the grill and serve warm or at room temperature.

sautéed ramps, fiddleheads, and spring onions

Serves 4

This dish is spring in a pan. You can substitute asparagus for the fiddleheads, and you can add morels or other well-flavored mushrooms. The wonderful spring flavors will shine no matter what you do.

¾ pound fresh fiddlehead ferns

½ pound fresh ramps

½ pound fresh, small spring onions

2 tablespoons salted butter

2 tablespoons extra-virgin olive oil

Sea salt

2 tablespoons chopped fresh mint

Freshly ground black pepper

Trim the tough long stem from the ferns, leaving a coiled portion with about a 1-inch tail. Using your fingertips, rub the rough, papery brown skin from the coil. Rinse the cleaned ferns in cold running water.

Bring a medium saucepan of salted water to a boil over high heat. Add the ferns and boil for about 5 minutes or until tender. Test frequently, as the ferns must be fully cooked for their true flavor to shine. Drain well and set aside.

Slip the first layer of skin from the ramps and remove and discard any yellow or wilted leaves. Rinse well under cold running water.

Cut the ramps crosswise at the point where the stem meets the leaves. If the bulbs are very small, keep them whole. If not, cut them in half lengthwise. (You can discard the green leaves or cut them into julienne and add them to the dish.) Set aside.

Trim off and discard the top tough greens and outer skin from the spring onions. Rinse the onions under cold running water. Cut the onions in half lengthwise. Set aside.

Combine the butter and oil in a large sauté pan over medium heat. Add the ferns, ramps, and onions. Season with salt to taste, cover, and cook for 4 minutes. Uncover and sauté for about 3 minutes or until tender.

Remove from the heat. Add the mint, and pepper to taste, stirring to blend. Serve warm or at room temperature.

"What interests me about Michael's cooking is the freshness and simplicity of the food itself. It isn't oversauced. It's cooked to perfection. There's just a clean presentation."

—MIKE MEDAVOY, CHAIRMAN AND COFOUNDER, PHOENIX PICTURES

peas

Once upon a time, fresh peas were available for a couple of weeks in the spring, and for the rest of the year a cook had to be satisfied with gray-green mushy peas from a can. That changed when supermarkets began to sell frozen baby peas picked at the height of their season—the only frozen vegetables I use besides French fries. Then, as ingredient availability expanded in supermarkets, we began to see edible peas in their pod, such as snow peas or sugar snaps. Now even sweet, crisp, fresh pea shoots and pea sprouts are available to home cooks.

I love fresh English or garden peas during the spring. They are generally so sweet and tender that they can be eaten raw, straight from the pod. They are also wonderful in quick sautés or in a creamy risotto or orzo mix. The pods should be bright green, moist, and dense, with the peas firm and just as green. *Petits pois* are simply baby peas, taken from the pod before they have a chance to plump up. When using peas alone as a side vegetable, you should allow about ¾ pound of peas in the pod (about ¾ cup shelled peas) for every serving.

When spring peas are not in the market, I rely on frozen Green Giant Le Sueurs. They are a terrific substitute, sweet, tender, and delicious!

sautéed peas, morels, ramps, and peewee potatoes
Serves 4

I use this mix as a side dish for grilled meat or poultry all through the spring. The peas and potatoes are buttery, and the ramps sweeten as they cook, which leaves the earthy morels to make the perfect balance.

½ pound peewee potatoes

¼ pound fresh morels, cleaned thoroughly and trimmed

3 tablespoons salted butter

3 ramps, trimmed and cut crosswise into thin slices

2½ pounds fresh peas in the pod (about 2¼ cups peas)

Sea salt and freshly ground black pepper

2 tablespoons chopped fresh chives or flat-leaf parsley

To speed the preparation, place the potatoes in a medium saucepan with cold, salted water to cover by 1 inch. Place over medium-high heat and bring to a boil. Lower the heat and simmer for about 10 minutes or until the point of a small sharp knife easily pierces the center. The cooking time will depend upon the density and age of the potatoes. Remove from the heat and drain well. Pat dry and set aside until cool enough to handle.

When cool, cut the potatoes in half. Set aside.

If the morels are very large, cut in half lengthwise. Set aside.

Heat the butter in a medium sauté pan over medium heat. Add the morels and sauté for about 5 minutes or until slightly colored. Add the ramps and sauté for an additional 2 minutes. Stir in the peas and potatoes and season with salt and pepper to taste. Sauté for about 5 minutes or until the peas are tender and the potatoes have colored slightly. Remove from the heat, sprinkle with chives, and serve.

potatoes

Although my guests on both coasts love the mountains of French fries I serve, I also love to cook potatoes in many other ways. "Heirloom," "artisanal," "specialty," "gourmet," and "baby" are some of the terms now used to identify a group of, for the most part, small, delicately flavored, buttery potatoes. Many of them have made the trip from European markets, while others have been nurtured by small farmers here in the States.

Among the heirlooms, I mainly use fingerlings, rattes, and peewees. There are myriad types of fingerlings, but they all generally have fairly oblong shapes (hence their name) and thin skins. Some are smooth to the touch while others are quite knobby. They range in color from creamy yellow to purple. Rattes (also known as *la ratte, la reine,* or *la princesse*) are used in France to make a very rich, buttery potato purée. Peewees are tiny, round gems that cook up quickly either in the roasting pan or on the grill.

I most frequently grill or roast small potatoes. For grilling, I season whole potatoes with olive oil, salt, and pepper and place them on the outer edge of the grill so that they will have time to cook through without burning. It will usually take about 30 minutes.

For simple roasting, I place whole small potatoes in a roasting pan along with unpeeled garlic (usually 2 cloves per person), rosemary, and salt and pepper to taste. I roast them in a preheated 450°F oven for about 30 minutes or until I can easily insert the point of a small sharp knife into the center. You can't beat a potato seasoned with a little purée-soft caramelized roast garlic squeezed from its skin. And, finally, I like to sauté peewees in butter, then season them with chopped parsley, salt, and pepper, to serve as a side with a great steak or fish.

I generally grill or roast at least 1 pound of potatoes (or other root vegetables) for 4 people. Of course, if you want leftovers or are feeding a hungry crowd, adjust the amount accordingly.

"The thing that's really impressed me about Michael's over the years is that the service is always the same, excellent, with no favoritism. No one is bending over backward to give a celebrity his meal before anyone else."

—Jamie Niven,
VICE-CHAIRMAN, SOTHEBY'S

> "The great family favorite is the *frites*. There's nothing comparable to them anywhere. Particularly when we're with younger members of the family, Michael will order two or three extra servings."
>
> —RHETT AUSTELL,
> MICHAEL'S STEPFATHER

pommes frites

Serves 4

Believe this! I use frozen French fries to make my world-famous Michael's *pommes frites*. (Lamb's Supreme Mor-Fries is my brand of choice, but any good-quality shoestring cut will do.) I find frozen fries to be extraordinarily dependable for making crisp, golden deep-fried potatoes. This is not to say that you can't make great fries from scratch, but you have to cut them, soak them, and then triple-fry them. There is one more secret to great *pommes frites:* I use a mixture of rendered beef suet and canola oil for frying. (You can use only canola oil if you prefer.)

Enough rendered beef suet and canola oil, in equal amounts, to fill a deep-fat fryer to a depth of at least 5 inches

2 pounds fine-quality frozen French-fried potatoes

Sea salt

Line a baking pan with a double layer of paper towel. Set aside.

Place the suet and oil in a deep-fat fryer over high heat. Bring to 375°F on an instant-read thermometer.

Working in batches, add the potatoes to the hot fat without crowding the pan. Fry for about 5 minutes or until crisp and golden brown.

Transfer the potatoes to the paper towel–lined pan to drain off excess fat. Continue frying until all of the potatoes are cooked. If necessary, place clean paper towel on the baking pan to keep the potatoes from reabsorbing the oil. Sprinkle with sea salt just before serving.

matchstick potatoes

Serves 4

These are my favorite potatoes to serve with sautéed soft-shell crab, shad roe, or grilled quail. They are light, crisp, and so delicious. You need a mandoline or a Japanese vegetable slicer to make the ultrathin, matchstick strips—hand cutting is much, much too difficult. Again, I use a mixture of beef suet and canola for frying, but feel free to use all canola oil if you prefer.

Enough rendered beef suet and canola oil, in equal amounts, to fill a deep-fat fryer to a depth of at least 5 inches

2 large (about 1 pound) Idaho potatoes, peeled

Sea salt

Line a baking pan with a double layer of paper towel. Set aside.

Place the suet and oil in a deep-fat fryer over high heat. Bring to 375°F on an instant-read thermometer.

Using a mandoline, cut the potatoes into matchstick-sized strips.

Working in batches, add the potatoes to the hot fat without crowding the pan. Fry for about 2 minutes or until crisp and golden brown.

Transfer the potatoes to the paper towel–lined pan to drain off excess fat. Continue frying until all of the potatoes are cooked. If necessary, place clean paper towel on the baking pan to keep the potatoes from reabsorbing the oil. Sprinkle with sea salt just before serving.

gratin de pommes de terre

Serves 4

I like my potato gratins as simple and pure as possible. Use sweet, buttery potatoes, properly seasoned, and enough cream and milk to keep them rich and moist.

3 tablespoons salted butter plus more for buttering dish

2 pounds Idaho potatoes, peeled and cut crosswise into thin slices

1¼ cups heavy cream

1¼ cups whole milk

Sea salt and freshly ground black pepper

Preheat the oven to 350°F.

Generously butter the interior of a gratin dish or 2-quart casserole. Set aside.

Combine the potatoes with the cream and milk in a large shallow saucepan (a rondeau) and season with salt and pepper to taste. Place over medium heat and bring to a simmer. Simmer for about 5 minutes or just until the liquid begins to thicken slightly from the potato starch.

Remove the potatoes from the heat and carefully pour the mixture into the prepared dish.

Using a rubber spatula, carefully smooth the top, pressing lightly to submerge all the potatoes in the liquid. Place pats of butter on top and transfer to the preheated oven.

Bake for about 1 hour or until the potatoes are cooked through, the top is golden brown, and the edges are bubbling. Remove from the oven and allow to rest for about 10 minutes before cutting and serving.

potato galettes

Serves 4

Thin, crispy, golden brown potato cakes make a great base for my Filet Mignon with Seared Foie Gras, Black Truffle–Armagnac Sauce, and Potato Galettes (page 134). Its texture is a perfect foil for that rich dish. It is very helpful to use a mandoline or Japanese vegetable slicer to make thin, uniform potato slices. A knife works just fine too, but you need a steady hand.

> "Michael's got a giant, happy personality, and I think it shows in his food. He entertains people with his honesty and his smile. He is always on point, always there, always the constant gentleman, always. People respect that. If he wasn't as happy a person, his food wouldn't be as good."
>
> —DONNIE MADIA, CO-OWNER, BLACKBIRD, CHICAGO

4 medium (about 2 pounds) Idaho potatoes, peeled

¼ cup clarified butter (see Note, page 48)

Salt and freshly ground black pepper

1 teaspoon whole fresh thyme leaves

Line a baking pan with a double layer of paper towel. Set aside.

Using a sharp knife or a mandoline, cut the potatoes crosswise into slices about ⅛ inch thick.

Place a piece of parchment or waxed paper on a flat work surface. Using a pastry brush, lightly coat a 4-inch circle with some of the butter. Form the first galette by placing a slice of potato in the center of the circle. Arrange 8 or more slices around the center slice, overlapping in a circular pattern and with the edge of each slice touching the very center of the first slice. Using the pastry brush, lightly coat with clarified butter and season with salt, pepper, and thyme. Form 3 more galettes in the same way.

Heat the remaining clarified butter over medium-high heat in a frying pan large enough to hold the galettes without crowding. When very hot but not smoking, using a wide spatula, carefully transfer the galettes, one at a time, to the hot pan. Fry for 30 seconds and then lift the cakes slightly with the spatula to keep them from sticking. Continue to fry for about 2 minutes or until the bottom is golden brown. Using the spatula, carefully turn each galette and fry for 3 to 4 minutes or until golden brown.

Remove from the frying pan and transfer to the paper towel–lined pan to drain. Serve immediately or place on a parchment paper–lined baking sheet in a preheated low oven until ready to serve.

roasted potatoes and other root vegetables

Serves 4

Perhaps because I spend so much time in sunny California, I don't often roast vegetables. The grill is handy and the weather is usually welcoming, so there is no need to turn on the oven. However, around the fall and winter holidays, I retreat to my childhood in the east and fire up the oven.

Potatoes (usually fingerlings, peewees, or other small specialty potatoes, though larger Yukon Golds or russets will do if quartered), beets, onions, and white turnips are the root vegetables that I most often roast. I don't usually peel potatoes or beets. The potato skins roast up nicely, and if the beets are bigger than babies I just slip the skins from them after roasting. However, this recipe also works very well with winter squash, parsnips, carrots—in fact all dense vegetables. Roasting caramelizes the sugars, making it a terrific cooking method to bring out the most flavor in vegetables.

1 pound peewee or other small heirloom potatoes or root vegetables

Extra-virgin olive oil

6 cloves garlic, unpeeled (optional)

2 tablespoons chopped fresh rosemary (especially for potatoes), chives, flat-leaf parsley, basil, or mint

Coarse salt and freshly ground black pepper

Freshly grated zest of 1 lemon or orange (optional)

½ cup chopped hazelnuts or pecans (optional)

Preheat the oven to 400°F.

Place the vegetables in a baking dish. Add enough oil to coat the vegetables generously and leave a residue in the dish. If using garlic and rosemary, add them now. (If using softer herbs, add them once the vegetables have been removed from the oven.) Season with salt and pepper to taste.

Place in the preheated oven and roast until the point of a small sharp knife easily penetrates the thickest part, about 30 minutes for small vegetables and 45 for larger ones. If using the citrus zest and/or nuts, toss them in about 5 minutes before the vegetables are ready.

Remove from the oven. If garlic was used, push the flesh from the skins and toss it into the potatoes. Serve immediately.

arugula mashed potatoes

Serves 4

Arugula purée adds real zest to rich and creamy mashed potatoes, a great side dish for steaks and roasts. You can also make mashed potatoes without the arugula, following the same recipe.

3 ounces arugula leaves

Pinch sea salt plus more to taste

1 tablespoon plus 1 teaspoon olive oil

1 pound Yukon Gold potatoes

¾ cup heavy cream

2½ tablespoons salted butter, at room temperature

4 large cloves roasted garlic, or to taste

Freshly ground black pepper

Have ready a large bowl of ice water.

Bring a small saucepan of water to a boil over high heat. Add the arugula leaves along with a pinch of salt. Blanch for 15 seconds. Immediately drain and place in the ice water bath to stop the cooking.

When cool, drain well. Using your hands, squeeze out any excess water. Transfer the arugula to a blender or food processor fitted with the metal blade. With the motor running, slowly add the oil, processing to make a bright green purée. Transfer to a container, cover, and refrigerate. Bring to room temperature just before using.

Peel and quarter the potatoes. Place in a medium saucepan with cold salted water to cover by at least 2 inches. Place over high heat and bring to a boil. Lower the heat and simmer for about 15 minutes, or until the point of a small sharp knife easily penetrates the thickest part. Remove from the heat and drain well.

When the potatoes are almost ready, combine the cream and butter in a small saucepan over medium-low heat. Cook until the butter has melted and the mixture is very hot. Remove from the heat and keep warm.

Place the hot potatoes in a ricer and push through into a mixing bowl. Add the hot cream and beat with a wooden spoon until creamy. Add the garlic along with salt and pepper to taste, beating to incorporate. (Potatoes may be made up to this point and kept hot in the top half of a double boiler over very hot water.)

When ready to serve, gently fold the arugula purée into the potatoes. Do not incorporate it completely; you want bright green clouds scattered throughout the potatoes.

"Michael's is the grown-up equivalent of the junior high school luncheonette you went to after school. There they are, in their self-assigned seats: the football captain and the prom queen, the newspaper editor and the leading actors. And, in the back, the bright kid doing homework with the girl in glasses. That's Michael's."

—JESSE KORNBLUTH, AUTHOR, EDITOR, AND CREATOR OF HEADBUTLER.COM

spinach

Spinach is my wife Kim's favorite vegetable. It is available all year long, both the curly dark green and the smaller, paler "California" type. I think spinach always requires a touch of acid to bring out the best, highlighting its bright, refreshing flavor. Kim likes spinach plain; I always add a good dose of melted butter.

"I was on a TV show once where they set you up with a blind date. And I asked them to do my date at Michael's in Santa Monica. If the date didn't work out, at least I knew the food would be great."

—Phyllis Diller, comedienne

kim's spinach

Serves 4

Kim likes to eat this spinach as a first course, plain and simple, with a little lemon. I add butter. The spinach also goes very well with a piece of steamed or grilled fish.

2 pounds fresh spinach leaves, tough stems removed

Sea salt and freshly ground black pepper

Juice of 1 lemon

3 tablespoons melted salted butter or extra-virgin olive oil (for my half—Kim eats hers "au naturel")

Wash the spinach in a deep sink filled with cold water, splashing the water to agitate the leaves and remove any dirt. Wash as many times as necessary until the water is absolutely clear. Do not dry.

Place about ¼ cup water in a 12-inch sauté pan over medium-high heat. Add the wet spinach leaves. Season with salt and pepper to taste and continue to cook, tossing frequently, for about 4 minutes, or until just wilted.

Remove the spinach from the heat and, using a spatula, push out excess liquid. (You can also cover and tilt the pan to drain off excess liquid.)

Transfer to a serving plate, add the lemon juice, and season with more salt and pepper to taste. If using, pour melted butter or olive oil over the spinach and toss to coat. Serve warm or at room temperature.

squash blossoms

I have always enjoyed eating squash blossoms in the south of France and Italy and tried, in vain, for some years to get American farmers to bring them to market. They are now available during the summer when those wild and crazy zucchini plants are going nuts with multiplying madness. There are male and female blossoms, the females being those that have the tiny little squash attached; I like them because you get to eat the vegetable along with the blossom. Generally the blossoms will be zucchini flowers. If you have a garden, plant extra squash so you can eat the blossoms for weeks during the growing season.

stuffed squash blossoms
Serves 4

Squash blossoms are most often stuffed and deep-fried (my ale batter, page 103, makes a great coating). But I also simply grill them. Their flavor is so delicate that I think the grilling produces just the right pleasing touch of caramelization. Always season with lemon juice before serving.

20 squash blossoms with tiny squashlets attached

Approximately 1 cup fresh goat cheese, with or without herbs

Extra-virgin olive oil

Salt and freshly ground black pepper

Juice of 1 lemon (preferably Meyer)

Preheat and oil the grill.

Have ready a large bowl of ice water. Carefully open the petals of the squash and, one at a time, dip them into the ice water. Place the washed blossom, stem side up, on a double layer of paper towel to drain. Do all of this carefully, as the petals are fragile.

Cut the goat cheese into portions small enough to fill the blossoms generously. Place a portion of the cheese in each drained blossom, gently twisting the petals together to seal.

When all of the blossoms are filled, brush them lightly with the olive oil and season with salt and pepper to taste.

Place the blossoms on the preheated grill and cook, using tongs to turn occasionally, for about 5 minutes, or until the cheese has melted and the squashlets are crisp-tender.

Using tongs, transfer the blossoms to a serving plate. Drizzle with lemon juice and additional oil and serve warm.

tomatoes

Seasonality is the only thing that matters when talking tomatoes, for there is nothing to compare when they are summer-ripe, fresh from the vine. No matter how much agribusiness has tried, no one has duplicated their taste and smell.

At home and in the restaurants, we use a wonderful assortment of "heirloom" tomatoes—the term, now known by just about everyone who loves good food, refers to traditional old varieties that have been revived by enterprising farmers. They can be red, yellow, candy-striped, orange, gold, green, spotted, purple . . . you get the picture. They are usually oddly shaped, with their physical imperfections part of their beauty. Some are quite large, while others are almost the size of a cherry tomato. They are generally juicy and meaty, make wonderful salads and sandwiches, and taste amazing.

We also use cherry tomatoes, both regular and heirloom, quite frequently. I especially like to cook them on the grill. Cherry tomatoes can now be found in different hues as well, red, yellow, orange, deep gold, and pale green.

But don't forget those great big deep red meaty homegrown or farmers' market beefsteak tomatoes. I eat them peeled, quartered, and seeded, with a vinaigrette of balsamic vinegar, extra-virgin olive oil, sea salt, and pepper, plus lots of fresh basil.

heirloom tomatoes with burrata cheese

Serves 4

This very simple recipe depends more than anything on the sweetness and maturity of the tomatoes and burrata, little bites of cheese with a mozzarella-like exterior and a creamy interior reminiscent of fresh ricotta. If you can't find burrata, garnish the tomatoes with a soft, fresh goat cheese or buffalo mozzarella. But burrata is the gold standard for this salad. I also offer sliced sweet onions on the side, for those guests who like to add them to their salad.

1½ to 2 pounds heirloom tomatoes of mixed colors

4 cups arugula leaves

Sea salt and freshly ground black pepper

1 pound burrata cheese, quartered

1 cup Balsamic Vinaigrette (page 39)

¼ cup julienned fresh basil leaves

Core the tomatoes, trim both ends, and cut them crosswise into ¼-inch slices. Arrange a bed of arugula on each of 4 luncheon plates. Arrange the tomatoes overlapping on top of the arugula, alternating colors. Sprinkle the tomatoes with salt and pepper. Place the cheese, rind side down, alongside the tomatoes on each plate. Drizzle with the vinaigrette and sprinkle with basil.

beefsteak tomato and basil salad

Serves 4

At the height of summer, when great beefsteak tomatoes are in the farmers' market, I like to make this incredibly simple salad. As with all tomato salads, I offer sliced sweet onions on the side. A thanks to Mark Rudkin, who first made this for me in Paris in 1972.

6 firm but ripe beefsteak tomatoes (about 2 pounds)

Sea salt and freshly ground black pepper

1 cup Balsamic Vinaigrette (page 39)

¼ cup fresh basil leaves, torn into small pieces

With a small sharp knife, score the bottom of each tomato with a shallow X. Have ready a large bowl of ice water. Bring a large saucepan of water to a boil over high heat. Drop the tomatoes into the boiling water and boil until the skins begin to wrinkle, about 45 seconds.

Using a slotted spoon, transfer the tomatoes to the ice water. Let stand for 1 minute. Then lift the tomatoes from the water one at a time and, with your fingertips, peel them. Using a paring knife, cut out and discard the stem end of each tomato. Halve the tomatoes crosswise and remove their seeds with your fingertips. Cut each half in quarters and put them in a bowl. Sprinkle with salt and pepper to taste and toss with the vinaigrette and fresh basil. Cover the bowl and chill in the refrigerator for 20 to 30 minutes, then serve.

"I've introduced a lot of people to Michael's. I remember being the first person to take Ann Richards there, or Bill Clinton, or Liz Smith, or Jean Kennedy Smith. Peter Jennings, Elton John, Carly Simon, Eric Idle, Robin Williams, Billy Crystal. I love turning people on to Michael's because I've never met anyone who didn't have a good time there.

"There's always a surprise. You'll always run into someone you've wanted to see, or someone you don't get to see enough of, or somebody you don't know but have always admired. It's fun and it feels like a club . . . and Michael's is the only club I've ever wanted to be in."

—JOE ARMSTRONG, MAGAZINE PUBLISHER AND TV EXECUTIVE, "THE MAYOR OF MICHAEL'S"

wild mushrooms and truffles

Terroir, terroir, terroir—the taste of the earth, the smell of the forest. I love cooking with morels, porcini, chanterelles, and black and white truffles. To me, the simplest dish can be elevated to grand cuisine with the addition of wild mushrooms or truffles.

Fresh wild morels are one of my favorite signs of spring. They pop up in abandoned apple orchards, in woody glens, and under old gnarly trees. They are also cause for organized hunts and celebrations throughout the Northwest, Midwest, and Appalachia, areas of the country where they are bountiful. I am particularly taken by their slight nuttiness and ability to absorb sauces. Morels are now raised in hothouses, so they are available almost all of the time, but I also use dried ones to add their nutty oomph to a great winter meal.

I was introduced to porcini in France, where they are known as *cèpes*. At one time available only dried, they now can be found fresh in the spring and fall in specialty markets throughout the United States. They have a wonderfully pleasing earthy flavor that, once experienced, remains readily identifiable. Porcini range in color from cream to chocolate brown; they may be long and tall or short and squat, moist or dry, and they exhibit a variety of other characteristics. No matter the size, all porcini are bulbous, with a spongy mass that replaces the gills. Both the caps and stems are edible.

Chanterelles (and their smaller cousins, *girolles*) are trumpet-shaped mushrooms with a delicate, almost spicy, fruity flavor. They range in color from golden yellow to black. The best are the little *girolles* at the first sign of summer. Just as white asparagus leaves us, *les girolles* arrive! Wild chanterelles are still brought to market or to

"God forbid when the white truffles from Alba would come in. We'd have a very dire financial situation that month because Michael couldn't keep his hands off them. We tried desperately to control his truffle consumption, but Michael would call a busboy and have him bring a truffle and a truffle shaver to his table and Mike would joyously shave truffles all over his plate."

—DAVID ROSOFF, GENERAL MANAGER OF MICHAEL'S SANTA MONICA, 1996–2001, AND MANAGING PARTNER OF PIZZERIA MOZZA AND OSTERIA MOZZA, LOS ANGELES

the restaurant door by professional foragers.

I think black and white truffles are the supreme rulers of the mushroom universe. They make a brilliant bridge between food and wine (along with sauce, of course); try a great Chardonnay with any dish containing white truffles, and a great big Cabernet with a dish featuring black truffles.

The best black truffles come from the Périgord region of France, while the best white truffles are from the Piedmont in Italy. Black truffles smell very much of damp, flowery earth. White truffles are somewhat more pungent, with a strong, sexy aroma that many say has

more than a hint of garlic and vanilla in it. The availability of both types depends on the weather, the moon, the stars, and whatever other climatic variation a truffle hunter can conjure up. Truffles are now also found in Oregon and China.

I usually call for truffles to be shaved over the top of a dish. To do so properly, you really do need a kitchen device called a truffle shaver. It's a small metal slicer with an adjustable blade that you usually hold at a 45-degree angle as you press down on the truffle and over it to make tissue-thin, even slices. If you don't have one, you can use a mandoline; or, if not, use a small, sharp knife, though the

slices won't be quite as neat and thin.

I also frequently use the standard *champignons de Paris* (good old everyday button, or white, mushrooms), particularly in salads. They should be firm and pure white with no blemishes. The undercap should be white and tightly sealed.

I will grill big flat portobellos for a mixed grill or for sandwiches or salads. They also make an informal first course or side dish, drizzled with a balsamic vinaigrette and sprinkled with fresh garlic and thyme.

And, finally, shiitakes are great in vegetable sautés.

white truffle risotto

Serves 4

I love to make risotto. I like mine moist: I've always considered moisture the key to life and good food! So I include enough stock in the ingredients to ensure a moist finished product, bearing in mind that some risotto rice varieties may be drier than others.

Risottos are simple to do, and if you have an open kitchen you can chat with and toast your guests as you cook. In this version, I like to dish up the risotto and then shave the truffle over each serving. It's awesome on its own or alongside a pan-seared chicken breast or veal chop. The smell is heavenly. When truffles are not available, I'll make a wild mushroom risotto, sautéing porcini or chanterelles separately and then folding them into the rice at the last moment.

If you don't have time to make risotto, by the way, try the rice-shaped pasta known as orzo, cooked al dente in boiling salted water, drained, tossed with Chardonnay Cream Sauce (page 73), and then topped with white truffle shavings.

This basic risotto, sans the truffles, can be made with the addition of lobster and asparagus (with basil), porcini and quail (with thyme), and scallops, shrimp, and clams (with chervil).

5 to 6 cups chicken stock

5 tablespoons salted butter

2 shallots, minced

1 clove garlic, minced

Pinch sea salt plus more to taste

2 cups Arborio or other medium-grain rice

½ cup champagne

2 tablespoons heavy cream, at room temperature

¾ cup freshly grated Parmesan cheese

Freshly ground white pepper to taste

2 ounces fresh white truffles

Place the stock in a medium saucepan over medium heat. Bring to a simmer. Immediately lower the heat to keep the stock very hot but not boiling.

Heat 2 tablespoons of the butter in a large shallow saucepan over medium heat. Add the shallot and garlic along with a pinch of salt. Cook, stirring frequently with a wooden spoon, for about 4 minutes or until the shallot is soft and translucent.

Stir in the rice and cook, stirring frequently, for about 5 minutes or until the rice is almost chalky in color and glistening. Add the champagne and cook, stirring constantly, for about 5 minutes or until the wine has been absorbed by the rice.

Begin adding the hot stock, about 1 cup at a time, and cook, stirring constantly, until the liquid has been absorbed by the rice. Do not add additional stock until the previous cup has been absorbed. Keep adding stock and stirring until the rice is al dente and a creamy "sauce" has formed. Stir in the heavy cream. Add the remaining 3 tablespoons butter along with the Parmesan. Season with salt and white pepper to taste.

When ready to serve, ladle out equal portions into large shallow soup bowls and shave the truffles over the top of each one.

NOTE: I am a big fan of Knorr chicken bouillon cubes. They are readily available and easy to use. When I don't have homemade chicken stock on hand, the cubes are my choice.

fettucine with chardonnay cream sauce and black truffles

Serves 4

In this quick, luxurious appetizer, fresh pasta is a fine base for a rich cream sauce and elegant truffles. It also makes a terrific side dish, served with a pan-seared chicken breast or veal chop. To make this recipe with morels or chanterelles instead of truffles, simply sauté the mushrooms and add them to the sauce just before tossing with the pasta.

Chardonnay Cream Sauce
(recipe follows)

2 ounces fresh black (or white) truffles

1 pound fresh fettuccine

½ cup freshly grated Parmesan cheese

Sea salt and freshly ground white pepper (optional)

2 tablespoons chopped fresh flat-leaf parsley

First prepare the Chardonnay Cream Sauce. Shave half the truffles into the pan of sauce, stir gently, and keep warm.

Meanwhile, bring a large pot of salted water to a boil over high heat. Add the pasta and cook according to package directions until al dente. Remove from the heat and drain.

Return the pasta to the hot pan. Stir the Parmesan into the sauce, then add the sauce to the pasta and toss to coat well. Taste and, if necessary, season with salt and white pepper. Transfer to a warm serving platter or individual pasta bowls. Shave the remaining truffles over the pasta and garnish with parsley. Serve immediately.

------

chardonnay cream sauce

¾ cup Chardonnay

1 medium shallot, minced

2 cups heavy cream

½ teaspoon fresh lemon juice

Sea salt and freshly ground white pepper

Place the wine and minced shallot in a small, heavy saucepan over medium-high heat. Bring to a boil and reduce the liquid to 1 tablespoon, about 7 minutes. Stir in the cream and bring to a simmer. Continue simmering until the sauce has reduced by about a third and is slightly thickened but still fluid, about 10 minutes.

Keep the sauce warm. When ready to serve, stir in the lemon juice and season to taste with salt and white pepper. Serve warm as a sauce for pasta, chicken, veal, or seafood.

seafood

It's so easy to get good, fresh fish nowadays. Develop a relationship with a good fish source, whether it's a shop dedicated to seafood or a supermarket with its own fish department, and you're almost home free. As often as possible, try to purchase fish that are labeled "wild," which I find have much better flavor than farm-raised fish.

I generally cook seafood very simply at home. I save the fancy dishes for the restaurants. Many of my recipes can be used with various types of fish or shellfish. For instance, both types of lobster—Maine and West Coast spiny—can be used interchangeably in any of my lobster recipes. If you can't find the fish I call for in a recipe, use one that is available to you. Don't limit yourself: experiment with what you do have.

"Every generation has its literary feeding trough. In the twenties and thirties, it was the Algonquin; in the forties and fifties, it was Toots Shor's; in the sixties, it was the Lion's Head; in the seventies and eighties, it was Elaine's; and since the nineties, Michael's has been the place for media and publishing types to eat."

—DAVID HIRSHEY, SENIOR VICE PRESIDENT AND
EXECUTIVE EDITOR, HARPERCOLLINS

oysters

With their sweet, slightly briny flavor, oysters are completely addictive. I've been eating them all of my life and never tire of their extraordinary succulence.

In Rhode Island, where I spent my early summers on Misquamicut Beach at Watch Hill, my mom would buy a big sack of oysters from the Portuguese fishermen down at the dock. These oysters were straight from the ocean and were absolutely delicious with just a squeeze of lemon. Later I was introduced to oysters from Washington State by my wife Kim's aunt, who lives on the Hood Canal. From her windows, you think you are looking at a sandy beach, but you are actually seeing huge wild oyster beds. It's so amazing! We pull them off of their rocks and then barbecue them. Some Lemon-Basil Butter (see page 78; substitute basil for the parsley) and ice-cold vodka make dinner!

When I opened Michael's in Santa Monica, very few oysters were available, and those that were came mostly from Atlantic waters for just a few weeks of the year. Because I had grown up on the East Coast and feasted on them since childhood, and then experienced their particularly wonderful brininess at the famous La Coupole in Paris, I very much wanted to include a variety of oysters on my menu. The San Franciscan Bill Marinelli, who was instrumental in getting the northwestern oyster industry back on track, greatly helped me in this endeavor.

Fall and winter are the best seasons for oysters, though you can also get great ones in spring and summer. To me, nothing beats slurping down fresh oysters with a crisp chilled glass (or many) of the most recent vintage of Sancerre or New Zealand Sauvignon Blanc.

I consider myself an equal-opportunity oyster eater—I enjoy them no matter what part of the world they may come from. The European oyster is found along the coasts of France, England, and Ireland, with the most well known being the meaty, sweet belon. Pacific oysters, native to Korea, Japan, and China, are found all along the western coast of the United States. They are fast-growing and they quickly reproduce, making them highly desirable for commercial cultivation. Native to Washington State are Olympia oysters. Kumamotos, native to Japan, are now cultivated in the Pacific Northwest. Eastern oysters reproduce in the cold waters of Canada, down the Mid-Atlantic coast to the southern coastal states and the Gulf of Mexico. So although the flavor of each is quite distinct, all of the oysters found along the eastern seaboard are the same species, whether called Malpeque, Wellfleet, bluepoint, and so on.

Oysters derive their particular flavor and texture from their environment, from the temperature and salinity of the water in which they have grown, the tidal forces, and the nutrients on which they feed. Oysters from icy waters tend to be sweeter, plumper, and more delicately flavored; salty water produces oysters with a sharp, briny taste. To me, for flavor, texture, and meatiness, there is nothing better than a Pacific Northwest oyster fresh from October's chilly waters. In the restaurants, we usually serve Olympia, belon, Quilcene Bay, Hog Island, Westcott Bay, and Kumamoto oysters; however, when others have better flavor they will make it onto the menu instead. My staff and I constantly test new oysters (yes, it's hard work, but somebody has to do it) to determine when they're at their peak.

Whether serving oysters raw or cooking them, you should scrub them well and keep them very cold until you're ready to work with them.

opening raw oysters

If you follow my directions, and wear an oyster glove and use a good oyster knife, opening oysters will be a snap.

1. Using a stiff brush, scrub the oysters under cold running water to remove any clinging debris. Place the oysters on a platter and refrigerate for 30 minutes. Oysters don't particularly like being manhandled, so they will tightly close in protest. This cold resting period allows them time to relax, which will then make opening easier.

2. Wearing an oyster glove, place the oyster, flat side up, in your nonwriting hand. (If you don't have an oyster glove, fold a clean kitchen towel into thirds and place it on a flat surface with the oyster in the center.) Firmly holding an oyster knife in your other hand, place the tip into the hinged end of the oyster, slightly wiggling the knife as you prod and push. As quickly as possible, jab the knife point into the oyster and give it a fast half turn to snap the shell open and break the seal. Then move the blade around the edge of the shell to separate the two halves.

3. Slightly turn the knife to an upward angle and slice across the interior of the top shell to separate the muscle from the shell, taking care that you do not spill the liquid (known as oyster liquor). Discard the top shell. Holding the bottom shell firmly in the palm of your hand to keep the juices from leaking out, carefully pry the meat loose from the shell. Place the oyster on a flat plate or platter and refrigerate while you continue to open oysters. If, like me, you sample as you go, it will take a bit of time to open enough oysters for a crowd.

All the while that I am opening oysters, I marvel over the fact that a good shucker can open a couple of dozen oysters every two minutes. Start practicing—and enjoy eating your homework and washing it down with that glass of young Sancerre!

Freshly shucked oysters are delicious in their natural juices, but in the classic French style, raw oysters must be served with a wedge of lemon for squeezing or with a mignonette sauce. The sauce recipe is so simple that I will pass it along should you be in the mood to do the French thing: Combine ½ cup of the very best vinegar (my favorites are sherry or Banyuls, but you can use champagne vinegar or a good-quality red wine vinegar) with 1 minced shallot and 1 tablespoon freshly ground black pepper and let rest for about an hour before spooning lightly over raw oysters. This recipe makes enough for at least 2 dozen oysters. Be sure to serve these oysters with hot, thinly sliced, toasted and buttered Walnut Bread (see page 188).

sautéed belon oysters with lemon-parsley butter

Serves 4

After I've eaten my fill of fresh, cold, raw belon oysters, I'm ready to move on to the next course: this recipe. I'll also move on in what I drink, from Sancerre or Sauvignon Blanc to a rich Chablis or California Chardonnay.

24 belon oysters

1 cup all-purpose flour

Sea salt and freshly ground black pepper

3 tablespoons clarified butter (see Note, page 48)

¼ cup dry white wine

Juice of 1 lemon

½ cup (1 stick) salted butter, cut into 8 pieces, at room temperature

2 tablespoons chopped fresh flat-leaf parsley

Shuck the oysters (see page 77) and put them in a bowl. Spread the flour on a dinner plate, season well with salt and pepper, and stir briefly to mix. One at a time, turn the oysters in the flour to coat them evenly, then transfer to a clean plate.

Heat the clarified butter in a large nonstick sauté pan over medium-high heat. Working in batches of 4 to 6 oysters at a time (depending on size) to avoid overcrowding, sauté the oysters until crisp and golden brown, turning them once with a spatula, about 3 minutes per batch. Transfer to a baking sheet and keep warm while you cook the remaining oysters.

Add the wine and lemon juice to the pan and stir and scrape with a wooden spoon to deglaze the pan deposits. Boil the liquid until it has reduced to a few tablespoons, then add the pieces of butter and half the parsley and swirl the pan until it forms a thick sauce. Season to taste with salt and pepper. Place 6 oysters in each of 4 shallow soup bowls. Drizzle with the warm sauce and sprinkle with the remaining parsley. Serve immediately.

"I go to Michael's in New York to make a deal. It's always been lucky for me. I've never had lunch there when I didn't make the deal. My Bravo deals, my Court TV deals, my *Today* show deal— every deal I've made in the last three years has happened at Michael's."

—JOAN RIVERS, COMEDIENNE

oyster stew

Serves 4

My mom always made this recipe on Christmas Eve, and it's still my favorite. For a basic oyster chowder, you can add one pound of cooked, cubed potatoes and half a pound Bacon Lardons (see page 98). Either way, I sometimes like to hit my bowl with a shot of Worcestershire sauce before eating.

½ cup (1 stick) salted butter, softened

½ cup finely diced sweet onion

3 dozen oysters, shucked (see page 77), juices reserved

2 cups heavy cream

Sea salt and freshly ground black pepper

2 tablespoons chopped fresh chives

Heat 6 tablespoons of the butter in a large shallow saucepan over medium-low heat. Add the onion and sauté for about 4 minutes or until very soft and translucent. Add the oysters along with their juices and cook, stirring occasionally, for about 3 minutes or just until the oysters begin to curl around the edges.

Add the cream, stirring to blend. Season with salt and pepper and cook, stirring frequently, for about 4 minutes or just until the mixture begins to boil and thicken.

Remove from heat and ladle into 4 shallow soup bowls. Place 1½ teaspoons of the remaining butter on top of each bowl, allowing it to melt. Sprinkle the top of each bowl with the chives. Serve immediately.

"Michael's New York is a little like a play being staged every day, with actors and scenery and a sense of energy. The place has a total sense of energy. It's a fun, lively joint. You always go in there and run into somebody you know. It's got a lot of pizzazz that way. It feels a little bit like home and a little bit like a party, with hot, interesting guests and a real frisson."

—JANN WENNER,
FOUNDER, PUBLISHER, EDITOR,
ROLLING STONE

clams

Clams are terrific party food. They're tasty either raw or cooked. At home, they are constants in my kitchen. I use them on a raw bar, in chowders, with pasta, baked as Clams Casino (page 82), or as a big bowl of steamers (page 81), my absolute favorite.

I use three types of clams: Atlantic littleneck, Manila, and steamers from Long Island to Maine. Littlenecks are the smallest of the hard-shell, native, Atlantic quahog clams and are at their best served raw, on the half shell, much like oysters. To ensure that my littleneck clams are always tender and sweet, I use those that are about 1 inch in diameter when serving raw or when baking clams casino.

Manila clams have become one of the most important Pacific varieties. Smaller Manilas about 1 inch across are the most tender and sweet. I like them in chowders or pasta sauces.

Because I grew up in the east, steamers—also known as Ipswich or pisser clams—were part of my summer ritual. They are called soft-shells because their shells are thinner and more brittle than those of quahogs. Be careful when handling soft-shells so you don't crush the shells. They also have a wrinkled, rubbery, necklike siphon that protrudes from one side of the shell, which is funky-looking but practical, as it offers a handle for dipping the clams into butter or sauce.

On the East Coast, clams are available all year long, but in California the season runs from November through April. Hard-shell clams should be tightly closed. If gaping, give a tap. If the shell closes, the clam is alive; if not, discard it. A simple touch to the siphon of a soft-shell clam is all you need to test it—if it moves, the clam is alive; if not, discard it.

Hard-shell clams that are to be eaten raw are shucked in much the same way as oysters (see page 77), although they are usually easier to open. However, when you cut through the hinge that holds the shell together, take care not to push the knife through the clam or you will cut the meat in half. It is a good idea to shuck over a bowl so you can catch any juices that drain off.

To clean soft-shell or steamer clams, put them in a sink and wash in at least three or four changes of cold water until there is no sand settling on the bottom. Even after this soaking, the cooking liquid will usually have to be strained through cheesecloth or left undisturbed in the serving bowl so that the grit will settle to the bottom before the clam or bread is dunked into the broth. I often strain off the liquid and transfer the steamed clams to a clean pan along with a bottle of commercial clam juice; I heat them up and serve them with melted butter and lemon. Hard-shell clams, like oysters, are generally quite clean and need to be scrubbed only on the outside (see page 77).

To serve clams on the half shell, shuck them and place them on an ice-lined platter. Serve with sherry wine vinegar mignonette (see page 77) or lemon wedges.

"Michael's is the only place I know of where you find the entire media business in one room at one time: television, newspaper, magazine, book, agents; you've got the talent and the agents, and the suits are making deals. It's the whole cloth of the entire media industry in a few hundred square feet. That's probably unique of its kind on the planet. The gang's all here, so to speak."

—PETER PRICE, PRESIDENT, NATIONAL TELEVISION ACADEMY

soft-shell steamers

Serves 4

In my family, steamers mean serious eating. Using this recipe, you can steam any clam, but my favorite is the good old pisser clam, found from Long Island to Maine. Insist on small to medium-sized clams, as they are the sweetest and tenderest. If your guests are unfamiliar with steamers, please explain that they must remove the siphon, or "sock," on each clam before eating. It's also important to "rinse" each clam, swishing it back and forth in the broth before you dip it into the clarified butter. A good crusty bread is the perfect accompaniment. If you have any steamed clams left over, remove the meat from the shells, pull off the socks, and refrigerate the clams; later that day or the next, fry them following the instructions in my recipe for Sautéed Belon Oysters (page 78) or deep-fry them in the same beer batter I use for shrimp (page 103).

½ cup fresh lemon juice

2 cloves garlic, sliced

1 lemon, quartered, seeds removed

8 pounds steamer clams, well cleaned

Sea salt and freshly ground black pepper

1 cup clarified butter (page 48)

2 tablespoons chopped fresh basil

Combine the lemon juice, garlic, and lemon quarters in a large, deep pot over high heat. Add enough cold water to cover the bottom of the pot with 1¼ inches of liquid. Bring to a boil and cook for about 3 minutes to allow the flavors to meld. Add the steamers, cover, and cook for about 5 minutes or until some of them begin to open. Gently move them around so that the open clams don't continue to cook in the liquid, taking care not to push the meat from the shells. Continue cooking for an additional 5 minutes or until all of the clams have opened and the liquid is richly seasoned with clam flavor.

Remove from the heat and portion the clams into each of 4 large shallow soup bowls. Strain the broth through a fine-mesh sieve lined with a double layer of cheesecloth into a clean container, discarding the solids. Taste and, if necessary, add salt and pepper. Pour an equal amount of the broth over the clams in each bowl. Pour the clarified butter into individual ramekins and add some of the chopped basil to each one. Serve the ramekins alongside the bowls of clams. Pass crusty bread for dunking.

baked clams casino

Serves 4

"Clams Casino!" is one of my favorite Michaelisms, something I yell when I feel like I'm living the high life. This recipe never goes out of fashion; it is just too, too good. Perfect for serving on the deck with a glass of white wine or around the holidays with martinis.

> "Michael conveys a great warmth. The number one thing with him is that he really loves life. He comes in and sits down for lunch and has seven or eight courses and loves everything and talks to everyone around him. He's the ultimate appreciator of good food and people and having a good time."
>
> —PAUL KAHAN, EXECUTIVE CHEF AND CO-OWNER, BLACKBIRD, CHICAGO

5 tablespoons salted butter

2 cloves roasted garlic

1½ tablespoons minced fresh flat-leaf parsley

1 teaspoon chopped fresh thyme

1 tablespoon fresh lemon juice

Sea salt and freshly ground black pepper

2 dozen littleneck clams, well scrubbed

6 tablespoons julienned crisp bacon (about 6 slices)

¼ cup fresh bread crumbs

Combine the butter, garlic, parsley, thyme, lemon juice, and salt and pepper to taste in the bowl of a food processor fitted with the metal blade. Process until blended, then scrape from the bowl into a clean container. Set aside.

Preheat the broiler.

Shuck the clams and place them on the half shell.

Line a large baking pan with loosely crumpled aluminum foil. Nestle the clams into the foil so that they will stay flat and anchored.

Spoon about a teaspoon of the lemon-herb butter on top of each clam. Sprinkle each with an equal portion of the bacon, followed by the bread crumbs. Place under the preheated broiler about 6 inches from the heat and broil until the bread crumbs are golden brown, 3 to 4 minutes.

Remove from the broiler and serve.

lobster

Lobster is one of those foods that immediately say "luxe."

I use two types of lobster, Maine and West Coast Channel Island spiny. The defining difference is that the latter has an exceptionally hard shell and lacks claws. Maine lobster is harvested from the waters of the Atlantic off the Maine shore and express-shipped all over the world. Spiny lobsters are generally available only fresh, in the areas from which they have been harvested. At the restaurants, we use California spiny lobster taken fresh from the Channel Islands and Maine lobster that is delivered to our door soon after being caught.

When shopping on my own, I want to find my purchase in a big tank of bubbling water, feisty, mean, and raring for a fight. I like to pick my lobster from the tank myself, always by holding on to both sides of its head to make sure that it will flap about in a fit of temper. If a lobster is mellow, it's not worth eating. I prefer lobsters on the small side, 1½ pounds for an entrée, 1 pound (known as chicks) for appetizers. I buy "culls," lobsters that have lost a claw or have one small claw, for salads and soups. I prefer female lobsters because, more often than not, they contain the coral, the rich-tasting roe or caviar of a lobster. And I always cook a lobster on the same day I purchase it.

I either boil or grill lobster. If I am serving it simply, I usually opt for the grill.

spiny lobster with creamy orzo and black truffles

Serves 4

California's spiny lobster season runs from the first Wednesday in October into the middle of March, and the cooler weather gives me the perfect excuse to ratchet it up with richer sauces and luxury garnishes. This recipe calls for orzo to accompany the lobster, but I also recommend angel hair pasta or risotto (page 72). Shaved white truffles or a spoonful of caviar also works very well in place of the black truffles. Needless to say, I also make this dish with Maine lobster.

Two 1½-pound spiny lobsters

½ pound orzo pasta

2 tablespoons clarified butter (see Note, page 48)

Sea salt and freshly ground white pepper

Chardonnay Cream Sauce (page 73)

2 ounces fresh black truffles

1 tablespoon chopped fresh flat-leaf parsley

1 tablespoon fresh chervil leaves

1 tablespoon chopped fresh chives

Place the lobsters in a large pot of heavily salted boiling water. Cover and return to the boil. Boil the lobsters for 6 minutes. Remove from the heat and drain well. Set aside until cool enough to handle. This blanching makes it easy to remove the meat from the shell. It only slightly cooks the meat so you don't overcook it on the grill.

Preheat and oil a grill.

When the lobsters are cool enough to handle, carefully crack the shells lengthwise and remove the intestinal tract at the top of the tail. Remove the meat in one piece. Cut each body crosswise into medallions about ¾ inch thick. Set aside.

Bring a large pot of salted water to a boil. Add the orzo and cook according to the package directions until al dente, about 8 minutes.

While the orzo is cooking, grill the lobster meat. Using a pastry brush, lightly coat each side of the lobster medallions with clarified butter. Season with salt and white pepper to taste. Place on the preheated grill and cook, turning once, for about 1 minute or until lightly colored. Do not overcook or the meat will be very tough! Remove from the grill and keep warm.

Drain the orzo and place it back in the pan. Add the cream sauce, stirring to coat. Spoon the orzo into the center of each of 4 shallow pasta bowls. Place an equal portion of lobster medallions on top of each serving. Shave the truffle over each serving. Sprinkle with chopped parsley, chervil, and chives.

"Michael shows you that entertaining at home is about not being conventional, not being stuck with clichés, boxes, do's and don'ts. Get free from that. Free yourself from any sort of intimidation. Be spontaneous and generous. Make a party an experience. Michael shouts and he acts crazy, and the moment you start speaking and laughing with him, you are at a party."

—RÉMI KRUG, PRESIDENT, KRUG CHAMPAGNE

"Michael's approach to cooking is very muscular. One time, in the early 1980s, Michael and I and a group of people were at a hotel that should probably remain nameless—oh, all right, at Two Bunch Palms. It was somebody's birthday, and Michael had brought these marvelous steaks and lobsters and he wanted to grill them, but there was no firewood. He brought out furniture and smashed it up and proceeded to cook the best steaks I've ever eaten. We've been barred from there ever since. The hotel asked us kindly never to darken its door again."

—MARTIN VON HASELBERG, AKA HARRY KIPPER, PERFORMANCE ARTIST

grilled maine lobster with lime-basil-garlic butter

Serves 4

Grilled lobster makes a great party dish. I split the lobsters in half, throw them on a hot grill, cover, and have a cocktail while they cook to perfection.

I also grill spiny lobster (which is first blanched, see page 85) in this fashion and serve it with a Meyer lemon–thyme butter made in the same way as the butter in this recipe, replacing the limes with Meyer lemons and the basil with fresh thyme.

Six 1½-pound live Maine lobsters

Lime-Basil-Garlic Butter (recipe follows)

Preheat and oil a grill. At the same time, bring a large pot of heavily salted water to a boil on the stove.

Place a lobster on a clean surface. Working quickly, push the blade of a large sharp knife into the lobster's head about 1 inch behind its eyes. Plunge the knife down into the head, pushing toward the front to cut the head in half lengthwise. Then, quickly and smoothly, continue to slice back to cut the lobster completely and evenly into two lengthwise halves. Twist off the arms and claws. Repeat with the rest of the lobsters.

Place the lobster halves on the grill, shell side down. Cover and grill for 10 to 12 minutes or until the meat is cooked through. There is no need to turn the lobsters, as the closed grill gives off enough heat to cook them fully. Plus you don't want to risk losing all the good stuff! (If you're cooking a female, the dark green roe will turn bright red and delicious.) After the lobster halves have been grilling for a few minutes, add the arms and claws to the pot of boiling water in the kitchen and cook until bright red, 6 to 9 minutes.

Remove the lobster halves from the grill, and drain the claws and arms. Serve with lobster crackers (to help extract the meat from the claws and arms) and warm Lime-Basil-Garlic Butter, into which you can dip the meat.

―――

lime-basil-garlic butter

1 cup (2 sticks) salted butter

1 tablespoon finely minced garlic

Juice of 2 limes

2 tablespoons fresh basil chiffonade (see Note)

Sea salt and freshly ground black pepper to taste

Place the butter and garlic in a small saucepan over medium-low heat. Cook, stirring occasionally, for about 5 minutes or until the butter has melted and is infused with the garlic. Add the lime juice and heat for another minute.

Remove from the heat and stir in the basil. Season with salt and pepper to taste and keep warm until ready to serve.

NOTE: "Chiffonade" is a French term describing herbs or vegetables (usually leafy greens) cut into fine strips.

"One lesson you can learn from Michael is: if you want to entertain at home, use the best ingredients and keep it simple, lobster, or beef, or corn on the cob. And any guests who want to, Michael always gives them a job. It's organized chaos. It's fun. And Michael always has a good attitude."

—Steve Wallace, president, Wally's Wines & Spirits, Los Angeles

crab

Although there are hundreds of types of crab, my three favorites are Dungeness, soft-shell, and Atlantic Florida stone. Fresh Dungeness crab was unknown to me during my East Coast childhood. We had only soft-shells and stone crab claws. After I tasted the sweet Dungeness on a trip to San Francisco, however, I was hooked. You really don't need a recipe for a Dungeness crab; just boil it, clean it, crack it open, and dig right in, pulling out those hunks of succulent meat. With, of course, chilled Sancerre, Sancerre, and more Sancerre!

Pacific Dungeness crab is now available throughout the country thanks to express shipping. Dungeness weighs in at anywhere from one to four pounds, and although most people assume that it's a San Francisco delicacy, it's actually found all up and down the Pacific coast.

Between May and October, blue crabs molt their hard shells and become what is known as "soft-shell crabs." They used to be available only along the eastern seaboard but are now shipped all across the country. I think that they are best early in the season when they are smaller, sweeter, and at their most tender. The really tiny ones (fondly called "roaches") are perfection. Soft-shell crabs must be live when purchased. You can have the fishmonger clean them, but if so you should cook them within a few hours. If you wish to clean them yourself, first use kitchen scissors to cut the "face" section from the crab, which will instantly dispatch it. Then gently pry up the shell flap from the back,

scrape off the gills, and remove the sand receptacle that is located near the mouth. Rinse the cleaned crab under cold running water and pat dry.

Florida stone crabs are one of nature's peculiarities. When a stone crab loses one of its claws, a new claw grows in its place. So stone crabs, whose claws alone are eaten, are harvested simply by removing their claws and leaving the crabs free to grow new ones for the next harvest. Because the meat is difficult to extract from the shell, stone crab claws are always sold cooked. In Florida, you can get them hot from the pot. Elsewhere, the claws are sold cooked and chilled and are best eaten that way. Stone crab is in season from November through May in Florida. Remember that the tastiest come from Atlantic waters.

warm dungeness crab with meyer lemon–herb butter

Serves 4

Herb butter accents Dungeness crab's sweet and juicy meat wonderfully. True to its San Francisco roots, this crab goes well with hot, crusty sourdough rolls, which you can use to soak up every last drop of butter. This recipe makes a great casual first course or lunch dish.

2 large live Dungeness crabs

Meyer Lemon–Herb Butter (recipe follows)

Good-quality sourdough rolls, heated in the oven

Bring a large pot of cold salted water to a boil over high heat. Add the crabs and return to a boil. Boil for 19 minutes or until the shells are bright red-orange. Remove from the heat and drain well.

Place the crabs, belly up, on a clean kitchen towel. Pull off the "apron" and pull out and discard the white intestine that runs along the back. Turn over the crab and pry loose and discard the top shell. Pull out and discard the gills from the body.

Using a sharp knife, cut each crab into quarters. Rinse the crabs under hot running water for no more than a second or two, shaking out any "insides."

Place 2 quarters on each of 4 plates. Place a small ramekin of the Meyer Lemon–Herb Butter on each plate, add a hot sourdough roll, and serve.

meyer lemon–herb butter

1 cup (2 sticks) salted butter

Juice of 2 Meyer lemons

2 tablespoons chopped fresh chives

1 teaspoon chopped fresh tarragon

1 teaspoon chopped flat-leaf parsley

Sea salt and freshly ground black pepper

Melt the butter in a small saucepan over medium-low heat. Stir in the lemon juice and heat for another minute.

Remove from the heat and stir in the chives, tarragon, and parsley. Season with salt and pepper to taste and keep warm until ready to serve.

"I don't go to Michael's to have a special favorite dish. I don't think I've ever eaten anything there I didn't like, and it's rare that I can say that. His entire menu has a freshness and an ingredient sensitivity and a clarity that is light and refreshing."

—TIM ZAGAT, COFOUNDER, COCHAIR, AND CEO, ZAGAT SURVEY

deep-fried soft-shell crabs
with ponzu sauce and asian slaw

Serves 4

Soft-shell crabs are truly one of the world's great delicacies. I like to jazz them up by serving them with Asian ponzu sauce and slaw.

Another great way to cook them is to grill them until crisp and serve them with Aïoli (page 103).

> "When Michael has soft-shell crabs in season, there's no better. He's got some sort of secret batter that does something with soft-shells that even the best fish restaurants don't seem to master in the same way."
>
> —CHRIS MEIGHER,
> PUBLISHER, *QUEST*

Peanut oil for frying

3 cups all-purpose flour

3 tablespoons cornstarch

½ teaspoon sea salt

½ teaspoon freshly ground black pepper

3 cups Bass ale

Seltzer water (optional)

12 small soft-shell crabs, cleaned

Ponzu Sauce (recipe follows)

Asian Slaw (recipe follows)

Place enough oil in a deep-fat fryer to fill the fryer by at least three-quarters. Turn the heat to medium-high and bring to 375°F on an instant-read thermometer.

While the oil is heating, combine the flour, cornstarch, salt, and pepper in a large mixing bowl. Whisk in the Bass ale, mixing just until the batter is smooth. If the batter is too thick, thin it with a little seltzer water.

When the oil reaches the desired temperature, working with one piece at a time, use tongs to dip the crabs carefully into the batter, allowing any excess to drip off. Drop the crabs into the hot oil and fry for about 4 minutes or until golden brown and crisp.

Transfer the crisp crabs to a paper towel–lined platter as you fry them. Serve hot with Ponzu Sauce for dipping and Asian Slaw.

---

ponzu sauce

1 cup light soy sauce

1 cup sour orange or yuzu juice (see Note)

¼ cup mirin (see Note)

One 2-inch piece kombu (see Note)

1 tablespoon bonito flakes (see Note)

Combine the soy sauce, juice, and mirin in a container. Stir in the kombu and bonito flakes. Cover and refrigerate for 2 days.

Remove from the refrigerator and strain through a fine-mesh sieve.

asian slaw

½ head green cabbage

1 tablespoon sea salt plus more to taste

1 cup rice wine vinegar (see Note)

2 teaspoons nuoc mam or nam pla (see Note)

1 teaspoon soy sauce

1 teaspoon light brown sugar

2 tablespoons minced fresh lemongrass (see Note)

1 tablespoon minced fresh ginger

1 teaspoon minced fresh green chili pepper or to taste

1 green mango, peeled and julienned (or 1 Granny Smith apple, peeled, cored, and julienned)

1 large carrot, peeled, trimmed, and julienned

1 daikon radish, peeled, trimmed, and julienned (see Note)

¼ cup chopped fresh cilantro

2 tablespoons chopped fresh mint

Using a food processor fitted with the shredding blade, shred the cabbage. Place the shredded cabbage in a colander that is placed in a bowl. Add 1 tablespoon salt and toss to coat. Place another dish or plate on top of the cabbage and weight it down with heavy object(s), such as several cans or a 5-pound bag of flour. Let drain, pouring off the liquid from time to time, for 2 hours.

Combine the vinegar, nuoc mam, soy sauce, and sugar in a small mixing bowl, stirring to dissolve the sugar. Add the lemongrass, ginger, and chili. Set aside.

Rinse the cabbage under cold running water. Pat dry.

Transfer the cabbage to a mixing bowl. Add the mango, carrot, and daikon and toss to combine. Add the dressing and again toss to combine. Cover and refrigerate for at least 1 hour to allow flavors to blend.

When ready to serve, add the cilantro and mint and toss to combine. Taste and, if necessary, season with additional salt.

NOTE: Sour oranges are available from specialty produce, Latin American, or Caribbean markets. Yuzu juice, kombu (dried kelp), and bonito flakes are available from Japanese markets and some specialty food or health food stores. Mirin is available from Asian markets, specialty food stores, and many supermarkets.

Ready-made ponzu sauce may be purchased from Asian markets; the best brand is Mikusan.

Rice wine vinegar, nuoc mam or nam pla (fish sauce), lemongrass, and daikon are available from Asian markets and some specialty food stores. Lemongrass and daikon are generally also available from specialty produce markets.

> "Michael broke the mold of the traditional restaurant. He changed the theme of how we do things when he brought in fashion and design and style, all part of the Californiazation of dining that now permeates America."
>
> —DREW NIEPORENT, OWNER, MYRIAD RESTAURANT GROUP

sautéed soft-shell crabs with giant spanish capers

Serves 4

I have been making this dish every spring for years and years. It is so perfect that I've never felt the urge to change it. I love to serve the crab with crunchy Matchstick Potatoes (page 61) on the side. The two different yet compatible crispy textures are the ideal combo. All that's needed to round out the meal is a bunch of watercress.

1½ cups all-purpose flour

Sea salt and freshly ground black pepper

Eight 2- to 3-ounce soft-shell crabs, cleaned

Approximately ¾ cup clarified butter (see page 48)

Juice of 1 lemon

2 lemons, cut into segments (see page 156)

½ cup giant Spanish capers, rinsed and well drained

2 tablespoons chopped flat-leaf parsley

Matchstick Potatoes (page 61)

2 bunches watercress, tough stems removed

Line a sheet pan with a double layer of paper towel. Set aside.

Combine the flour with salt and pepper to taste on a platter.

Dredge the crabs in the seasoned flour.

Place half the clarified butter in a large flying pan over high heat. When very hot, add 4 of the crabs, shell side down, and fry for 2 minutes. Using tongs, turn and fry the other side for 2 to 3 minutes more or until golden brown and crisp. Transfer the crabs to the prepared baking sheet. Discard the butter in the pan and wipe it clean with paper towels.

Return the frying pan to high heat and add the remaining clarified butter. When very hot, fry the remaining crabs.

Transfer all the crabs from the baking sheet to a platter.

Add the lemon juice to the pan and, using a wooden spoon, scrape up the browned bits from the bottom to incorporate them into the browned butter. Stir in the lemon segments, capers, and parsley. Pour the sauce over the crabs. Serve immediately with Matchstick Potatoes and watercress.

chilled stone crab claws with pommery mustard sauce

Serves 4

Because stone crab claws are always sold cooked, they make an easy meal for entertaining. The meat is quite firm and very sweet, so that the spiciness of the mustard sauce is a very enticing accent. When making the mustard sauce, make sure all of the ingredients are at room temperature so that the finished sauce emulsifies.

1 large egg yolk

1 tablespoon Pommery mustard

1 tablespoon Dijon mustard

1 tablespoon champagne vinegar

1 cup peanut oil

Juice of 1 lemon

Sea salt and freshly ground black pepper

1 bunch watercress, tough stems removed

12 cooked, chilled stone crab claws

1 lemon, quartered, seeds removed

Combine the egg yolk, mustards, and vinegar in a small bowl. Using a wire whisk, beat the mixture until pale yellow and well blended. Whisking constantly, begin adding the oil in a slow, steady stream. Increase the flow slightly as the sauce thickens.

When thick, whisk in the lemon juice and season with salt and pepper to taste. If the sauce seems too thick (it should resemble mayonnaise), whisk in up to ½ tablespoon cool water.

Place an equal portion of the watercress on each of 4 luncheon plates. Because stone crab shells are extremely hard, you'll need a hammer to crack them open before serving. To do this, wrap a claw in a kitchen towel and then lightly tap each crab with the hammer; have lobster crackers on hand for guests to help them finish the extraction. Pour the sauce into a ramekin on each plate and garnish with a lemon wedge.

scallops

In Europe, scallops are sold still in their shells, complete with the flavorful, deep orange roe, or coral. Virtually all scallops sold in America come already shelled and only very rarely with the coral still attached. So your scallop choices in America are between products that are generally known as "wet" or "dry." At the risk of contradicting my rule that "moisture is the key to life," I say go for the "dry" product, which has not been treated with a preservative solution. A "dry" scallop will cook to a gorgeous caramel brown finish, losing none of its natural juices.

Maine, Nantucket, and Long Island bay scallops are the ones I use most often, with their season running from November through March. Maine sea scallops are the largest; when shucked, they are anywhere from 1 inch to 1¾ inches in diameter. Nantucket bay scallops are ½ to ¾ inch in diameter and delicately flavored. Long Island Sound scallops, only ¼ to ½ inch in diameter, are great for ceviche. However, delicious scallops are now also being cultivated in Washington, California, and Baja California. The term "day boat" or "diver" scallops, most often applied to sea scallops, identifies those caught in the wild and brought to market within a day.

long island bay scallop ceviche
with walla walla onion, cilantro, and lime

Serves 4

I affectionately call Long Island bay scallops "little guys" because they're so tiny and tasty. Ceviche (also spelled "seviche" or "cebiche") is simply a Latin American method of "cooking" raw seafood in acid, usually citrus juice, with herbs, chilies, and onion. Because the seafood is not heated, it is necessary that it be absolutely pristine and then handled with extreme care.

With my ceviche, I love to serve margaritas (page 209) made following the method taught to me by my good friend Robert Del Grande, Southwestern chef par excellence and a margarita connoisseur.

1 pound tiny, fresh Long Island bay scallops, trimmed

1 Walla Walla or other sweet onion, peeled and diced

½ teaspoon finely diced fresh green chili (such as serrano or jalapeño) or to taste

½ cup fresh lime juice

Sea salt and freshly ground black pepper

¼ cup chopped fresh cilantro

Combine the scallops, onion, and chili with the lime juice in a container, tossing to coat. Cover and refrigerate for 15 minutes.

Remove from the refrigerator. Uncover and season with salt and pepper to taste. Toss in the cilantro and serve in small bowls, on toothpicks, or in clean scallop shells. Enjoy with a margarita.

"When Michael's Santa Monica opened, I was among his first customers with my best friend, Bruce Paltrow. We used to eat there once a week for years, each trying to stick the other with a higher-priced bottle of wine. My dinners with Bruce are the most lasting memory of Michael's. Of course, Michael was always there. He just added another level of laughter to the table."

—TONY BILL, ACTOR, WRITER, DIRECTOR, PRODUCER

nantucket bay scallops with bacon-watercress cream sauce

Serves 4

The secret to this dish is the quick searing of the scallops—you just want to give them some color. They are so delicate that they will continue to cook in the warm sauce.

I love lardons, which are crisp little pieces of slab bacon cut into julienne strips.

½ cup dry white wine

½ cup champagne vinegar

2 tablespoons minced shallots

3 tablespoons heavy cream

1 cup (2 sticks) salted butter, chilled and cut into cubes

1 tablespoon fresh lemon juice

Sea salt and freshly ground black pepper

2 bunches watercress, tough stems removed and leaves chopped

40 Nantucket bay scallops, trimmed

3 tablespoons clarified butter (see Note, page 48)

Bacon Lardons (recipe follows)

3 tablespoons chopped fresh chives

Combine the wine and vinegar with the shallots in a medium saucepan over medium heat. Bring to a boil and cook for about 12 minutes or until the liquid has reduced to 1 tablespoon. Whisk in the cream and lower the heat. Cook, whisking constantly, for 1 minute. Begin whisking in the butter, a cube at a time, adding fresh butter as each addition is incorporated into the sauce. Do not allow the mixture to simmer; if it begins to bubble, lift from the heat for a few seconds. When all of the butter has been incorporated, whisk in the lemon juice and season with salt and pepper to taste. Fold in the watercress and place over a bowl of hot water to keep warm (or transfer to the top half of a double boiler over hot water).

Heat a large nonstick skillet over high heat. Using a pastry brush, lightly coat the scallops with clarified butter. Season with salt and pepper and place in the hot pan. Sear on one side for about a minute or until just golden.

Pour the sauce over the scallops, gently spooning the liquid over them to finish the cooking.

Using a slotted spoon, transfer 10 scallops to each of 4 dinner plates. Fold the lardons and half of the chives into the sauce. Spoon the sauce over the scallops and sprinkle with the remaining chives. Serve immediately.

bacon lardons

Three ¼-inch-thick slices (about ¼ pound) lean, smoked slab bacon

Using a sharp knife, cut the bacon crosswise into ¼-inch strips.

Place the bacon in a large frying pan over medium heat. Fry, stirring and turning frequently, for about 5 minutes or until the bacon is golden and crisp.

Remove from the heat and place on a double layer of paper towel to drain.

NOTE: If you have the grill going, place the whole piece of bacon on a hot grill and grill until very crisp and cooked through. Remove from the grill and cut into ¼-inch julienne. The grill flavor adds a nice touch.

> "I don't like overly decorated, opulent places. Michael's is very simple, without pretense, and that makes it very comfortable."
>
> —AHMET ERTEGUN, COFOUNDER, ATLANTIC RECORDS

shrimp and santa barbara spot prawns

Everyone loves a classic shrimp cocktail or a big batch of shrimp deep-fried in beer batter. I also love the Santa Barbara spot prawn, a ridgeback shrimp that is the pride of its namesake Southern California town and close cousin to the also excellent Alaska and Texas spot prawns.

"Michael certainly rocks that restaurant. It's a reflection of him and his joy and his love of the game and love of the food."

—JANN WENNER, FOUNDER, PUBLISHER, AND EDITOR, *ROLLING STONE*

shrimp cocktail

Serves 4

Now, you tell me, is there anything that says celebration more than a perfect meaty shrimp cocktail? I remember the thrill of being able to order one when I was a kid, and I still enjoy finding one on a menu. Shrimp cocktails seem so old-fashioned that they've become a restaurant rarity—except at a big, splashy fish house. I still serve them at home for the holidays.

If you have special shrimp cocktail bowls, by all means use them, and tightly pack them with shaved ice. If not, use martini glasses or other small bowls.

The key to great cocktail sauce is fresh horseradish. Use it, and you'll taste the difference in one bite.

20 cooked jumbo shrimp, peeled, deveined, and partially butterflied

Cocktail Sauce (recipe follows)

4 lemon wedges

If using shrimp cocktail dishes, fill them with shaved ice. Hang 5 shrimp around the edge of each of 4 dishes. Place a small dish of cocktail sauce in the center and garnish with a lemon wedge.

cocktail sauce

1 cup ketchup

¼ cup freshly grated horseradish

Juice of 1 lemon

Combine the ketchup, horseradish, and lemon juice in a small bowl.

NOTE: You can buy cooked shrimp at most fish markets. However, I prefer to prepare mine at home to ensure that they are not overcooked. First peel, devein, and partially butterfly the shrimp. Place the shrimp in boiling salted water for about 3 minutes or until firm, opaque, and curled. Immediately drain and rinse under cold running water.

bass ale beer-battered shrimp

Serves 4

Served with aïoli or ponzu sauce, this recipe is a real crowd-pleaser, great as a passed hors d'oeuvre or as a sit-down first course. Everyone loves shrimp. Ask the market to peel, devein, and butterfly the shrimp for you. The key to a light batter is combining the right amount of flour and cornstarch. If you add too little cornstarch, the batter will be thick and cakey; too much and the batter will absorb too much oil and become soggy.

Peanut oil for frying

3 cups all-purpose flour

3 tablespoons cornstarch

½ teaspoon sea salt

½ teaspoon freshly ground black pepper

3 cups Bass ale

Seltzer water (optional)

16 medium-sized raw shrimp, peeled, deveined, and butterflied

Aïoli (recipe follows) or Ponzu Sauce (page 92)

Place enough oil in a deep-fat fryer to fill the fryer by at least three-quarters. Turn the heat to medium-high and bring to 375°F on an instant-read thermometer.

While the oil is heating, combine the flour, cornstarch, salt, and pepper in a large mixing bowl. Whisk in the ale, mixing just until the batter is smooth. If the batter seems too thick, thin with a little seltzer.

When the oil reaches the desired temperature, working with one piece at a time, use tongs to dip the shrimp carefully into the batter, allowing any excess to drip off. Drop the shrimp into the hot oil and fry for 2 to 3 minutes or until golden brown and crisp.

Transfer the shrimp to a paper towel–lined platter as you fry them. Serve hot with Aïoli or Ponzu Sauce.

aïoli

2 large egg yolks

4 cloves garlic, peeled and chopped

1 cup olive oil

1½ teaspoons Meyer lemon juice

Sea salt and freshly ground black pepper

Combine the egg yolks and garlic in the bowl of a food processor fitted with the metal blade. Process until light and smooth. With the motor running, begin adding the oil in a very slow stream just until the mixture begins to hold and thicken. Then add the oil in a faster stream, making sure that it is continuously incorporated. Add the lemon juice and process just to blend. Season with salt and pepper to taste. The mixture should be the consistency of a thick mayonnaise. If too thick, loosen with a bit of cold water. Serve immediately.

"A great magazine is like a circus. In one ring is the bareback rider and in another is the trapeze artist and in another the clowns. The magic is in the mix. That's true of a great restaurant like Michael's, too. It's a mix of a great menu and great people."

—CHRISTIE HEFNER,
CHAIRMAN AND CEO, PLAYBOY ENTERPRISES

grilled santa barbara spot prawns with purslane salad

Serves 4

One of the great things about Santa Barbara spot prawns is that you can buy them with the head on, an advantage not only for your presentation but because you get even more flavor out of each prawn. Forget about the knife and fork. This is finger food, messy but tasty and fun.

2 dozen Santa Barbara spot prawns, heads on

1 cup extra-virgin olive oil

3 cloves garlic, peeled and chopped

1 tablespoon chopped fresh rosemary

Purslane Salad (recipe follows)

Juice of 1 Meyer lemon

Place the prawns in a single layer in a shallow baking dish. Combine the oil, garlic, and rosemary in a small bowl and, when blended, pour the seasoned oil over the prawns. Toss to combine. Cover with plastic film and set aside for 20 minutes.

Preheat and oil the grill.

Place the prawns on the grill and cook, turning occasionally, for about 4 minutes or until brightly colored.

Remove from the grill.

Mound the Purslane Salad in the center of a large, white platter. Lay the prawns on top, drizzle with Meyer lemon juice, and serve.

purslane salad

1 pound purslane, tough stems removed

1 bunch fresh flat-leaf parsley, tough stems removed

1 small sweet onion, julienned

¼ cup extra-virgin olive oil

1 tablespoon freshly squeezed Meyer lemon juice

Sea salt and freshly ground black pepper

Combine the purslane, parsley, and onion in a medium mixing bowl.

Combine the oil and lemon juice, whisking with a fork to blend. Season with salt and pepper to taste. Drizzle the dressing over the salad, tossing to combine.

Serve at room temperature.

"What Michael brings to the restaurant world is a lack of pretense. Things don't have to be complicated to be impressive. Simple really is better, and letting the ingredients star in the dish makes the cook look like a star as well."

—BARBARA FAIRCHILD,
EDITOR IN CHIEF, *BON APPÉTIT*

"I've been told that I'm the only person to have had four meals at Michael's New York in one day. It just happened. I had breakfast with a book agent, lunched with one of my authors, hosted a book signing party that evening in the garden room, and stayed for a sit-down dinner for ten with more friends and colleagues. What a day! I maybe spent two hours at my office. At the end of the evening, Michael's offered to roll up a bed for me. But I said, 'No thanks. I can walk home from here . . . See you tomorrow for breakfast.'"

—LARRY ASHMEAD, FORMER EXECUTIVE EDITOR, HARPERCOLLINS

squid

The best squid I ever ate was grilled over a driftwood fire under a full moon on Paradiso Beach on the Greek island of Mykonos back in the early 1970s. Years later when I opened Michael's, grilled squid was one of my first specials. Even without the moonlight or the driftwood, it was a knockout—sweet, smoky, tender, and very Southern California.

Try to find the smallest fresh squid you can and use both the bodies and the tentacles. Most stores preclean them. Cook them the same day you buy them.

herb-grilled calamari with micro greens

Serves 4

Grilled calamari is a sensational first course or light lunch. Served over a bed of delicately flavored micro greens as I do here, it is heavenly. For grilling, I prefer very small squid that can be cut in half.

This simple recipe can be jazzed up in a million ways. The vinaigrette is my standard. You can change the vinegar, citrus accent, or the oil to put your own stamp on it.

1 pound small squid, cleaned and halved lengthwise

¼ cup extra-virgin olive oil

2 cloves garlic, peeled and minced

½ tablespoon fresh thyme leaves

Sea salt and freshly ground black pepper

8 cups micro greens

8 to 10 cherry tomatoes, halved lengthwise

½ cup Michael's Vinaigrette (page 30)

Place the squid in a shallow baking dish. Add the olive oil, garlic, thyme, and salt and pepper, tossing to coat.

Preheat and oil the grill.

Place the squid on the grill and cook, turning once, for about 2 minutes or until the squid is cooked through and colored. Remove from the grill.

Place the greens in a bowl and drizzle lightly with the vinaigrette. Toss to coat.

Place an equal portion of the greens and tomatoes in the center of each of 4 luncheon plates. Place an equal amount of the grilled squid on top of each salad and drizzle the squid and plate with a bit of the vinaigrette. Serve immediately.

bass ale beer-battered calamari

Serves 4

Once you have tried my version of fried calamari, you will know just how good the dish can be. So good, in fact, that you don't need anything more than a spritz of lemon juice to enjoy it. If you want to add some zip, serve with Ponzu Sauce (page 92) or Aïoli (page 103).

Peanut oil for frying

3 cups all-purpose flour

3 tablespoons cornstarch

½ teaspoon sea salt plus more to taste

½ teaspoon freshly ground black pepper

3 cups Bass ale

Seltzer water (optional)

1¼ pounds cleaned squid, cut crosswise into rings, tentacles left whole

Meyer lemon wedges

¼ cup freshly grated Parmesan cheese

Place enough oil in a deep-fat fryer to fill the fryer by at least three-quarters. Turn the heat to medium-high and bring to 375°F on an instant-read thermometer.

While the oil is heating, combine the flour, cornstarch, salt, and pepper in a large mixing bowl. Whisk in the ale, mixing just until the batter is smooth. If the batter seems too thick, thin with a little seltzer.

When the oil reaches the desired temperature, working with one piece at a time, use tongs to dip the squid carefully into the batter, allowing any excess to drip off. Drop the squid pieces into the hot oil and fry for about 1 minute or until golden brown and crisp.

Transfer the squid to a paper towel-lined platter as you fry them.

When all of the squid have been fried, sprinkle with sea salt, Meyer lemon juice, and grated Parmesan. Serve immediately.

NOTE: To make Crispy Maui Onions, cut large Maui onions crosswise into ¼-inch-thick slices. Pull the slices apart into rings, reserving the smaller centers for another purpose. Prepare the batter as above. Dip the rings into the batter, a few at a time, and fry, drain, and salt as directed above. Everybody loves these, so figure at least 1 large onion per person.

"Michael has become a master at knowing a little bit about everybody. When you're a host, to be able to walk over to any table and know just enough about your guests to start the conversation so that people feel welcome, that makes an enormous difference . . . The Yiddish word is *heimisch,* homey. Michael has this ability to be very *heimisch.*"

—Jonathan Tisch, chairman and CEO, Loews Hotels

dover sole

Dover sole is the king of white fish. Imported from Europe, it was once found only on the menus of fine "continental" or four-star hotel restaurants. Although there are a number of fish sold as "sole" (lemon sole, rex sole, Petrale, and so on), they are actually members of the flounder family and are not true sole. Dover sole is the most desirable "true" sole, and it can be found only in European waters. Even today, with improved distribution and shipping methods, Dover sole is available only through fine fishmongers. It is expensive but worth every penny.

Dover sole has a very sweet, firm flesh with a delicate flavor. It has an elongated body with very dark, tough top skin, which must be removed before cooking unless grilling whole. It is often served whole and then filleted at the table, and it is traditionally served *meunière,* that is, lightly dusted with flour, seasoned, and cooked in butter. It is then served with a *beurre meunière,* brown butter with lemon juice and chopped parsley.

dover sole with white mushrooms and caviar

Serves 4

The elegance of Dover sole is only heightened with a sauce containing delicately flavored button mushrooms and caviar. Although I love the classic *meunière,* this recipe gives the sole the extra oomph that it deserves. Blanching the mushrooms helps set their pale white color and keeps them from exuding liquid into the sauce.

2 tablespoons salted butter

1 teaspoon fresh lemon juice

Sea salt and freshly ground white pepper

½ pound white mushrooms, cleaned, trimmed, and cut lengthwise into ⅛-inch-thick slices

1 large shallot, minced

⅓ cup Chardonnay

2 cups heavy cream

Freshly ground white pepper to taste

½ cup clarified butter (see Note, page 48)

2 whole Dover soles, filleted (8 fillets total, 6 to 8 ounces per piece)

1 cup all-purpose flour

2 ounces caviar

1 tablespoon chopped fresh chives

Place just a touch of water in a medium saucepan. Add 1 tablespoon of the butter and the lemon juice and season with salt and white pepper. Bring to a simmer over medium-high heat. Add the mushrooms, cover, and bring to a boil. Cook, covered, for about 4 minutes or until the mushrooms are fully cooked. Remove from the heat and drain well.

Heat the remaining tablespoon of butter in a medium saucepan over medium heat. Add the shallot and cook, stirring frequently, for about 2 minutes or until the shallot has softened. Add the Chardonnay and bring to a boil. Cook for about 3 minutes or until the liquid has evaporated.

Stir in the cream and bring to a simmer. Season with salt and white pepper and cook, stirring frequently, for about 5 minutes or until the mixture coats the back of a metal spoon. Fold in the mushrooms and keep warm.

Heat the clarified butter in a large sauté pan over high heat. Season the sole with salt and white pepper to taste. Spread the flour on a dinner plate and turn the fillets in the flour to coat them evenly. Place in the hot pan and cook for about 3 minutes or until the fish is set around the edges. Using a fish spatula, turn and cook the remaining side for about 2 minutes or just until golden brown. Remove from the heat.

Spoon an equal portion of the sauce and mushrooms on each of 4 dinner plates. Place 2 fish fillets on top. Place a small dollop of caviar on each fillet. Sprinkle with chives and serve.

"Michael played a pivotal role in creating what we think of as modern American cuisine. He was instrumental in elevating the status of the chef in our culture, creating a sense that chefs were every bit as important as leaders in the visual arts or other art forms. In his early work with the American Institute of Wine and Food, his passion for food was always wrapped up in his passion for the larger arts world."

—Greg Drescher, Culinary Institute of America, Greystone Campus, Napa Valley

loup de mer, rouget-barbet de roche, wild striped bass, and sardines

Both *loup* and *rouget* are Mediterranean fish that are available in the United States through fine fishmongers. *Loup* is actually a bass and, in fact, the only fish for which the single name "bass" is appropriate. It has a rich, firm white flesh that has, for generations, been prized on classic French menus. The Italians call their version *branzino,* and in the States we have great wild, striped bass that is delicious. The French Atlantic wild bass, cousin to Mediterranean *loup de mer,* is called *bar de ligne,* which refers to the fact that it's line-caught.

Rouget is red mullet, which can be found only in the Mediterranean. In Europe, it is considered quite a delicacy. Its firm, bright reddish pink flesh is very lean and is used throughout the region in stews as well as in *escabèche* (a dish in which cooked fish is seasoned in a savory marinade and then served cold as an appetizer or snack) or prepared on the grill. In France, the fish is often grilled intact, innards and all, and the diner pulls off the charred skin at the table.

Fresh sardines from Europe or North America are a great warm-weather treat. I love to grill them and eat them on a salad.

On America's East Coast, line-caught striped bass is a favorite catch of weekend fisherman. The fish is very delicate and sweet, and I look forward to it every summer.

The following recipes can be used for each of the fresh fish, including sardines (which are also a common Mediterranean fish). I like to prepare *rouget* or sardines as a first course, but I usually serve *loup de mer* as a main course.

grilled loup de mer

Serves 4

This recipe can be used for any of my favorite fish. Leave the skin on for a very nice, crunchy finish. I like to garnish the simply grilled fish with a slightly sweet Tomato-Basil Vinaigrette, but it is important that the tomatoes be very ripe and redolent with the scent of summer.

Tomato-Basil Vinaigrette is one of my signatures. It makes a terrific garnish for all types of grilled vegetables, fish, poultry, and meats.

Four 6-ounce skin-on *loup de mer* fillets (or striped bass or whole *rouget* or sardines, cleaned)

2½ tablespoons extra-virgin olive oil

Sea salt and freshly ground black pepper

6 cups baby arugula leaves

Tomato-Basil Vinaigrette (recipe follows)

Preheat and oil a grill.

Using a pastry brush, lightly coat the fish with 1 tablespoon of the oil. Season with salt and pepper to taste.

Place fish on the grill, skin side down, and grill for 1 minute. Rotate the fish to make crosshatch marks on the skin and grill for an additional minute, or until the fish is cooked around the edges. Turn and grill the flesh side as above for an additional 1 to 2 minutes or until the fish is just barely cooked through.

Season the arugula with the remaining oil and salt and pepper. Place a mound in the center of each of 4 dinner plates. Place a fillet on top of the arugula on each plate. Spoon an equal portion of the vinaigrette over each piece of fish. Serve immediately.

tomato-basil vinaigrette

2 very ripe red or yellow tomatoes, about ½ pound

½ cup medium extra-virgin olive oil

½ cup balsamic vinegar

Sea salt and freshly ground black pepper

2 tablespoons fresh basil chiffonade

With a small sharp knife, score the bottom of each tomato with a shallow X. Have ready a large bowl of ice water.

Bring a saucepan of water to a boil over high heat. Drop the tomatoes into the boiling water and boil until the tomato skins begin to wrinkle, about 45 seconds. Using a slotted spoon, transfer the tomatoes to the ice water. Let stand for 1 minute.

Then lift the tomatoes from the water and, with your fingertips, peel them. Using a paring knife, cut out and discard the stem end of each tomato. Halve the tomatoes crosswise and remove their seeds with your fingertips

Cut the tomatoes into ½-inch cubes and place them in a bowl. In a separate bowl, whisk together the oil, vinegar, and salt and pepper to taste. Stir the dressing into the tomatoes. Set aside until ready to serve. Just before serving, fold in the basil.

line-caught striped bass
with baby pea sauté

Serves 4

When spring arrives, with it come fresh English peas along with their shoots and, if you're lucky, some wild mushrooms. I have devised this subtle sauté as the perfect bed for a wonderful piece of striped bass. The sauté offers the hint of fresh flavor that highlights the sweetness of the fish. Striped bass can also be simply served with Tomato-Basil Vinaigrette (page 110) as its sauce. And it is also terrific on the grill.

1½ pounds fresh young English peas in the pod

¼ cup salted butter

½ pound wild mushrooms (chanterelles, morels, or shiitakes), cleaned and, if large, quartered

2 bunches spring onions, quartered

Pinch sea salt plus more to taste

Four 6-ounce skin-on wild striped bass fillets

Freshly ground black pepper

All-purpose flour for dusting

¼ cup peanut oil

¼ cup chopped fresh mint leaves

2 tablespoons chopped fresh chives

Shell the peas, discarding the pods. You should have about 1½ cups. Blanch in boiling salted water for 2 to 3 minutes; drain, immediately plunge into a bowl of ice water, drain again, and set aside.

Heat 2 tablespoons of the butter in a medium saucepan over medium-high heat. Add the mushrooms and sauté until lightly browned, 3 to 5 minutes. Remove from the pan and set aside. Add the remaining 2 tablespoons of butter to the pan and, when melted, add the onions, season with a pinch of salt, and sauté for 2 minutes. Add the mushrooms and the peas, stir to blend well, and sauté for 3 to 5 minutes more.

Remove from the heat and keep warm.

Season the fish with salt and pepper to taste and dust lightly with the flour.

Heat the oil in a large frying pan. When very hot, but not smoking, add the fish, skin side down. Fry for about 3 minutes or until the skin has crisped and the fish is just cooked around the edges. Turn and fry for another 2 to 3 minutes or until the fish is cooked through. Remove from the heat and place on a double layer of paper towel to drain off excess oil.

Add the mint to the vegetable sauté, tossing to blend the whole mixture. Place an equal portion on each of 4 dinner plates. Place a piece of fish on top, sprinkle with chives, and serve.

salmon

Salmon is, without a doubt, the most popular fish in the United States. I await summer's marvelous run of wild salmon with their incomparable deep, rich flavor.

Almost all of the best wild salmon comes from Pacific waters, primarily northern California, Oregon, Washington, Canada, and Alaska. Salmon are usually caught at the mouths of the great rivers that give the fish their names, such as Copper River, Klamath, and Columbia. I generally use either sockeye or king salmon. Copper River wild sockeye has deep red flesh and glistening silver skin. It is usually quite small, ranging from six to twelve pounds. King salmon, also known as Chinook, is the largest of all salmon. It has the fattiest meat, which is a rich orange in color. Its best season is the height of summer, but my favorite, Columbia River king, is available through the early winter.

Even though I specify a particular type in the following recipes, you can use any salmon. Farm-raised salmon is reasonably priced and widely available. It works very well on the grill or with a quick sear during those periods when the wild varieties are not in the market.

gravlax

Makes 1½ pounds for 8 to 12 servings

I first tasted gravlax at Café des Artistes, the renowned Manhattan eatery run by the famed Hungarian restaurateur George Lang. At Michael's I was determined to make my own California-style version. The traditional Scandinavian curing calls for aquavit, but I choose to eliminate the alcohol so that the sweet salmon flavor dominates. Gravlax is one of the great first courses, and it also makes a terrific hors d'oeuvre when placed on brioche toast.

One 1½-pound skinless salmon fillet, pinbones removed

4 cups chopped fresh dill

⅓ cup sea salt

⅓ cup sugar

⅓ cup freshly ground white pepper

Mustard-Dill Mayonnaise (recipe follows)

Line a shallow glass dish large enough to hold the salmon with enough plastic film to enclose the salmon completely. Set aside.

Using a small sharp knife, lightly score the skin side of the salmon with diagonal lines about 1 inch apart. Set aside.

Combine the dill, salt, sugar, and white pepper. Place half of the mixture in the bottom of the plastic film–lined dish. Place the salmon on top of the dill mixture. Spoon the remainder of the dill mixture over the salmon, taking care to pack it evenly over the top and around the sides. Pull the plastic film up and over the fish to enclose it tightly. Place a piece of aluminum foil snuggly over the wrapped fish.

Place another dish that is small enough to fit into the fish-filled dish on top of the salmon. Weight the dish down with filled cans or any other clean, heavy implement that will keep the salmon submerged in the curing mixture and the juices that form as the fish cures.

Place in the refrigerator for at least 48 hours.

Remove the salmon from the refrigerator. Uncover and unwrap. Using your fingertips, push off the curing mix.

To serve, cut the salmon using a carving knife, almost parallel against the flesh, into long, tissue-thin slices.

Serve with Mustard-Dill Mayonnaise and toasted brioche.

mustard-dill mayonnaise

1 large egg yolk, at room temperature

1 tablespoon Dijon mustard, at room temperature

1 tablespoon champagne vinegar, at room temperature

1 cup peanut oil

1½ teaspoons fresh lemon juice

Sea salt and freshly ground white pepper

3 tablespoons chopped fresh dill

Combine the egg yolk, mustard, and vinegar in the bowl of a food processor fitted with the metal blade, processing until smooth and light yellow. With the motor running, begin adding the oil in a slow, steady stream, increasing the flow as the mixture begins to thicken. Add the lemon juice and salt and white pepper to taste. (If you don't have a processor, use a wire whisk, beating rapidly until the egg mixture is light yellow; then whisk in the oil.)

Scrape the mixture from the processor bowl into a clean container. Fold in the dill.

NOTE: This presentation may also be used to serve smoked salmon. I prefer Irish or Scottish cold-smoked Atlantic salmon, which I believe to be the absolute best on the market, with a robust smoky flavor and silky texture that makes perfect hors d'oeuvres or appetizers. However, there are now many great American smokehouses producing their own salmon. Like gravlax, smoked salmon must be cut into almost paper-thin slices for service.

pan-seared king salmon with blood orange vinaigrette

Serves 4

King salmon has a lovely rose color and a high fat content, making its flavor very rich and sweet. The acidic vinaigrette offsets the sweetness perfectly, and the colors are an absolute symphony on the plate. Tomato-Basil Vinaigrette (page 110) is another great sauce for this salmon. Alternatively, you can grill the salmon, but again take care not to overcook.

My favorite accompaniments for this dish are steamed spinach and mashed fingerling potatoes; prepare the potatoes following the recipe on page 64 but omit the arugula. Or not!

2 cups fresh blood orange juice

⅓ cup white wine vinegar

1¼ cups extra-virgin olive oil

Sea salt and freshly ground white pepper

1 cup blood orange segments, well drained of excess juice

2 tablespoons clarified butter (see Note, page 48)

Four 6-ounce boneless, skinless king salmon fillets

1 tablespoon chopped fresh chives

Place the blood orange juice in a small saucepan over medium heat. Bring to a simmer and cook for about 30 minutes or until reduced to ⅔ cup. Remove from the heat and set aside to cool.

Combine the vinegar with the reduced orange juice. Whisk in the oil. Season with salt and white pepper to taste. Fold in the orange segments and set aside.

Heat the butter in a large nonstick sauté pan over high heat. When very hot but not smoking, add the salmon and sear for about 4 minutes or until just set around the edges. Turn and sear for an additional 4 minutes or until the fish is just barely cooked through.

While the fish is cooking, put the vinaigrette in a small saucepan and gently warm it over low heat.

Spoon the warm vinaigrette on each of 4 dinner plates. Place one piece of salmon in the center of each plate. Garnish with chives and serve immediately.

> "I'm an investor in Michael's. Why? I just like the guy so much. He's a great human being. He's fun, he's got ideas, he makes things happen, he's got good taste, and his dishes all look good. There's a whole gestalt. I eat whatever Michael tells me to eat. He tells me what the special is, and I say, 'Yeah. I'll have one of those.' But it's the friendly lovingness of Michael that's the biggest appeal for me, that feeling of family. And I think he's got a great wife, too."
>
> —FRANK GEHRY, ARCHITECT

"Michael has always been one of the pioneers of what has been called California cuisine. In the late 1970s, when I started working at *Bon Appétit,* Michael's (along with Chez Panisse) defined it. These days, we talk about cooking from the farm, or cooking fresh with the seasons, or letting the ingredients shine; but back then it was a new concept. The fact that Michael's endures is really a testament to his talent and his flair for this type of cooking."

—BARBARA FAIRCHILD, EDITOR IN CHIEF,
BON APPÉTIT

grilled copper river sockeye salmon with fava bean, white corn, and wild mushroom succotash

Serves 4

The arrival of early spring means sockeye salmon to me. Its ruby flesh has almost no fat and is highly prized in Japan for sashimi. It is best served rare, as the flavor is incomparable. The succotash is the perfect base, combining some of spring's sweetest vegetables.

"Michael's New York is like a well-told story. The story has a great beginning and a middle, and a good plot: to open a restaurant in the most important city in the world and be instantly successful. It's the story of a hero who came into his own. And I don't think the end of the story is in sight."

—HELEN GURLEY BROWN,
AUTHOR AND LEGENDARY
EDITOR IN CHIEF, *COSMOPOLITAN*

Four 6-ounce thin, skin-on, sockeye salmon fillets

Sea salt and freshly ground black pepper

Fava Bean, White Corn, and Wild Mushroom Succotash (page 49)

1 tablespoon finely chopped fresh flat-leaf parsley

Preheat and oil the grill.

Season the salmon with sea salt and pepper to taste.

Place the salmon on the hot grill, skin side down, and grill for about 3 minutes or just until the flesh is set. Turn and grill for about 1 minute or just until the fish is lightly colored. Remove from the grill. Take great care not to overcook!

Spoon equal portions of the succotash in the center of each of 4 dinner plates. Place a salmon fillet on top. Sprinkle the entire plate with parsley and serve

Shad roe has always been considered one of the great spring delicacies, and you can count on it to be on my menu, both at home and in the restaurants. It is available only during the spawning season of late March through May, when Atlantic shad make their way up the coast to their spawning grounds from the Carolinas to the Hudson River.

Shad roe comes in two sacs, called a pair, that are encased in a thin, edible membrane. The sacs are elongated ovals tightly filled with tiny brownish pink eggs. They are best when sautéed in butter.

Shad roe is, I admit, an acquired taste. When getting your friends to try it, think, "A really great hamburger." And for the record, shad roe is best served with an ice-cold Bombay Sapphire Martini Straight Up with Five Olives (page 209). You'll find it a perfect marriage!

sautéed shad roe with pommery mustard cream sauce, grilled sweet onions, and bacon lardons

Serves 4

I have served shad roe every spring since I opened the restaurant in Santa Monica. We fly it out from the East Coast and then watch transplanted easterners get all nostalgic on us. Of course, you can get it each spring at Michael's New York, too.

Grilled Sweet Onions (recipe follows)

¾ cup Chardonnay

2 tablespoons minced shallots

2 cups heavy cream

2 tablespoons Pommery mustard

1 tablespoon lemon juice

Sea salt and freshly ground black pepper

1 cup all-purpose flour

2 whole shad roe, each separated into 2 pieces

3 tablespoons clarified butter (see Note, page 48)

3 tablespoons extra-virgin olive oil

½ cup Bacon Lardons (page 98)

Matchstick Potatoes (page 61)

1 bunch watercress, tough stems removed

1 tablespoon chopped fresh flat-leaf parsley

First make the Grilled Sweet Onions.

While they are grilling, start to prepare the mustard cream sauce. Put the Chardonnay and shallots in a saucepan. Bring to a boil over high heat, reduce the heat slightly to maintain a brisk simmer, and cook until almost all of the wine has evaporated but the shallots are still moist, about 6 minutes. Stir in the cream and bring it to a simmer. Reduce the heat and cook at a bare simmer for about 12 minutes or until the cream has thickened and reduced by about one-third. Whisk in the mustard and lemon juice. Season with salt and pepper to taste. Keep warm.

Spread the flour on a dinner plate. Season with salt and pepper and stir lightly to combine. One at a time, dredge the shad roe pieces in the seasoned flour to coat them evenly, tapping off excess flour, and set them aside. Heat the clarified butter and oil in a large sauté pan over medium-high heat. Carefully place the shad roe in the pan. Cook, turning once, for about 2 minutes per side or until slightly crisp and golden brown; this method will result in shad roe that are still pale pink and moist inside, like a medium-rare burger.

Place one piece of shad roe on each of 4 dinner plates. Spoon the sauce over and around the shad roe. Separate the grilled onions into rings and arrange them on top of the roe. Sprinkle with Bacon Lardons. Mound the Matchstick Potatoes and the watercress alongside the roe. Sprinkle with parsley and serve immediately.

NOTE: I also like to serve shad roe with brown butter sauce and giant Spanish capers. To make the sauce, put 1 cup (2 sticks) room-temperature butter in a small sauté pan over low heat. Cook, stirring frequently, for about 4 minutes or until the butter foams and begins to turn brown. It should smell almost nutty. Watch carefully, as it will blacken quickly. Remove the butter from the heat and stir in ½ cup drained giant Spanish capers and 2 tablespoons lemon juice. Fold in 2 tablespoons chopped flat-leaf parsley, season to taste with salt and black pepper, and spoon the sauce over the roe before hitting the plate with Matchstick Potatoes and watercress.

grilled sweet onions

4 large ½-inch-thick slices sweet onion

¼ cup olive oil

Sea salt and freshly ground black pepper

Preheat and oil the grill.

Using a pastry brush, lightly coat both sides of the onion slices with the oil. Season with salt and pepper to taste.

Place the seasoned onions on the hot grill and cook, turning occasionally and moving to cooler parts of the grill as the onions begin to char, for about 10 minutes or until cooked through and slightly crisp.

Alternatively, you can sauté the onions in a little butter until just barely cooked.

Remove from the heat and serve warm or at room temperature.

"In the late 1970s, I was in Los Angeles, and Michael took me to see this really dilapidated house on Third Street in Santa Monica, with a patch of weeds in the back. And he said, 'This is it. This is my restaurant.' "

—TIM KITTLESON, DIRECTOR, UCLA FILM & TELEVISION ARCHIVE, AND LONGTIME FRIEND AND FAN

tuna carpaccio with white mushrooms

Serves 4

My first introduction to raw tuna was a revelation. It was stupendous—meaty yet delicate, with extraordinary texture and flavor. I immediately determined to use it at Michael's, and thought, What better way than in the style of a classic beef carpaccio. It worked so well that I still offer it frequently, with white truffles in the fall and early winter and pristine white mushrooms at other times of the year.

I prefer to use ahi tuna, but if you can't find it use whatever sushi-grade tuna you can find.

One 1-pound block ahi tuna

4 bunches baby arugula, tough stems removed

Sea salt and freshly ground black pepper

¼ cup fruity green extra-virgin olive oil

One ¼-pound piece Parmesan cheese

Fresh white truffles *or* 4 large pristine white button mushrooms, stems removed

1 lemon, quartered, seeds removed

Wrap the tuna in plastic film and refrigerate for about 45 minutes, or until firm enough to slice easily.

Place 4 flat luncheon plates in the freezer.

Unwrap the tuna and, with a very sharp slicing knife, cut it across the grain into ⅛-inch-thick slices. Working with one cold plate at a time, lay the tuna, barely overlapping, around the plate to cover the center completely, leaving about ¼ inch around the rim.

When all of the plates have been arranged, place arugula leaves over the tuna. Season with sea salt and pepper. Drizzle an equal portion of oil over the tuna and shave the cheese over the top.

Freely shave white truffles over the top at the last minute or use a knife to cut the button mushrooms into very thin slices and scatter them over each serving. Place a lemon wedge on each plate and serve.

Although there are a number of different types of tuna, I generally use only ahi, the Hawaiian name for bigeye tuna. Because of its high fat content, which brings with it big flavor and a rich texture, it is the most desirable tuna for eating raw. Ahi is at its best during the winter months, although it is also available during other times of the year. Yellowfin tuna (also sometimes called ahi) and bluefin are both really great fish, but not quite so rich as bigeye.

Fresh tuna was almost nonexistent when I opened Michael's Santa Monica. The standard *salade niçoise* featured canned tuna. Thank God I found the Japanese fish market in downtown Los Angeles. Today fresh tuna is available all across the country.

Although I prefer ahi, bluefin comes a close second. It is the largest of the tunas and, during the summer months, can be found in cold Atlantic waters off the New England coast. Its deep red color looks beautiful on the plate, and its richness makes for sublime eating.

The best tuna looks as beautiful as it tastes. When shopping for tuna, always ask for sushi-grade. To get the best, I advise going to a busy Japanese market or a top-notch seafood shop where you know the tuna will be absolutely fresh. "Toro," the belly cut, offers the richest of all tuna-eating experiences.

salade niçoise

Serves 4

This recipe is my take on the French classic. Using seared fresh tuna takes this salad to new heights. All of the ingredients should be as flawless as the tuna—garden-fresh lettuce, tomatoes, and beans are fitting companions to the fresh fish. See the method on page 69 for tips on peeling and seeding tomatoes.

One 2-pound piece yellowfin tuna, cut into smaller 2- by 2-inch pieces

Sea salt and freshly ground black pepper

2 tablespoons peanut oil

4 very ripe beefsteak tomatoes, peeled, cored, seeded, and roughly chopped

½ pound *niçoise* olives, pitted and roughly chopped

¼ pound picholine olives, pitted and roughly chopped

1 tablespoon fresh tarragon leaves

⅔ pound mesclun or other mixed baby greens

1 cup Balsamic Vinaigrette (page 39)

2 ounces cooked fingerling potatoes, cut crosswise into thin slices

4 fertile organic free-range eggs, boiled for no more than 9 minutes, peeled and quartered

¾ pound haricots verts, trimmed and blanched

Large chunk Parmesan cheese for shaving

Lightly score one side of the tuna. Season both sides with salt and pepper to taste.

Heat the oil in a medium-sized heavy sauté pan over high heat. When the oil is smoking, add the tuna, scored side down. Sear for 40 seconds, then turn and sear the remaining sides for about 20 seconds or just until colored. Remove from the heat and place on a double layer of paper towel to absorb any oil. Allow to cool slightly.

Combine the tomatoes, olives, and tarragon, stirring to blend well.

Place the greens in a large bowl. Add just enough vinaigrette to season lightly, tossing to blend. Using tongs, transfer the dressed greens to a serving platter. Place mounds of the tomato mixture at 3 equidistant points around the greens. Place a mound of potatoes on one side of the tomatoes and a few pieces of egg on the other.

Using a sharp knife, cut the tuna into ¼-inch-thick slices. Place the slices, slightly overlapping, around the edge of the greens. Place the haricots verts on top of the greens in an attractive pattern. Shave a few pieces of Parmesan cheese over the top, drizzle some vinaigrette over the plate, and serve.

> "What I describe as a defining moment is when Michael went from gel in his hair to the dry look. He knew he'd arrived."
>
> —TOM BROKAW,
> NBC NEWSMAN

tuna tartare with cucumber and cilantro

Serves 4

This dish is very simple but sensational. It is easy to make, as the broth can be prepared early in the day and the tuna can be diced and kept refrigerated until ready to mix at the last minute. You don't want to chop too far in advance, or it will get mushy. One note of caution: Let the tuna shine. Do not overseason it.

3 ounces ice-cold sushi-grade tuna, finely diced

2 tablespoons chopped fresh chives

1 teaspoon soy sauce, or to taste

¼ teaspoon sesame oil, or to taste

¼ teaspoon wasabi oil, or to taste

Cucumber Broth (recipe follows)

Approximately ½ cup loosely packed kaiware (see Note) or other fresh sprouts

Place the tuna in a medium bowl. Add the chives and carefully season with soy sauce and the oils. You want the seasonings to accent the sweet, oily tuna, not overpower it.

Assemble 4 shallow soup bowls. Place a 2-inch ring mold in the center of one bowl. Fill the ring about ¾ full with the tartare, patting it down with the back of the spoon to make a neat, even circle. Carefully lift the ring and continue making circles of tartare in each of the remaining 3 bowls.

Ladle about ¼ cup of the Cucumber Broth around the tuna and garnish the top with the sprouts.

———

cucumber broth

2 hothouse cucumbers, peeled and chopped

1 bunch fresh cilantro

1 bunch fresh basil

½ bunch fresh mint

2 tablespoons yuzu juice (see Note)

1 tablespoon pickled ginger with its juice, or to taste

Combine the cucumbers, cilantro, basil, mint, and yuzu juice with the ginger and its juice in a blender. Process on high until very smooth. Do not overprocess, as you want the liquid to be bright green.

Pour the purée through a fine sieve into a clean container. Cover and refrigerate for about 1 hour or until well chilled.

NOTE: Kaiware sprouts (from daikon radish seeds) and yuzu juice (the juice of a very tart Japanese citrus fruit) are available from Asian markets and some specialty food or health food stores.

If you can't find yuzu juice, you can substitute a mixture of equal parts lemon and tangerine juices or just plain lime juice.

seared sesame tuna on a sesame crisp

Serves 4

This hors d'oeuvres is one of my favorites, with its knockout combination of crispy sesame-coated potatoes, rich tuna, and a cool-hot hit of wasabi cream sauce. The components can be prepared in advance and put together at the last minute. Keep this dish in your entertaining repertoire. It's a real crowd-pleaser.

One 8-ounce, 1-inch square block ahi tuna loin

Togarashi to taste (see Note)

Sea salt

Approximately 3 tablespoons clarified butter (see Note, page 48)

Sesame Crisps (recipe follows)

Wasabi Cream (recipe follows)

Chives for garnish

Season the tuna with togarashi and salt.

Heat the clarified butter in a large heavy-bottomed sauté pan over medium-high heat. When very hot, add the tuna and sear for about 20 seconds per side or until nicely colored but still rare. Remove from the heat and place on a double layer of paper towel to drain off excess butter.

Cut the tuna crosswise into ¼-inch-thick squares. Working with one piece at a time, place one square of tuna on top of a Sesame Crisp. Place a dollop of Wasabi Cream on top and garnish with chives. Serve immediately.

sesame crisps

Approximately ¼ cup clarified butter (see Note, page 48)

Sea salt

Sesame seeds

1 large russet potato, peeled and cut into 1½-inch square pieces

Preheat the oven to 325°F.

Line a baking sheet with parchment paper. Using a pastry brush, lightly coat the parchment with clarified butter. Sprinkle with salt and sesame seeds. Set aside.

Using a mandoline, cut the potato crosswise into paper-thin slices. Place the potato slices in a single layer on the buttered and seasoned parchment. Using the pastry brush, lightly coat the top of each potato slice with clarified butter and sprinkle with salt and sesame seeds.

Using the pastry brush, again lightly coat a piece of parchment cut to fit the baking sheet with clarified butter. Place the parchment, buttered side down, on top of the potatoes. Cover with another baking sheet to keep the potatoes from curling up as they cook.

Place in the preheated oven and bake for about 6 minutes or until golden brown. Remove from the oven and, using a spatula, carefully transfer the crisps to wire racks to cool before serving.

wasabi cream

½ cup crème fraîche

Wasabi paste

Squirt fresh lime juice

Combine the crème fraîche, wasabi to taste, and lime juice in a small dish. Cover and refrigerate until ready to use.

NOTE: Togarashi is a traditional Japanese seven-spice seasoning that usually includes red chili pepper, white and black sesame seeds, orange zest, Japanese pepper, seaweed flakes, and ginger. It is available from Japanese markets, as is wasabi paste.

"The most inspiring thing about Michael is that he runs a restaurant as if he were running a party that happens every day and every night. When people walk into that room, they have to feel they're at the right place at the right time. There has to be an electricity in the air. The same is true when you're cooking at home. What are the ingredients that make a great dinner party? Food is definitely a component. But it's also the group of people you put together, the music, the flowers—all the little twists on what you do."

—CLARK FRASIER, CO-CHEF AND CO-OWNER
(WITH MARK GAIER) OF ARROWS RESTAURANT AND
MC PERKINS COVE, OGUNQUIT, MAINE

meat, poultry, and game birds

Charbroiling, barbecuing, grilling: These terms kept coming back to me every day I spent in French cooking school. *Pourquoi?* Because in France at that time, the primary cooking methods were roasting, braising, and sautéing. *Les pauvres mecs!*

One of my most vivid memories of childhood is the sight, sound, and smell of the fantastic meat and poultry that my dad, J. T. McCarty, cooked on our outdoor wood-burning grill in Briarcliff Manor, New York; over driftwood fires on the beaches of Misquamicut, Rhode Island; or over glowing oak log embers in our fireplace during winter breaks in Manchester, Vermont.

Wherever we cooked meat or poultry, my mother, Carol, always insisted on starting with the best quality. She was the first one to teach me the all-important cooking truth that your meal is only as good as the ingredients you start with. J.T.'s effortless mastery of the grill showed me

> **"Whether it's a meal at Michael's or a great dinner party at home, it's a little like the duck on the pond, paddling like hell beneath the water but looking serene on the surface. You've got to work hard to make it look effortless."**
>
> —CHRISTIE HEFNER, CHAIRMAN AND CEO, PLAYBOY ENTERPRISES

how that absolutely simple cooking method can efficiently maximize the taste and texture of whatever food you throw on the fire. No surprise, then, that grilling has been, from the start, the preferred cooking method for meats, poultry, and game birds at Michael's.

In America today, we are blessed with the finest-quality beef, veal, pork, lamb, chicken, duck, quail, and squab. You can get great stuff virtually everywhere today, from your neighborhood supermarket to specialty butchers to Internet sources. See www.welcometomichaels.com. Fire up that grill and have a great meal!

"Michael has been a relentlessly positive influence on other restaurateurs, and he's never been arrogant or piggish about his success. He always has this air of 'Aren't I fortunate?' while you also know he's very shrewd and hardworking."

—CORBY KUMMER, SENIOR EDITOR, *THE ATLANTIC MONTHLY*

beef

Americans love beef. Nothing defines American beef better than a juicy, prime, twenty-eight-day-dry-aged New York strip steak, followed closely by a well-marbled rib-eye, an intensely meaty rare hanger steak, or a delicately tender filet mignon.

Those steaks are the bestsellers in my restaurants. They will be the big winners when you entertain at home, too.

"When we moved to Houston to open up Cafe Annie in 1981, we called Michael and he started sending people. Then he showed up. Michael is a restaurateur who shares. He's so generous, and he wants to spread the word. He's not like the usual competitive restaurateur."

—MIMI AND ROBERT DEL GRANDE, COFOUNDERS, CAFÉ ANNIE, HOUSTON

new york strip steak with arugula mashed potatoes, crispy maui onions, and cabernet sauvignon sauce

Serves 4

A great dry-aged New York strip is my steak of choice. And it seems to be the choice of our customers on both coasts. It is the boneless top loin muscle from the short loin, the tenderest part of the steer. Always make sure that your grill is really hot and the wire grid is brushed thoroughly clean before you put the steaks on; that will keep them from sticking. You can also sear them on a stovetop grill pan with great results. To enjoy maximum tenderness and juiciness, make sure you let your steaks rest for at least ten minutes before serving.

Four 12-ounce New York strip steaks, each at least 1¼ inches thick, trimmed of excess fat

Sea salt and freshly ground black pepper

Arugula Mashed Potatoes (page 64)

Cabernet Sauvignon Sauce (recipe follows)

Crispy Maui Onions (see Note, page 107)

1 tablespoon whole thyme leaves

Preheat the grill.

Season the steaks with salt and pepper to taste. Place the steaks diagonally on the hot grill and leave them undisturbed for 3 minutes; then rotate them 90 degrees to make a crosshatch pattern on their undersides and leave undisturbed for about 3 minutes more. Turn over the steaks and grill the other side for a total of 6 minutes more, again rotating them halfway through that time to make crosshatch grill marks. The steaks will be medium-rare. (You can also use an instant-read thermometer to gauge the interior temperature, noting that the grill time will depend on the thickness of the steaks.) Transfer the steaks to a platter, tent them with aluminum foil, and leave them to rest for 10 minutes so their hot juices can settle.

Place a steak on each of 4 dinner plates. Spoon an equal portion of the potatoes on one side. Drizzle with Cabernet Sauvignon Sauce and garnish with Crispy Maui Onions. Sprinkle with thyme and serve.

cabernet sauvignon sauce

1 clove garlic, peeled

¾ cup Cabernet Sauvignon

¼ cup black currants (see Note)

2 tablespoons cassis syrup (see Note)

2 cups veal stock or reconstituted Knorr beef bouillon

1 teaspoon fresh thyme

1 tablespoon salted butter, at room temperature

Sea salt and freshly ground black pepper

Place the garlic in a small saucepan of cold water over high heat. Bring to a boil and immediately remove from the heat and drain. Repeat the process one more time. This blanching produces garlic that is milder and sweeter than raw. Set aside.

Combine the wine, currants, and syrup in a small saucepan over medium-high heat. Bring to a boil and cook for about 7 minutes or until the mixture has reduced to about ¼ cup and is syrupy.

Stir in the stock and bring to a simmer. Lower the heat and simmer, skimming frequently, for about 15 minutes or until the mixture coats the back of a metal spoon and has reduced to 1½ cups. Add the thyme along with the reserved garlic, stirring to blend. Swirl in the butter until totally incorporated. Season to taste with salt and pepper and keep warm until ready to serve.

NOTE: Until recently in the United States, black currants were available only frozen. The frozen product is good, but currants are now raised here, and you can purchase fresh ones from specialty produce stores in the early summer. You can use either fresh or frozen currants in this recipe.

Cassis syrup is available from liquor stores and some specialty food stores.

hanger steak with syrah sauce

Serves 4

I learned to love this inexpensive French bistro meat during my student days in Paris. The classic preparation is *aux échalotes* (with shallots and red wine sauce), and I like to do it with California Syrah, a red whose robust quality matches that of the meat. Hanger steak's name, by the way, comes from the fact that the cut hangs between the rib cage and loin. It was once known as a "butcher's cut" because there is only one per cow and butchers knew that it was extremely flavorful so kept it for their own tables.

I once had a hard time getting our purveyors to provide me with hanger steaks, but they finally stepped up to the plate. Now hanger steaks can be found on menus everywhere, from bistros to four-star spots, not to mention your local market. They go especially well with Pommes Frites (page 60) and a side of Dijon mustard to swirl with the Syrah sauce. The steak should be served rare because if it is overcooked it becomes quite tough. To round out the plate, add a mound of steamed spinach.

simmer and cook for about 7 minutes or until reduced by three-quarters. Stir in the stock and simmer until reduced by half, about 10 minutes. Whisk in the butter and season with salt and pepper to taste. Cook for a minute. Remove from the heat and serve.

NOTE: You may be able to find 4 dressed hanger steaks of equal size, but, most often, fine butchers sell whole hanger steaks. They are in one piece with a vein running lengthwise down the center. Once the vein is removed, you will have 2 pieces of meat of unequal size. Two whole hanger steaks will more than adequately feed 4 people.

2 hanger steaks, center vein removed (see Note)

Sea salt and freshly ground black pepper

Syrah Sauce (recipe follows)

Preheat the grill.

Season the steaks with salt and pepper to taste.

Place the seasoned steaks on the hot grill and cook for 2 minutes. Turn and grill the other side for 2 minutes just to sear the meat. Continue grilling, turning occasionally, for about 12 minutes for medium-rare (140°F on an instant-read thermometer) or until the meat is cooked to the desired degree of doneness.

Remove from the grill and place a steak on each of 4 dinner plates. Spoon the Syrah Sauce over the top and serve.

———

syrah sauce

2 cups Syrah

2 shallots, minced

1 cup veal stock or reconstituted Knorr beef bouillon

½ cup (1 stick) salted butter, chilled and cut into pieces

Sea salt and freshly ground pepper

Combine the wine and shallots in a small saucepan over medium heat. Bring to a

"Michael's *steak frites* is perfect—simple in its elegance."

—KEN HOM, CHINESE CHEF, AUTHOR, TEACHER, AND TELEVISION PERSONALITY

côte de boeuf with herb butter

Serves 4

I always serve this steak, a bone-in rib-eye, with grilled peppers, which make the perfect accompaniments. But if you prefer your steak with potatoes, I suggest a big batch of fries (see page 60) or grilled peewees.

The herb butter makes a versatile garnish for meat, poultry, or fish.

Both Niman Ranch in California and Four Story Hill Farm in Pennsylvania have succeeded with a terrific côte de boeuf. (See Sources, page 223.) They were both early providers of organic free-range meats to the general public.

Two 2½-inch-thick bone-in rib-eye steaks

Sea salt and freshly ground black pepper

1 pound peewee or other tiny specialty potatoes, grilled (see page 59)

Grilled Bell Peppers (page 45) or other grilled peppers

Herb Butter (recipe follows)

1 tablespoon chopped fresh basil

Preheat the grill.

Season the steaks with salt and pepper to taste. Place the steaks diagonally on the hot grill and leave them undisturbed for 5 minutes; then rotate them 90 degrees to make a crosshatch pattern on their undersides and leave undisturbed for about 5 minutes more. Turn over the steaks and grill the other side for a total of 10 minutes more, again rotating them halfway through that time to make crosshatch grill marks. The steaks will be medium-rare. (You can also use an instant-read thermometer to gauge the interior temperature, noting that the grill time will depend on the thickness of the steaks.) Transfer the steaks to a platter, tent them with aluminum foil, and leave them to rest for 10 minutes so their hot juices can settle.

Cut the meat from the bone on each steak. With a sharp knife, cut each steak on the diagonal into slices ¼-inch-thick and place them overlapping slightly in the center of each of 4 dinner plates. Place an equal portion of the potatoes and peppers on each plate. Place a pat of Herb Butter in the center of each steak, sprinkle on the basil, and serve immediately as the butter begins to melt.

herb butter

½ cup (1 stick) salted butter, at room temperature

1 shallot, finely minced

1 tablespoon minced fresh flat-leaf parsley

1 tablespoon minced fresh thyme leaves

1 teaspoon fresh lemon juice

Sea salt and freshly ground black pepper

Put the butter, shallots, herbs, lemon juice, and salt and pepper to taste in a food processor fitted with the metal blade. Process until blended. With a rubber spatula, transfer the butter to the center of a piece of plastic wrap. Fold the plastic wrap over the butter and, with your hands, form it into a neat log shape about 1½ inches in diameter. Refrigerate until ready to serve.

Before serving, unwrap the log and cut it crosswise into slices about ¼ inch thick and bring to room temperature.

filet mignon with seared foie gras, black truffle–armagnac sauce, and potato galettes

Serves 4

Make this recipe when you want a knockout main course for an elegant dinner party. Both the sauce and the galettes can be prepared in advance, and the steaks take just a few minutes to pan-sear, giving you time to enjoy your guests.

¾ cup Armagnac

2 shallots, minced

2 cups veal stock or reconstituted Knorr beef bouillon

2 tablespoons salted butter

Sea salt and freshly ground black pepper

2 ounces fresh black truffles

1 tablespoon peanut oil

Four 6-ounce filets mignons

Four 2-ounce pieces duck foie gras

Potato Galettes (page 62)

1 tablespoon fresh thyme leaves

Combine the Armagnac with the shallots in a small saucepan over medium-high heat. Bring to a boil and boil for about 5 minutes or until reduced by three-quarters and syrupy.

Stir in the stock and bring to a simmer. Lower the heat and simmer, skimming frequently, for about 15 minutes or until the mixture coats the back of a metal spoon and has reduced to 1½ cups. Swirl in the butter until totally incorporated.

Season with salt and pepper to taste. Shave half of the black truffles into the sauce, stir gently to incorporate, and keep the sauce warm until ready to serve.

Pour the oil into a heavy-duty skillet, swirling to coat the bottom of the pan. Place over high heat. Season the filets with salt and black pepper to taste. When the oil is very hot but not smoking, add the steaks. Sear for 3 minutes. Turn and sear for another 3 minutes for rare. (Add a minute per side for medium-rare and 2 minutes per side for medium.) Remove from the pan and allow to rest for 10 minutes before serving.

A few minutes before the steaks are done resting, heat a nonstick sauté pan over medium-high heat. Season the foie gras pieces with salt and pepper and sear them in the hot pan for 30 to 45 seconds per side.

With a spatula, transfer them to paper towels to drain.

Place a galette in the center of each of 4 dinner plates. Place a filet in the center of each galette. Place one piece of foie gras on top of each steak. Drizzle the reserved sauce over the steaks and around each plate. Shave the remaining black truffle over the steaks and garnish with fresh thyme leaves. Serve immediately.

"The exuberance of Michael's lifestyle, where only the best is good enough, shows up in his recipes from the beginning to the present day. There is no boring meal with Michael. It's always a great party."

—WOLFGANG PUCK,
CHEF AND RESTAURATEUR

veal

Ever since I first ate it pan-seared in Italy, I've always loved the sweet flavor and tender texture of milk-fed veal. It is one of the great wine-friendly meats, marrying well with robust Chardonnays.

My enthusiasm for veal also extends to crispy sweetbreads, which are great on salads or pasta or paired with foie gras.

Two pioneers of natural veal are Four Story Hill Farm in Pennsylvania and Summerfield Farm in Virginia . (See Sources, page 223.) You may have to search around to get top-quality veal and sweetbreads. But the search is well worth the effort.

pan-seared veal chops with white truffle risotto

Serves 4

A big, meaty veal chop tastes best when given a rich brown sear that caramelizes its naturally sweet juices. Add risotto with a garnish of white truffles, and perfection is on the plate. When they're in season, porcini or chanterelles make a wonderful addition to the risotto. Or make it with black truffles and morels for a dish that goes beautifully with red wine.

Four 12-ounce veal rib chops, trimmed of excess fat

2 tablespoons olive oil

Sea salt and freshly ground black pepper

White Truffle Risotto (page 72)

Place a large heavy frying pan over high heat.

Lightly coat both sides of the chops with the oil. Season with salt and pepper to taste.

Place the seasoned chops in the hot pan. (Alternatively, you can cook them on a hot grill.)

Sear for about 10 minutes or until golden brown. Turn and sear the remaining side for 10 minutes or until golden brown and cooked to medium.

Remove from the heat, transfer to a platter, tent with aluminum foil, and let rest for 10 minutes.

Place an equal portion of the risotto on each of 4 dinner plates. Place a veal chop next to the risotto and finish by shaving the truffle over all as directed on page 71. Serve immediately.

"I love the fried sweetbreads when they have them at Michael's. I never was a sweetbread lover as a kid. My father was, but I found them disgusting. Then one day I saw them going by at Michael's, and I ordered them. I adored them and felt as though posthumously I was admitting to my father that he was right. I was grateful to Michael's for enabling that discovery."

—KURT ANDERSEN,
NOVELIST AND JOURNALIST

crispy sweetbreads with giant spanish caper–lemon brown butter

Serves 4

With their mild, creamy flavor, smooth interior texture, and crispy surfaces, sweetbreads are not only delicious but extremely versatile. Make this recipe, one of my absolute favorites, and you'll see—and taste—exactly what I mean. Besides this classic treatment with capers-and-lemon-butter sauce, you can cook the sweetbreads the same way and serve a small portion on top of a salad of mesclun greens with sautéed wild mushrooms and a hot sherry-wine vinaigrette; or on top of a perfectly cooked risotto; or in one of the all-time best pairings, served alongside a slab of sautéed foie gras, pan-seared veal loin, and a sauté of fresh morels.

You do need to take some care with sweetbreads, as just the slightest overcooking will dry and toughen them. The frying oils must be very hot so that a quick sear will usually do the trick.

1 cup (2 sticks) salted butter, at room temperature

Juice of 1 lemon

½ cup giant Spanish capers, well drained

Coarse salt and freshly ground black pepper

1 cup dry white wine

1 cup water

2 pounds veal sweetbreads

½ cup all-purpose flour

¼ cup walnut oil

1 tablespoon clarified butter (see Note, page 48)

2 tablespoons chopped fresh chives

Place the salted butter in a small sauté pan over low heat. Cook, stirring frequently, for about 4 minutes or until the butter foams and begins to turn brown. It should smell almost nutty. Watch carefully, as it will blacken quickly.

Remove from the heat and stir in the lemon juice and capers. Season with salt and pepper to taste. Set aside and keep warm.

Combine the white wine and water in a medium saucepan over medium heat. Bring to a simmer and add the sweetbreads. Blanch for 3 minutes. Remove from the heat and drain well.

When the sweetbreads are cool enough to handle, using a small, sharp knife and your fingertips, carefully remove and discard the tough outer membrane along with any cartilage, tubes, or ducts.

Line a plate with plastic film. Place the sweetbreads on the plate and then cover with another piece of plastic. Place a plate on top and then weight the plate down with a heavy object so that there is pressure on the sweetbreads. Refrigerate for about 2 hours or until most of the water has drained out and the sweetbreads are quite firm and uniformly thick. Remove from the refrigerator, uncover, and carefully divide each one into 2 equal portions.

Place the flour on a plate. Season with salt and pepper to taste. Lightly dredge all sides of each sweetbread in the seasoned flour.

Combine the walnut oil with the clarified butter in a medium sauté pan over medium-high heat. When very hot, but not smoking, add the sweetbreads. Sear for 90 seconds or until golden. Turn and sear the remaining side for another 90 seconds or until golden. Do not overcook or the sweetbreads will toughen.

Divide the sweetbreads evenly among 4 dinner plates. Spoon the sauce over the meat and around each plate. Sprinkle with chives and serve.

lamb

Lamb is one of my favorites. It is terrific on the grill and is the perfect partner for wild mushrooms, black truffles, and rich wine sauces. I use marvelous natural lamb raised by the Jamisons on their bucolic farm in Pennsylvania or great lamb from Colorado. (See Sources, page 223.)

Almost all lamb that comes to market is between six and eight months old. The meat is a deep pink, very lean and compact, and the fat is almost pure white. The charring of the grill wonderfully accents lamb's sweetness.

grilled boneless leg of lamb with rosemary, garlic, roasted potatoes, and spinach

Serves 4

This dish is simple to put together. A boneless leg of lamb is an uneven piece of meat, so care must be taken when grilling to ensure that the thinner parts do not overcook. Yet it's still easy to make, is great with red wine, and even if everything cools a bit, will still taste terrific.

One 4-pound butterflied leg of lamb

½ cup plus 1 tablespoon extra-virgin olive oil

1 tablespoon minced garlic, plus 2 cloves, peeled and slivered

2 tablespoons chopped fresh rosemary

Freshly ground black pepper

Roasted Potatoes (see page 63)

Sea salt

1 tablespoon salted butter

8 cups California spinach leaves, tough stems removed

Place the lamb in a shallow dish large enough to hold it flat.

Combine ½ cup of the oil with the minced garlic. Whisk in the rosemary along with black pepper to taste. Pour over the lamb, turning to coat. Cover with plastic film and set aside to marinate for at least 1 hour, turning occasionally. The lamb may also be refrigerated and marinated for up to 24 hours. If so, bring to room temperature before grilling.

While the lamb is marinating, prepare the potatoes.

Preheat the grill.

Remove the lamb from the marinade, lifting it up to let the excess drip off. Season with salt to taste.

Place the lamb on the hot grill and sear for 5 minutes. Turn and sear the remaining side for 5 minutes. Move the lamb to the cooler portion of the grill, cover, and grill for about 15 minutes for medium-rare (150°F on an instant-read thermometer) or until it's reached the desired degree of doneness.

Remove from the grill and transfer to a platter. Let rest for 10 minutes before slicing.

While the lamb is resting, prepare the spinach. Heat the butter with the remaining 1 tablespoon oil in a large sauté pan over medium heat. Add the slivered garlic and sauté for 1 minute just to soften. Add the spinach and season with salt and pepper to taste. Cook, tossing with tongs, for about 4 minutes or until the spinach has wilted. Remove from the heat.

When ready to serve, using a sharp knife, cut the lamb on the bias into thin slices. Layer the slices in the center of a platter. Place the spinach on one side and the potatoes on the other and serve.

"Michael is irrepressible. He's always on. He's just this unfailing source of good cheer. I always feel better when I see him, and it's seldom that you feel that way about people."

—Corby Kummer, senior editor, *THE ATLANTIC MONTHLY*

grilled lamb racks

Serves 4

I prefer to grill individual chops, as I think that the quicker cooking allows the meat to remain juicier and more flavorful and gives more surface caramelization. I always use baby lamb— the chops offer just a couple of bites of succulent meat and then a delicious little bone to chew on for passed hors d'oeuvres—but big Colorado chops are great for a main course.

3 tablespoons chopped fresh thyme plus whole leaves for garnish

3 tablespoons chopped fresh rosemary

½ cup extra-virgin olive oil plus more for drizzling

Sea salt and freshly ground black pepper

2 racks (8 chops each) baby lamb, trimmed of excess fat

Preheat the grill.

In a dish large enough to hold all the lamb, combine the chopped thyme, rosemary, ½ cup oil, salt, and pepper. Cut the racks into individual chops, turn them in the oil mixture, cover, and leave to marinate at room temperature for about 30 minutes.

Place the chops on the hottest part of the grill and cook for about 2 minutes; then rotate them 90 degrees and grill 2 minutes more to create a crosshatch pattern; turn the chops and grill for about 4 minutes more, rotating them once midway through, until rare.

Remove the chops from the grill and place on a platter to rest for 5 minutes before serving with either Spring Vegetable Sauté (page 51) or Grilled Bell Peppers with Other Summer Vegetables (page 45). Drizzle with oil and sprinkle with the whole thyme leaves.

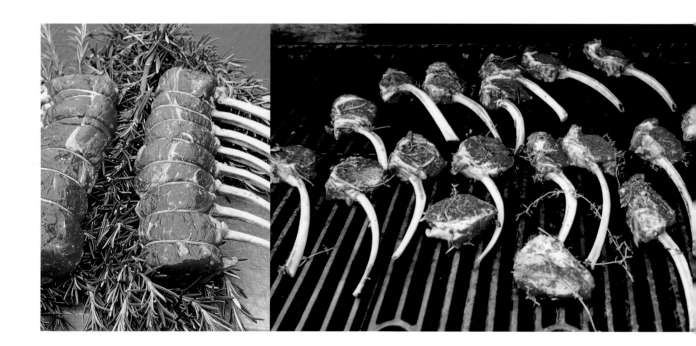

pork

Pork is incredibly versatile, providing us with perfect roasts, chops, belly, ribs, sucklings, and of course my beloved "party meats," aka charcuterie or salumi.

About twenty years ago, a California rancher named Bill Niman (with his then partner, Orville Schell) began raising pigs the old-fashioned way. Within a few years, Niman organized other ranchers into a commercial venture called Niman Ranch. (See Sources, page 223.) All pigs carrying the Niman Ranch label are raised on sustainable family farms on pastureland or in deeply bedded pens.

And don't forget the great Korabuto pork that comes from the Snake River area in Wyoming. Or the absolutely wonderful heritage strains, such as Berkshire and Ossabaw. The meat is well marbled, juicy, tender, and extremely flavorful. Ask for these fine-quality brands at your butcher or supermarket meat counter.

pork tenderloins with molasses barbecue sauce

Serves 4

Couldn't be simpler or more delicious. My Molasses Barbecue Sauce, a friends-and-family favorite, is a terrific have-on-hand barbecue sauce for quick summer grills. The delicately flavored pork tenderloin is great for entertaining, as it requires very little grilling to be cooked to perfection. The sauce is also tasty on chicken, baby back ribs, or country-style ribs.

Two ¾- to 1-pound pork tenderloins, cleaned of all silver skin and fat

Molasses Barbecue Sauce (recipe follows)

Place the tenderloins in a baking dish. Add the barbecue sauce, turning to coat. Cover with plastic film and refrigerate for 2 hours, turning occasionally.

When ready to cook, remove the meat from the refrigerator and bring to room temperature.

Preheat the grill to medium-hot.

Remove the tenderloins from the marinade and, using your hands, push off excess sauce. Place the tenderloins on the grill and cook, turning frequently, for about 15 minutes, or until an instant-read thermometer inserted into the thickest part registers 150°F. Using a pastry brush, lightly baste the meat with the remaining sauce from time to time.

Transfer any remaining sauce to a small saucepan over medium heat and bring to a simmer.

Remove from the heat and set aside.

Remove the meat from the grill and set aside to rest for 10 minutes before cutting crosswise on the bias into ¼-inch-thick slices. Drizzle with the warm sauce and serve.

molasses barbecue sauce

1 bottle KC Masterpiece Original Barbecue Sauce

¼ cup Worcestershire sauce

¼ cup dark molasses

3 tablespoons Dijon mustard

1 to 2 roasted jalapeño chilies, seeded (optional)

½ large sweet onion, such as Vidalia or Maui Maui, peeled and chopped

½ cup chopped fresh cilantro

Combine the barbecue sauce, Worcestershire sauce, molasses, and mustard in a bowl. Whisk in the chilies (if using), onion, and cilantro. Set aside to allow the flavors to mellow for 30 minutes before using.

NOTE: If you really want to chow down, this recipe makes a great sandwich. Take a sourdough baguette, slice it in half lengthwise, slather it with butter, and grill until crusty. Coat the hot buttered bread with Pommery mustard; pile on warm sliced pork, a few slices of sweet onion, a couple of handfuls of spicy watercress; mop with some sauce; and give a drizzle of lime juice over the whole mess. Cover with the top half of the baguette and go to heaven!

"party meats," aka charcuterie platter or salumi

I have always referred to this dish as "party meats," because everyone loves them. They're easy to pick up and eat, and there's something for every taste.

In the classic French vernacular, *charcuterie* refers to pork specialty meats, such as cured meats, rillettes, pâtés, and sausages, as well as to the market in which these types of meats are sold. An *assortiments de charcuteries* is a platter of cold cured or cooked sliced meats, sausages, and pâtés, generally served as an appetizer. Although I love all types of cured meats as well as pâtés, both rustic and elegant,

galantines, and other French specialties, when entertaining at home I usually put together a very simple, easy-to-purchase-and-assemble mix. I always aim to serve 2 or 3 slices of each party meat per person.

For starters, there is always prosciutto di San Daniele, a *prosciutto crudo* (or cured raw ham) from the San Daniele region of Italy, which I consider to be the best available. It is sliced paper-thin. It is joined by another marvelous European cured meat, Serrano ham (*jamón serrano,* or mountain ham) from Spain, a somewhat drier but equally delicious, thinly sliced, almost sweet ham. *Saucisson sec,* a French dried pork sausage reminiscent of Italian salamis, is sliced into thicker cuts, and *bresaola,* an air-dried Italian beef fillet, is thinly sliced to complete the meat section of the platter.

To these four temptingly tender meats I add chunks (about ¾ inch each) of exquisite Parmigiano-Reggiano cheese, bowls of green and black olives, cornichons (piquant French pickles), and Dijon mustard. A bottle of feisty green extra-virgin olive oil and lemon halves brighten the flavors, while some soft salted butter adds extra mellowness for those who seek it. And, of course, great, crusty baguettes. ¿*Un ración de jamón,* anyone? It's Cava time!

Armandino Batali (father of Mario of Babbo fame) has an outstanding salumi shop in Seattle, Salumi Artisan Cured Meats. And Paul Bertolli (former chef at Chez Panisse) is a stalwart of salumi, with his Berkeley, California, company Fra' Mani. (See Sources, page 223.) Plan in advance and have them ship you some great party meats.

grilled pork belly with pommery mustard

Serves 4

> "When Michael was seven or eight years old, his father and I were having a dinner party and I had planned on having beef Stroganoff. Michael came into the kitchen and saw that I had one of those brand-new electric skillets on the counter, and I was putting pieces of beef in and stirring them around. He really got into it, so we pushed a chair up to the counter, and he stood on the chair and made beef Stroganoff for twelve people. It was quite a production."
>
> —Carol Austell, michael's mom

Until very, very recently, pork belly was reserved for seasoning dishes or for "cheap eats" at home or in a corner bistro. Now it is available from the finest natural meat producers and has found its way onto menus high and low. I love its rich, fatty flavor, which is highlighted by creamy mashed potatoes (see my recipe on page 64 but omit the arugula) and a garnish of spicy watercress.

One 2-pound ¾-inch-thick piece pork belly

⅓ cup white wine vinegar

2 tablespoons Pommery mustard

1 cup olive oil

Sea salt and freshly ground black pepper

Preheat and oil the grill.

Cut the pork belly into pieces 3 inches long by ¾-inch thick. Set aside.

Combine the vinegar and mustard in a small mixing bowl. Whisking constantly, slowly add the oil, whisking until completely emulsified. Season with salt and pepper to taste. Set aside.

Place the pork belly on the hot grill and cook, turning frequently, for about 10 minutes or until brown and crisp.

Remove from the grill and place an equal portion on each of 4 dinner plates. Drizzle with the mustard vinaigrette and serve. Pass any remaining vinaigrette on the side.

marinated country-style ribs

Serves 4

Although I use the traditional spicy tomato sauce on pork tenderloins (see page 142), I prefer my ribs to be flavored with a simple mustardy marinade. I use meaty country-style ribs, but this recipe works for smaller baby back ribs as well. Grill them in the summer or bake them in the winter.

An ice-cold rosé is my beverage of choice with ribs.

5 pounds meaty country-style ribs

1½ cups olive oil

½ cup Dijon mustard

2 tablespoons dried *herbes de Provence*

Sea salt and freshly ground black pepper

If ribs are still in racks, cut them into individual ribs.

Place the ribs in a shallow baking dish large enough to hold them in a single layer.

Combine the oil, mustard, and *herbes de Provence* in a small bowl, whisking to combine.

Pour the marinade over the ribs and set aside to marinate for about an hour.

Preheat the oven to 375°F

Transfer the ribs to 2 baking pans, taking care that there is space around each rib so that it can brown evenly. Place in the preheated oven and bake for 30 minutes. Turn and bake for an additional 20 minutes or until the ribs are nicely browned and cooked through. Season with salt and pepper to taste.

Remove from the oven and serve hot.

NOTE: To grill big, meaty country-style ribs, make sure you cook each one on all 4 sides.

The great New York chef Larry Forgione coined the term "free-range chicken." That image of chickens puttering about outdoors in their natural setting, eating good stuff, remains vivid in our minds.

I use two types of free-range chicken almost exclusively: *jidori* and local free-range chickens such as Eberly Farms and Murray's on the East Coast, or Shelton's and Rocky's on the West Coast. Breeders in America are trying to replicate the great bluefoot, the French *poulet de Bresse. Jidori* chickens are free-range birds raised in natural settings in a manner based on a traditional Japanese method that is comparable to the extreme pampering of Kobe beef. In Japan, genuine *jidori* birds are produced by only a few select farmers in the town of Hinai in the Akita prefecture. A *jidori*-style chicken is now raised in Southern California.

Blackfoot chickens do, in fact, have black feet. They are raised in a fashion similar to the famous Bresse chickens of France, free-range, corn-fed, and pampered. Fat yellow birds, they are superb when roasted.

If you can't find either of these types, there are many other naturally raised birds available from fine butchers or through the Internet.

grilled chicken and goat cheese salad with jalapeño-cilantro-lime salsa

Serves 4

I have been making this salad for as long as I have been in the restaurant business. These ingredients work beautifully together. I always have Balsamic Vinaigrette on hand as well as the makings of the salsa. You can use whatever greens you like—the merrier the mix the better—or even a great ready-made mesclun mix.

4 skin-on chicken breast halves, boned, with the wing bone attached (see Note)

½-pound log goat cheese, cut crosswise into ¼-inch-thick slices

Sea salt and freshly ground black pepper

Leaves from 2 heads limestone lettuce, torn into bite-size pieces

Leaves from 1 head baby red leaf lettuce

Leaves from 2 bunches mâche

Leaves from 1 bunch arugula

Leaves from 1 head baby radic-chio, torn into bite-size pieces

Balsamic Vinaigrette (page 39)

Tomato Concassé (recipe follows)

2 red bell peppers, grilled and cut into 1-inch-wide strips (see page 45)

2 yellow bell peppers, grilled and cut into 1-inch-wide strips (see page 45)

1 large sweet onion, sliced and grilled (see page 45)

Jalapeño-Cilantro-Lime Salsa (recipe follows)

½ cup chopped fresh chives

Preheat the grill.

Using your fingertips, gently separate the skin from the meat along the length of each breast to make a pocket. Make sure that you leave the skin attached on the opposite side of the breast. Insert an equal portion of the goat cheese medallions, slightly overlapping, into each pocket. Gently press the pockets closed. Season both sides of the breasts with salt and pepper to taste.

Place the breasts, skin side down, on the preheated grill. Cook for 5 minutes or until nicely browned. Turn and grill for an additional 7 minutes or until cooked through and nicely browned on both sides. Using tongs, carefully transfer the breasts to a platter.

Combine the limestone and red leaf lettuces, mâche, arugula, and radicchio in a large bowl. Toss with enough of the vinaigrette to coat lightly.

Place an equal portion of the mixed greens in the center of each of 4 dinner plates.

Using a sharp knife, cut each breast on the bias into 4 or 5 slices. Keeping the breast slices together, place a breast on top of the greens on each plate. Place a spoonful of Tomato Concassé at 3 equidistant points around the greens. Arrange an equal portion of the grilled peppers and onion in an attractive pattern on each plate. Spoon some of the remaining vinaigrette over the onions and peppers. Spoon the salsa over the chicken and sprinkle the plates with chives. Serve immediately.

---

tomato concassé

4 medium (about 1⅓ pounds) red or yellow ripe tomatoes

2 tablespoons fresh basil julienne

1 cup Balsamic Vinaigrette (page 39)

Sea salt and freshly ground black pepper

With a small sharp knife, score the bottom of each tomato with a shallow X. Have ready a large bowl of ice water.

Bring a large saucepan of water to a boil over high heat. Drop the tomatoes into the boiling water and boil until the skins begin to wrinkle, about 45 seconds. Using a slotted spoon, transfer the tomatoes to the ice water. Let stand for 1 minute. Then lift the tomatoes from the water one at a time and, with your fingertips, peel them. Using a paring knife, cut

out and discard the stem end of each tomato. Halve the tomatoes crosswise and remove their seeds with your fingertips. Cut the tomatoes into ¼-inch dice.

Combine the tomatoes, basil, and vinaigrette in a medium bowl. Season with salt and pepper to taste.

Cover and refrigerate for at least 30 minutes to allow flavors to meld. Bring to room temperature before serving.

---

jalapeño-cilantro-lime salsa

Juice of 2 limes

2 jalapeño chilies, roasted, peeled, seeded, and finely chopped (see Note)

1 cup extra-virgin olive oil

Sea salt and freshly ground black pepper

2 tablespoons chopped fresh cilantro

Combine the lime juice and chilies in a small bowl. Whisk in the oil and season with salt and pepper to taste.

Just before serving, fold in the cilantro. Do not let the salsa sit around, or the lime juice will turn the cilantro brown.

NOTE: It is best to have a butcher prepare the boneless breasts, as it is difficult to find whole breasts with the wing attached. If you want to do this at home, purchase 2 whole

chickens and use the remaining pieces for another purpose. If you do find breasts with the wing attached, carefully remove the breast bone and then cut off the wing tip and second bone, leaving the larger bone as a handle.

Be very careful when roasting chilies, as their vapors are a killer. Wear gloves when peeling, seeding, and chopping to keep their virulent juices from burning your hands. Believe me, once you've rubbed your eyes with chili-tainted fingers, you will never do it again.

"Michael goes to great lengths to make every person in his restaurants feel comfortable. That translates into how you should welcome people into your own home."

—Carlos Lopes, general manager, hotel bel-air, los angeles

cobb salad

Serves 4

This is, without a doubt, the most frequently requested lunch dish at both restaurants. Our guests can't seem to get their fill—every time we take it off the menu, they demand it back! Because people seem to prefer it, we mix the salad in the kitchen, but I think it looks absolutely beautiful when arranged like a traditional French *salade composée*. I must say that after all these years, I still enjoy it myself, chopped and mixed beforehand.

1½ cups olive oil

½ cup balsamic vinegar

¼ cup chopped chives

Sea salt and freshly ground black pepper

1 pound chicken tenders, all fat and sinew removed

3 tablespoons peanut oil

¾ pound mesclun

10 ounces cherry tomatoes, halved lengthwise

2 avocados, peeled and diced

4 hard-boiled eggs, peeled and chopped

½ pound Bacon Lardons (page 98)

½ pound crumbled Maytag blue cheese

Combine the oil, vinegar, and chives in an attractive container with a tight-fitting lid. Season with salt and pepper to taste. Cover and vigorously shake to incorporate. Set aside.

Season the chicken with salt and pepper to taste.

Heat the peanut oil in a frying pan over medium-high heat. When very hot, add the chicken and sear, turning occasionally, for about 6 minutes or until cooked through and nicely browned. Transfer to a platter and set aside.

Place an equal portion of the mesclun in each of 4 large shallow soup bowls. Cut the chicken tenders crosswise into thin slices and arrange equal portions of the chicken down the center of the greens. Place a line of cherry tomatoes on one side of the chicken and a line of avocado down the other side. Place a line of chopped egg next to the tomatoes and a line of lardons next to the avocado. Sprinkle blue cheese over all.

Serve with the dressing passed on the side or drizzle a moderate amount over the top as you serve, asking diners to mix their salads immediately.

"One of my oldest friends, the late Bob Tisch, and I had been on four thousand diets together, and we were convinced that we could lose weight on the Cobb salad at Michael's, the biggest salad in the world."

—BEVERLY SILLS, LEGENDARY SOPRANO

OPPOSITE
Michael greeting guests in Santa Monica

ABOVE
The New York restaurant entrance on 55th Street

"The Cobb salad is what everybody eats at Michael's New York. I once sat down there with Henry Schleiff, and he was on this Joe DiMaggio streak, fifty-six straight Cobb salads."

—TIM ARANGO, MEDIA BUSINESS REPORTER, *FORTUNE*

"I nearly always have the Cobb salad. And I may split it with somebody because it's so huge and I tend to be a thrifty girl. I'm not trying to save money, but I don't like to waste money either."
—HELEN GURLEY BROWN, AUTHOR AND LEGENDARY EDITOR IN CHIEF, *COSMOPOLITAN*

roast chicken with herb butter

Serves 4

Every chef has a special method for making a perfect roast chicken. This version comes from our Michael's New York chef Robert Ribant. Use only the sweet leaves of the herbs. Once the chicken has been trussed, leave it to rest uncovered overnight in the refrigerator. The resting allows the herb butter to season the breast meat deeply. It also dry-ages the skin, allowing it to separate from the meat, keeping the juices in and letting the skin roast to an unbelievable crispness. And this preparation makes for a tender, juicy, perfectly roasted bird. Obviously you need to start with a very fresh chicken. A truffled roast chicken may also be prepared in this fashion if you eliminate the garlic and herbs and simply coat the breast meat with softened butter and a layer of truffle slices.

½ cup (1 stick) unsalted butter, softened

3 large cloves garlic, peeled

⅓ cup finely chopped fresh flat-leaf parsley

⅓ cup fresh lemon thyme leaves

One 3½- to 4-pound roasting chicken

Sea salt and freshly ground black pepper

Place the butter in a shallow bowl. Set aside.

Place the garlic on a cutting board and, using the side of a large knife, begin rubbing the garlic at a 45-degree angle, working to turn it into a paste. Scrape the garlic paste into the butter. Add the parsley and thyme and, using a spatula, press into the butter mixture to blend well. When blended, scrape the mixture into a pastry bag fitted with a small, plain tip.

Very gently work your fingertips between the chicken breast and skin so that the skin remains unbroken as it separates from the meat. Once the skin is fully separated, carefully begin piping the herb butter between the skin and meat, working the butter backward against the meat until it is completely covered with the butter.

Using kitchen twine, truss the chicken together. Place the trussed chicken on a rack in a small roasting pan. Cover with plastic film and refrigerate, undisturbed, for 3 days (or, to "cheat," overnight).

Preheat the oven to 450°F.

Remove the chicken from the refrigerator. Remove and discard the plastic film. Season the bird with salt and pepper to taste.

Place the seasoned chicken in the preheated oven and roast for 20 minutes. Reduce the oven temperature to 275°F. Roast for an additional 20 to 30 minutes or until the juices between the thigh and breast run clear when poked with the point of a small sharp knife and/or an instant-read thermometer registers 165°F when inserted into the thickest part (the chicken will continue to cook as it rests).

Remove the chicken from the oven and allow to rest for 10 minutes before cutting into 8 serving pieces: 2 legs, 2 thighs, and 2 breasts cut into halves.

"When you're hungry and want a great roasted chicken with *frites,* Michael's is the place in New York to get it. Nobody on the planet does chicken and *frites* like Michael. It's the finest organic field-raised poultry, spiced and cooked and presented beautifully. "

—JERRY INZERILLO, EXECUTIVE VICE PRESIDENT, KERZNER INTERNATIONAL

grilled chicken with tarragon butter

Serves 4

This dish was one of the most popular on our menu when we opened Michael's Santa Monica back in 1979. The tasty caramelized chicken breast, the hot tarragon butter, the mound of *pommes frites*, the crisp green watercress, and the side of Dijon mustard evoked fond memories of Parisian bistros.

> **"The fact that Michael can go from having a hit formula in Los Angeles, catering to a very different clientele, and then come to New York and hit the same high mark in a completely different arena is a sign of genius."**
>
> —DAN HALPERN, PUBLISHER, THE ECCO PRESS, AN IMPRINT OF HARPERCOLLINS

4 skin-on boneless chicken legs with boneless thighs attached

4 skin-on boneless chicken breast halves with the wing bone attached (see Note, page 147)

Sea salt and freshly ground black pepper

Pommes Frites (page 60)

6 tablespoons salted butter

2 tablespoons chopped fresh tarragon

2 bunches watercress, tough stems removed

Preheat the grill.

Lightly season all the chicken pieces with salt and pepper. Place the pieces on the grill, skin side down. Grill the leg-thigh pieces for 8 minutes, then turn and grill for an additional 8 minutes or until cooked through but still moist and pink near center. Grill the breasts for 5 minutes and then turn and grill for 2 minutes or until cooked through but still moist. Halfway through the grilling of the skin side, rotate the pieces about 90 degrees to create attractive crosshatch grill marks.

While the chicken is grilling, fry up the Pommes Frites.

Remove the chicken from the grill, place on a platter, and keep warm.

Place the butter in a small saucepan over medium heat. Add the tarragon and season lightly with salt and pepper. Cook just until the butter has melted. Remove from the heat and keep warm.

Place an equal portion of watercress in the center of each of 4 dinner plates. Place a big mound of *frites* at the top of each plate. Place a chicken leg-thigh and a breast at the bottom of each plate. Spoon some warm tarragon butter over the chicken on each plate and serve immediately with any remaining tarragon butter on the side.

pan-seared chicken with duck foie gras and morels

Serves 4

I first had a version of this dish at the famous Parisian restaurant Lasserre in 1972. The extravagant presentation takes simple chicken to extraordinary heights. If fresh morels aren't in season, you may replace them with chanterelles or porcini—or dried morels, reconstituted in water and well drained.

3 tablespoons olive oil

Four 8-ounce skin-on chicken breasts with wing bones attached (see Note, page 147)

Sea salt and freshly ground black pepper

2 shallots, finely chopped

¼ cup Madeira

2½ cups unsalted, defatted chicken stock

½ cup heavy cream

3 tablespoons salted butter

18 small to medium-sized fresh morels, cleaned thoroughly and trimmed

½ pound fresh duck foie gras, trimmed and cut into 4 equal pieces

2 tablespoons finely chopped fresh chives

Place the oil in a heavy sauté pan over high heat. When very hot and almost smoking, season both sides of the chicken with salt and pepper to taste and place it, skin side down, in the hot pan. Sear for about 5 minutes or until the skin is golden brown. Turn and cook for about 6 minutes more, until done. Remove the chicken from the pan to a plate, cover with foil, and keep warm.

Return the pan to the heat, add the shallots and the Madeira, and stir and scrape with a wooden spoon to deglaze the pan deposits. Add the stock and reduce by half, about 10 minutes. Stir in the cream and simmer until thickened, about 4 to 5 minutes. Season to taste with salt and pepper. Keep warm.

In a sauté pan over medium-high heat, melt the butter. Add the morels and sauté until crisp, 6 to 8 minutes. Stir them into the sauce.

Heat a nonstick pan over medium-high heat. Season the foie gras on both sides with salt and pepper and sear for 30 to 45 seconds per side. Transfer to paper towels.

Place a chicken breast in the center of each of 4 dinner plates. Lean a piece of foie gras alongside each breast. Spoon the sauce and morels over the top. Sprinkle with chives and serve immediately.

"My husband, John Gregory Dunne, and I lived nearby Michael's in Santa Monica, and it was just the most cheerful place to go. It was the first restaurant to look the way you wanted your house to look. It had great pictures on the walls and was always the right color. We used to go there for lunch whenever we were feeling sorry for ourselves. I would always have the grilled chicken, which was just wonderful, with its crisp skin, a little watercress, and terrific fries; and John always had the gravlax. It was a very sweet place and still is."

—Joan Didion, novelist, essayist, and journalist

duck

When I returned to the States from France, I faced a shortage of the great products that I had grown used to in my French kitchen. One of my first forays into quality production was a duck venture with Jean Bertranou, the chef-owner of L'Ermitage, a fantastic Los Angeles restaurant. We smuggled in the appropriate duck eggs and set up a duck farm so that we could not only have delicious duck to eat, but could also produce foie gras. It didn't take long before I was making foie gras in my basement in Malibu and shipping it to French chefs all across the country.

The most commonly available duck is a variety known as white Pekin or, more familiarly, Long Island duck. However, because of the demand from American chefs, you can now find Muscovy, Mullard, and domestic mallard ducks. Pekin ducks usually weigh about five pounds and have a mild flavor and juicy texture. Muscovy is larger, mallard smaller. The Muscovy is richer in flavor than the Pekin, and the mallard is even more so, having a memorable, almost wild taste. Mullards (mule ducks), a cross between the Muscovy male and Pekin female, are the best; they have a deep flavor and juicy texture, much like a New York strip steak. All of them are used interchangeably in most duck recipes. But a Pekin is best for roast duck, Mullard duck breasts (magret) for grilling.

I prefer duck foie gras to traditional French goose liver (not that I don't love goose foie gras when I find it placed in front of me). It has a richer, earthier, and more rustic flavor.

duck with blood orange sauce

Serves 4

This recipe is a simplified version of one of my favorite French dishes. Duck with blood oranges has always been a popular combo, a perfect marriage of rich meat and a sweet-and-sour sauce with just the right amount of acidity to pair up with a great Pinot Noir. Early on, I had to import the blood oranges from Malta, but now, of course, California growers provide a superb product. I even have a blood orange tree growing at my Malibu home. And don't forget to serve crispy confit of leg and thigh alongside the breast.

5 medium blood oranges

½ cup red wine vinegar

2 tablespoons minced shallots

2½ cups duck stock

¼ cup Grand Marnier

Sea salt and freshly ground black pepper

½ cup (1 stick) salted butter

Four 6- to 8-ounce duck breasts

Wild Rice (recipe follows)

Juice 2 of the oranges and set the juice aside.

Using a small sharp knife, carefully cut the top and bottom off each of the remaining 3 oranges. Working with 1 orange at a time, set the orange down on a flat surface and carefully cut downward from the top to remove all of the rind and white pith. Holding the orange in your hand, insert the knife tip into the orange at the point where the white membrane separates each segment. Free the segments by gently lifting them out and into a small bowl. Continue segmenting the remaining oranges. Set aside.

Combine the juice, vinegar, and shallots in a small saucepan over medium-high heat. Bring to a simmer; then lower the heat and simmer for about 12 minutes or until reduced to a thick, almost caramelized syrup. Stir in the stock, raise the heat, and bring to a boil. Boil for about 7 minutes or until the liquid has reduced by half. Stir in the liqueur and season to taste with salt and pepper. Swirl in the butter and keep warm.

Place a sauté pan over medium-high heat. Season the duck breasts with salt and pepper to taste and place the seasoned breasts, skin side down, in the hot pan. Sear for about 7 minutes or until almost all of the fat has been rendered out and the skin is very crisp. Turn the breasts over and continue cooking for 3 to 5 minutes more, until medium-rare (about 160°F on an instant-read thermometer). Allow the breasts to rest for a couple of minutes.

Using a chef's knife, cut each breast, at a 45-degree angle, into slices about ¼-inch thick.

Slightly fan a breast over the center of each of 4 dinner plates. Spoon an equal portion of the sauce over each breast and garnish with the reserved blood orange segments. Spoon an equal portion of the wild rice next to the duck and, if desired, finish with Steamed Haricots Verts (page 52) or Kim's Spinach (page 65).

wild rice

2 teaspoons peanut oil

½ cup chopped sweet onion

Pinch sea salt plus more to taste

⅔ cup wild rice

2 cups water

1 teaspoon salted butter

Freshly ground black pepper

¼ cup Bacon Lardons (page 98)

1 tablespoon finely chopped fresh flat-leaf parsley

Heat the oil in a medium saucepan over medium heat. Add the onion along with a pinch of salt. Sauté the onion for 2 minutes; remove half and set aside. Stir the rice together with the onion in the pan. Add the water and raise the heat. Bring to a boil and stir once. Lower the heat, cover, and cook for about 50 minutes or until the rice has absorbed the water and is fluffy.

Remove from the heat and uncover. Add the butter and season with salt and pepper to taste.

Just before serving, toss in the lardons, reserved onion, and parsley and serve.

"I find that people can sometimes be overimpressed by a great bottle of Krug champagne and worry if the moment is big enough to open that bottle. I tell them, my God, open that bottle and drink it and be happy! Then worship the empty bottle, if you wish, but drink it first! Go for it, enjoy it, and share it! Don't box yourself in. Don't set rules. Make it your own party. Be free. This is what Krug is all about, and it's also what Michael is all about. Michael has been a Krug lover for many, many years. Why does he love Krug? I think it's because his character and individuality and generosity made him adopt Krug as a reflection of himself. I think of Michael as a glass of Krug champagne. He has power, glamour, and energy at the same time."

—RÉMI KRUG, PRESIDENT, KRUG CHAMPAGNE

traditional duck confit

Makes about 3 cups

In France, confit has been made for hundreds of years. It began as a method to cure meat so that it would remain edible for long periods of time. To make a meat into confit, it is slowly cooked in its own rendered fat. In the French rural countryside, it was often made in the fall for the coming cold winter months. We serve seared duck breast accompanied by the confit leg and thigh—excellent with a crisp red wine.

One 3-pound box sea salt

4 large duck legs with thighs attached

2 quarts liquid duck fat (see Note)

Place a thick layer of sea salt in a dish large enough to hold the duck legs tightly in a single layer. Lay the duck legs in the salt and then add enough salt to cover them thickly. Cover the dish with plastic film and then place either another pan or a cutting board on top of the plastic and weigh it down with a filled 3-pound can (or a couple of smaller cans). Set aside to marinate at room temperature for 2 hours.

Preheat the oven to 325°F.

Remove the duck legs from the salt and rinse them under cold running water. (If using the marinating dish for roasting, wash and dry the dish.)

Lay the duck legs in a single layer in a small roasting pan. Add enough duck fat to cover the legs completely. Cover the entire pan with aluminum foil. Place in the preheated oven and roast for about 3 hours or until the meat is falling off the bone. You don't want the meat to cook too fast or it will become tough rather than meltingly soft.

Remove the meat from the fat and transfer it, skin side down, to an airtight container. Pour the fat through a fine sieve to cover the meat entirely.

When ready to serve, place the desired amount skin side down in a sauté pan. Cook over medium heat until hot and really crisp.

NOTE: Duck fat is available from fine butchers and most specialty food shops. If solid, melt it over low heat.

sautéed foie gras

Serves 4

This recipe tops my list of favorite hors d'oeuvres. Nothing could be simpler, and absolutely nothing is more luxurious. The complexity of flavors and textures comes from the crunchy nuttiness of the walnut toast, the silky-smooth richness of the foie gras, and the blast of spiciness from the final hit of pepper.

The skillet in which you fry the foie gras must be nonstick and very hot so that the liver immediately exudes fat and seals in the rich juices.

If you don't have homemade Walnut Bread on hand, many artisanal bakeries now make wonderful nut breads that work just fine.

Two ¼-inch-thick slices Walnut Bread (page 188), toasted and quartered

8 ounces grade-A duck foie gras, cut into eight ½-inch-thick rectangles

Coarse sea salt and freshly ground white pepper

Place the toast pieces on a serving platter. Set aside.

Heat a large, heavy nonstick skillet over medium-high heat.

Add the foie gras and sear for 30 to 45 seconds or until nicely browned. Using a spatula, quickly turn each piece and cook for an additional 30 seconds or until browned and slightly crisp.

Using the spatula, immediately transfer a piece of foie gras to each of the toast rectangles. Season with a touch of sea salt and a healthy grind of white pepper. Serve immediately.

"Michael came back from Paris loving French food but thinking, Why do we have to do it like the French? Why can't we do an American version of French cuisine? Let's find someone to make our own cheese, or grow our own foie gras. How can we do this American-style?"

—Robert and Scrantz Shapiro,
College Friends

foie gras terrine

Makes one 11½-inch terrine

There is an old adage that great chefs are measured by their ability to roast the perfect chicken. I add to that the ability to scramble eggs properly, roast a suckling pig, and, most of all, prepare a silken foie gras terrine. At Michael's New York, Chef Robert Ribant has developed a wonderful foie gras terrine, among the finest I've tasted. The recipe takes time, but the results are well worth it.

You will need a mold that is 11½ inches long, 3¼ inches wide, and 2¾ inches deep, a piece of heavy cardboard cut to fit the top of the mold precisely, a full 3-pound box of kosher salt, a baking pan large enough to hold the livers comfortably, an instant-read thermometer, kitchen tweezers, and ten clean, sturdy kitchen towels. And a little time!

This recipe makes a large terrine, but I suspect that home cooks will make a terrine only when entertaining: it is the perfect size for a cocktail buffet table, served with crisp slices of sweet brioche.

One 3-pound box kosher salt

4 grade-A duck livers (foie gras)

Sea salt and freshly ground white pepper

½ cup duck consommé (clarified duck stock) or canned beef consommé

¼ of a 0.25-ounce package unflavored gelatin

Line a baking pan with parchment paper. Set aside.

Cut a piece of heavy cardboard to fit the top of your terrine mold exactly. Cover it neatly with aluminum foil. Set aside, along with the mold, an instant-read thermometer, and 10 clean kitchen towels.

Completely cover a full, unopened 3-pound box of kosher salt with plastic film or aluminum foil. Place in the refrigerator.

Preheat the oven to 350°F.

Using a small sharp knife, gently remove any noticeable fat and sinew from the livers. Separate the smaller lobe from the larger on all of the livers; you will have 4 large and 4 small pieces. Place the lobes, flat side down, on a clean work surface. Working with one piece at a time, make an incision, lengthwise, down the center of the lobe, cutting about halfway into but not through the liver. Then cut

into each half to create flaps. Open the flaps to make one large, flat piece of liver. If one end of the liver seems much thicker than the other parts, use the same process to open it up so that the entire piece is of an equal thickness.

Using kitchen tweezers, begin carefully pulling out all of the veins, gently grabbing them from the bottom and pulling up and out. When all of the larger veins have been removed, squeeze the tweezers through every part of the liver to make sure that all of the unseen veins have been extracted. If the tweezers pull up nothing but liver, just push the meat back into the solid piece. It won't matter if the liver looks a bit mangled. Continue working until all of the liver has been cleaned.

Liberally season the open livers with salt and white pepper. Then carefully roll each lobe back together. Place the livers on the prepared baking pan. Cover with another sheet of parchment paper, tucking the top piece of paper under the bottom piece to enclose the livers.

Stack 5 of the kitchen towels on top of one another on a clean, flat surface. Stack the remaining 5 towels at the side.

Place the livers in the preheated oven and cook for about 10 minutes or until the internal temperature reaches 96°F on an instant-read thermometer. Immediately remove the livers from the oven and, using a slotted spatula, transfer the livers to the stacked towels. Cover with the remaining stack of 5 towels and, using the palms of your hands, gently press down on the livers for 1 minute.

Transfer the livers to the terrine, gently pressing them in. Cover with the piece of foil-covered cardboard and immediately invert onto the refrigerated box of salt. Let set for 24 hours.

Remove the mold from the refrigerator. Remove the cardboard and, using a small sharp knife, trim off any liver that has come up and over the cardboard to make a neat loaf.

Fill a pan large enough to accommodate the mold with very hot water to come up to the rim of the mold. Carefully run a sharp knife around the interior of the mold to loosen the contents slightly. Dip the mold into the hot water for 15 seconds. Immediately invert the mold onto a cutting board, banging slightly on the bottom to extract the foie gras. Lift the mold.

Fold a piece of parchment paper to fit the bottom of the mold and come up and over both of the narrow ends. Set the parchment aside.

Combine the consommé with the gelatin in a small saucepan. Set aside for about 3 minutes, stirring occasionally to soften the gelatin. Once softened, place over medium heat and cook, stirring constantly, for a minute or so or until completely dissolved. Remove from the heat and set aside.

Wash the mold and fill it with ice. Let stand for about 5 minutes or until very cold. Discard the ice and wipe the mold dry. Place the piece of parchment down into the mold.

Return the foie gras to the chilled, lined mold by inverting the mold over the terrine; then, holding the mold in place, invert the cutting board that it's resting on. The parchment paper extensions will serve as pull tabs at each end. Pour the reserved consommé over the liver to cover.

Cover the entire mold with plastic film and return to the refrigerator for at least 30 minutes or until set.

When ready to serve, remove the foie gras from the refrigerator. Using your hands, gently pull on the parchment tabs. The terrine should easily lift from the mold.

Place on a serving platter and serve with thin slices of brioche toast.

quail

While I had my duck farm with Jean Bertranou of L'Ermitage, our famous French foreman, Francis, had a great passion for quail. Like our ducks, his quail were the best. He fed them only whole grains—wheat, barley, and millet. While working the farm, we'd often grill those quail for lunch and wash them down with a great bottle of rosé or a crisp white wine.

Quail make a perfect appetizer, alone, on a risotto, or in a wonderful salad. You can purchase fine deboned birds all year long. They should weigh no more than about four ounces to be at their tastiest. The meat is very delicate, yet richly flavored and juicy. Quail are perfect for a fast grill and some finger licking, as they are very easy to eat with your hands. You should figure on at least two birds per serving. Although I generally grill them, quail are as good and quickly cooked by pan-searing.

risotto with pan-seared quail and foie gras, baby chanterelles, and pinot noir sauce

Serves 4

This is a real "restaurant" dish, elegant, luxurious, and delicious. It should be saved for a dinner at which you want to pull out all the stops. If you do a small portion of the risotto, this recipe will serve as a very satisfying first course.

Four 4-ounce quail, boned

Sea salt and freshly ground black pepper

2 tablespoons clarified butter (see Note, page 48)

Four 2-ounce grade-A pieces duck foie gras

2 tablespoons salted butter

2 cups baby chanterelle mushrooms

Risotto (without the white truffles; see page 72)

Pinot Noir Sauce (recipe follows)

2 tablespoons fresh thyme leaves

Cut each quail into 4 equal pieces. Season with salt and pepper to taste.

Heat the clarified butter in a heavy skillet over medium-high heat. Add the quail, skin side down, and sear for about 4 minutes or until crisp and golden brown. Turn and sear for another 3 minutes or until colored but still pink inside. Remove from the pan and set aside to rest for a few minutes.

While the quail are resting, sear the foie gras as directed on page 159.

Heat the salted butter in a medium sauté pan over medium heat. Add the chanterelles and cook, stirring frequently, for about 5 minutes or until just cooked. Season with salt and pepper to taste and remove from the heat. Set aside and keep warm.

Spoon an equal portion of the risotto into each of 4 shallow soup bowls. Place a piece of foie gras in the center of the risotto in each bowl. Surround the foie gras with 4 pieces of quail. Drizzle the Pinot Noir Sauce over all, sprinkle with thyme leaves, and serve.

pinot noir sauce

2 tablespoons salted butter

1 pound quail bones

½ cup chopped shallots

1 cup Pinot Noir

2 cups chicken stock or reconstituted Knorr chicken bouillon cubes (see note, page 72)

1 teaspoon fresh thyme leaves

Sea salt and freshly ground black pepper

Heat 1 tablespoon of the butter in a medium-sized heavy saucepan over medium heat. Add the quail bones and shallots and cook, stirring frequently, for about 5 minutes or until nicely colored. Add the wine, raise the heat, and bring to a boil. Lower the heat and simmer for about 30 minutes or until the pan is almost dry.

Stir in the stock, raise the heat, and bring to a simmer. Lower the heat and simmer, skimming frequently, for about 25 minutes or until the mixture coats the back of a metal spoon and has reduced to about 1 cup. Add the thyme and season with salt and pepper to taste. Swirl in the remaining tablespoon of butter until completely incorporated. Serve immediately or keep warm.

"Cecilia Chiang took me to Michael's in Santa Monica right after it first opened. She had told me that there was something going on in Los Angeles that I just had to see. Michael's defined the California look, and he the style. Though I cannot think that there is anyone there now who has the kind of personal style of Michael, who would even think of wearing Susan Bennis/Warren Edwards ocelot slippers around the restaurant or to a March of Dimes benefit. In 1986, it took Michael less than a second to recognize my $2,000 crocodile slippers from Bennis/Edwards, and smile. On that first day at Michael's restaurant, the chef was Jonathan Waxman. The dish I had, memorable and remembered even until now, was roast chicken with herb butter, watercress, and *pommes frites*—the best I ever had or have had since. Of course it was French bistro food at its best, much beloved by Jonathan, Michael, and me. Nothing new there, but perfect. New was the look and style of the place. One did expect Clark Gable to come in with his Sulka embroidered velvet slippers on."

—JEREMIAH TOWER, CHEF AND AUTHOR

grilled marinated quail

Serves 4

The real key to great grilled quail is to cook it quickly on the skin side and follow with a brief grilling on the other side. It is so low in fat and, once boned, so thin, that overcooking happens very easily.

I use two different marinades for my grilled quail—fresh Lime-Thyme and Meyer Lemon–Cilantro—and I include both here. They also work well with chicken and pork.

Matchstick Potatoes (page 61) and a green salad are the perfect dinner accompaniments. If serving as an hors d'oeuvre or snack, use the herb-citrus butter as a dipping sauce.

Eight 4-ounce quail, boned except for the leg and wing

1 recipe marinade (recipes follow)

½ cup (1 stick) salted butter, at room temperature

Juice of 1 lime or 1 Meyer lemon

Sea salt and freshly ground black pepper

3 tablespoons clarified butter (see Note, page 48)

1 tablespoon chopped fresh thyme (if using the lime) or cilantro (if using the Meyer lemon)

½ cup Onion Confit (page 55)

Place the quail in a single layer in a glass baking dish. Pour the marinade of your choice over the birds. Cover with plastic film and refrigerate for at least 12 hours or up to 2 days.

When ready to cook, remove the quail from the refrigerator. Using your hands, push off the excess marinade. Set aside to bring to room temperature.

Melt the butter in a small saucepan over very low heat. Add the lime or lemon juice and season with salt and pepper to taste. When the butter is melted, turn off the heat, but leave the pan on the burner to keep warm.

Preheat the grill.

Using a pastry brush, lightly coat the quail with the clarified butter. Season with salt and pepper to taste.

Place the quail on the grill, skin side down, and grill for about 3 minutes or until grill marks appear. Rotate the quail 90 degrees and grill for another 2 minutes or until brown and crisp and crosshatched with grill marks. Turn and grill for another 2 minutes or until colored slightly, but still pink inside. The breast meat should be springy to the touch.

Remove the quail from the grill and place 2 on each of 4 dinner plates. Place some of the Onion Confit on each plate. Add the thyme or cilantro to the melted citrus butter and spoon it over the quail. Serve immediately.

---

lime-thyme or meyer lemon–cilantro marinade

1 cup extra-virgin olive oil

¼ cup fresh lime juice or Meyer lemon juice

¼ cup minced sweet onion

1 tablespoon chopped garlic

1 large bunch chopped fresh thyme, leaves only (if using lime juice), or 1 large bunch chopped fresh cilantro, leaves only (if using Meyer lemon juice)

1 to 2 jalapeño chilies or to taste (if using Meyer lemon juice; no chilies for the lime)

Cracked black pepper

Combine the oil, citrus juice, onion, garlic, herb, and chilies if using. Whisk in the pepper. Leave at room temperature for 10 to 15 minutes before using.

pan-seared squab with huckleberries, onion confit, and wild rice

Serves 4

It seems that I have been cooking one version or another of this dish for years—especially for food-and-wine menus. Squab is so rich that it requires a bit of tartness to mellow it out, which is what the huckleberry sauce does here. Another great version replaces the huckleberries with black currants. Both berries work equally well in the recipe whether you get them fresh or frozen.

4 squabs, boned except for leg and wing, quartered

Salt and freshly ground black pepper to taste

1 cup plus 2 tablespoons extra-virgin olive oil

4 sprigs fresh thyme

2 cups Pinot Noir

¼ cup cassis syrup

2 tablespoons chopped shallots

2 cups huckleberries or black currants

1½ cups chicken stock

5 tablespoons salted butter, cut into several pieces

½ pound wild rice, cooked

½ cup Onion Confit (page 55)

3 tablespoons chopped fresh thyme

The night before you plan to serve the squabs, or up to 2 days before, put them in a dish or bowl. Season all over with salt and pepper, drizzle with 1 cup of the oil, add the thyme sprigs, and turn the squab pieces to coat them thoroughly. Cover with plastic film and refrigerate until about 30 minutes before cooking time.

When you're ready to cook the squabs, remove them from the refrigerator and let them come to room temperature.

For the sauce, put the Pinot Noir, cassis syrup, shallots, and 1½ cups of the huckleberries in a medium-sized saucepan over moderate heat. Bring to a boil, then reduce the heat and simmer until the liquid has reduced by about three-quarters, 15 to 20 minutes. Add the stock and continue simmering until the sauce is thick enough to coat the back of a spoon. Strain the sauce through a fine-meshed sieve into a clean saucepan, pressing down on the solids. Rewarm the strained sauce over medium heat, then remove the pan from the heat, add 3 tablespoons of the butter pieces, and swirl the pan until the butter is incorporated, thickening the sauce. Season to taste with salt and pepper. Cover and keep warm.

Wipe the marinade from the squabs and season them again with a little salt and pepper. Heat a large heavy skillet over medium-high heat and add the remaining 2 tablespoons oil and 2 tablespoons butter. When the butter starts to sizzle, add the squab pieces skin side down and sauté until the skin is golden brown and crisp, about 5 minutes. Turn the pieces over and continue cooking until medium-rare, 3 to 5 minutes more.

Stir the remaining huckleberries into the warm sauce. If necessary, gently rewarm the sauce.

To serve, mound some wild rice in the center of each serving plate. Place some of the onion confit on top of the rice. Arrange the squab quarters around the rice and spoon the sauce and berries over the squab. Garnish with fresh thyme leaves.

Squab is *très, très elegante,* yet rustic and earthy at the same time. Known as *pigeon* in France, where I first experienced it, squab is one of my favorite foods to serve with Pinot Noir. I've always been impressed with the squab from Gary Carpenter's Carpenteria Squab Ranch in Southern California; it's as close to the French product as possible.

Squab meat is dark red in color, extremely tender, and wonderfully succulent. To enjoy it at its best, you should cook it to medium-rare. Grill or sauté it, starting skin side down. One squab is sufficient for a main course; split it in two for an appetizer.

desserts

I like very simple sweets. In fact, my favorite dessert to serve and eat when I'm entertaining at home is vanilla ice cream with hot chocolate sauce and salted dry-roasted peanuts, or a selection of good ice creams or sorbets with fresh fruit and a couple of cookies on the side.

When it comes to ice creams and cookies, by the way, we always make our own at the restaurants. But at home, nothing beats pulling a few pints of Häagen-Dazs from the freezer. My favorites among their many flavors are vanilla chocolate chip, chocolate chocolate chip, dulce de leche, coffee, and vanilla—a small scoop of each, all together in one bowl. The cookies I serve at home with that assortment come straight out of the Pepperidge Farm bag: Brussels, Bordeaux, and Double Chocolate Milanos. Nothing succeeds like excess!

Everyone loves to order dessert when they're dining out. I'm happy to share with you here a few of my regulars' favorites.

"I always tell new pastry chefs at Michael's to be prepared for Michael to come through the kitchen. If he's going to stand there and talk to you, you'll notice all of a sudden that half of your ingredients are missing. Michael will eat all the chocolate on the cutting board before the recipe is finished. All of his chefs know that they need to prepare extra chocolate and bacon."

—DORTE LAMBERT,
MICHAEL'S PASTRY CHEF,
1985–1990 AND 1993–1998

flourless chocolate cake

Makes 1 large or 6 small cakes

When I first opened Michael's in Santa Monica, one of my goals was to transform great French pastries by removing the booze and lightening them up. Here's an example of that principle, a spectacular dessert when garnished with homemade Vanilla Bean Ice Cream (page 174), fresh raspberries, chocolate sauce, and a dollop of crème fraîche.

You can make one large cake or smaller individual cakes.

¾ pound bittersweet chocolate, chopped

¾ cup (1½ sticks) unsalted butter, at room temperature

6 very fresh large eggs, separated

1 cup sugar

2 teaspoons pure vanilla extract

¼ teaspoon salt

Chocolate Sauce (recipe follows, optional)

Preheat the oven to 350°F.

Generously butter a 9-inch round springform pan or six 6-ounce ramekins. Line the bottom with a circle of parchment paper cut to fit. Then butter the parchment. Place the prepared pan or ramekins on a baking sheet and set aside.

Combine the chocolate and butter in the top half of a double boiler over barely simmering water. Do not allow the water to touch the top half.

Heat, stirring occasionally, for about 5 minutes or until the chocolate has melted and is blended with the butter. Remove from the heat.

Place the egg yolks and ½ cup of the sugar in the bowl of a standing electric mixer fitted with the paddle. Beat on medium-high speed for about 3 minutes or until the yolks are very thick and pale yellow. Remove the paddle and fold the chocolate mixture along with the vanilla into the yolks. Set aside.

Using the standing mixer or a handheld mixer, beat the egg whites until foamy. Add the salt and continue beating until soft peaks form. With the motor running, gradually add the remaining sugar, beating until medium-firm peaks form. Fold the egg whites into the chocolate mixture.

Pour the batter into the prepared pan. Place in the preheated oven and bake for about 50 minutes or until the top is puffed and cracked and a cake tester inserted into the center comes out with moist crumbs.

Remove from the oven and place on a wire rack to cool slightly.

When cool enough to handle, run a small sharp knife around the inside of the pan to loosen the cake. Open the springform latch and remove the ring. Carefully transfer the cake to a cake plate, cut into wedges, and serve either warm or at room temperature, drizzled with Chocolate Sauce, if desired.

———

chocolate sauce

9 ounces bittersweet chocolate, chopped

½ cup plus 1 tablespoon (9 ounces) unsalted butter, at room temperature

½ cup hot heavy cream

Combine the chocolate and butter in the top half of a double boiler over barely simmering water. Do not allow the water to touch the top half. Heat, stirring constantly, for a few minutes or until the chocolate is melted and blended with the butter.

Remove the mixture from the heat. Pour the hot cream into the chocolate, gently whisking until combined.

strawberry-rhubarb cobbler

Serves 6 to 8

Rather than the traditional pie, this wonderful cobbler is a perfect welcome to spring. The biscuit topping can also be formed into individual cakes for fruit shortcake. I love to replace the strawberries and the rhubarb with white peaches.

1 pound fresh rhubarb, trimmed and cut crosswise into 1-inch pieces

2 pints fresh strawberries, hulled and halved lengthwise

¾ cup plus 1 tablespoon sugar

¼ cup all-purpose flour

Pinch salt

3 tablespoons fresh orange juice

Sweet Biscuit Topping (recipe follows)

1 large egg, at room temperature

1 tablespoon heavy cream

Preheat the oven to 375°F.

Combine the rhubarb, strawberries, and ¾ cup of sugar in a mixing bowl. Add the flour and salt, tossing to coat. Stir in the juice. Pour the mixture into a 13- by 9-inch baking dish.

Cover the surface of the fruit with the Sweet Biscuit Topping, leaving small holes and gaps so that the fruit juices can bubble up through the dough.

Whisk the egg and heavy cream together. Using a pastry brush, lightly coat the dough with the egg wash. Sprinkle with the remaining tablespoon of sugar. Bake in the preheated oven for about 55 minutes or until the top is golden brown and the juices have thickened slightly and are bubbling up.

Serve warm with Vanilla Bean Ice Cream (page 174), sweetened whipped cream, or crème fraîche, if desired.

---

sweet biscuit topping

1 cup all-purpose flour

2 tablespoons sugar

1½ teaspoons baking powder

¼ teaspoon salt

¼ cup (½ stick) cold unsalted butter, cut into ½-inch pieces

½ cup heavy cream

Combine the flour, sugar, baking powder, and salt in a mixing bowl. Add the butter and, using your fingertips, a kitchen fork, or a pastry cutter, cut the butter into the dry ingredients until the mixture resembles coarse sand. Add the cream and, using a wooden spoon, gently stir the mixture to form a wet dough.

desserts 171

apple tart

Serves 6 to 8

This recipe is a never-fail favorite. It is an easy-to-make and absolutely delicious end to any meal, fancy or family. The tart is best eaten on the day it is made or reheated the next morning and accompanied by a cup of espresso. You can jazz it up with ice cream, whipped cream, or, my favorite, crème fraîche.

One ⅛-inch-thick piece frozen puff pastry

1 large egg

2 tablespoons milk

3 medium Granny Smith apples

½ cup sugar

1½ teaspoons ground cinnamon

Pinch salt

2 tablespoons unsalted butter, cut into tiny pieces

3 tablespoons apricot preserves, no fruit pieces included

2 tablespoons water

Remove the puff pastry from the freezer. If it is folded, set aside to thaw until it is soft enough to unfold without breaking. However, it is important to keep the dough very well chilled or it will become difficult to work with.

Lightly flour a clean, flat work surface. Place the thawed dough on the floured surface and, using a small sharp knife, cut ½-inch-wide strips from each side of the dough. Set the strips aside.

Place the large piece of dough in the center of a parchment-lined baking sheet.

Combine the egg and milk in a small bowl, whisking to blend. Using a pastry brush, lightly coat the edges of the large piece of dough with the egg wash. Place the strips back on top of the egg-washed edges. Place the pastry in the refrigerator while you prepare the apples. Do not discard the egg wash.

Preheat the oven to 375°F.

Peel and core the apples. Working with one at a time, cut the apples in half lengthwise and, using a sharp knife or mandoline, cut them lengthwise into very thin slices.

Remove the pastry from the refrigerator and carefully place the apples slices, slightly overlapping, in rows with the slices all facing in the same direction.

Combine the sugar, cinnamon, and salt and sprinkle the mixture over the apple slices. Dot with the butter. Using a pastry brush, lightly coat the edges of the tart with the remaining egg wash.

Place on the lower rack of the preheated oven and bake for about 30 minutes or until the pastry is golden and the apples are glazed and cooked through. If the edges brown too quickly, cover them with aluminum foil and continue baking. Uncover just before the tart is ready.

Remove from the oven and place on a wire rack to cool slightly.

Place the apricot preserves and water in a small saucepan over low heat and cook, stirring constantly, for about 3 minutes or just until melted.

Using a clean pastry brush, lightly coat the top of the tart with the warm preserves. Cut into portions and serve, warm, with ice cream, whipped cream, or crème fraîche, if desired.

meyer lemon sorbet

Makes about 1 quart

I always have a selection of sorbets in a rainbow of colors—red, yellow, white, orange, green. I use whatever fruits might be in season along with a citrus. I generally serve a small oval scoop of each of two or three complementary sorbets, with cookies on the side. My all-time favorite sorbets are Meyer lemon, passion fruit, and strawberry, which make a great color combo when served together.

It is difficult to give a precise amount of sweetener or acid in a fruit sorbet recipe because of the variation in the inherent sweetness of the fruit. I have given the basic amounts, but it is important for you to taste before freezing; you may need to add more Simple Syrup or additional citrus juice to balance the flavors.

I have listed the ingredients for a variety of fresh fruit sorbets, but you can make almost any flavor. Pear, lime, and tangerine are just a few other ideas. For all sorbets, the ingredients are blended together and then frozen.

For a wonderful simple dessert, assemble a plate of three to five sorbets and six to eight different cookies, a light way to complete a tasty meal.

2¾ cups strained fresh Meyer lemon juice

2 cups Simple Syrup (page 176)

¼ cup light corn syrup

Combine the juice with the two syrups, mixing to blend well.

Place in an ice cream or sorbet machine and freeze according to manufacturer's directions.

SATSUMA SORBET:
Juice of 15 fresh satsuma tangerines, puréed and strained twice through a fine-mesh sieve; ½ cup Simple Syrup; 2 tablespoons light corn syrup; 2 tablespoons strained fresh lime juice or to taste.

STRAWBERRY SORBET: 6 cups fresh strawberries, puréed and strained twice through a fine-mesh sieve; ¾ cup Simple Syrup; 2 tablespoons light corn syrup; ¼ cup strained fresh lemon juice or to taste

PASSION FRUIT SORBET:
Flesh of 15 fresh passion fruit (seeds discarded), and 1 ripe banana and 2 tablespoons Simple Syrup, puréed and strained twice through a fine-mesh sieve; additional ¾ cup Simple Syrup; ¼ cup fresh orange juice; ¼ cup cold water; 2 tablespoons light corn syrup.

> "Michael's is very accommodating to guests. They once provided me with thirty quarters, so I could send them to an editor, sitting at one of the other tables, who had wronged one of my clients. You know, thirty pieces of silver."
>
> —ESTHER NEWBERG,
> SENIOR VICE PRESIDENT,
> INTERNATIONAL CREATIVE MANAGEMENT

warm berry compote
with vanilla bean ice cream

Serves 4 to 6

Wonderful homemade vanilla ice cream is one of the simplest treats imaginable. I love it with fresh berries or, as in this recipe, a warm berry compote. Ice cream is easy to make at home; or you can always use one of the high-quality brands available in markets everywhere. If you want to jazz up this dessert even more, you can use strawberry or raspberry sorbet in place of half of the vanilla ice cream.

1½ cups Simple Syrup (page 176)

¼ cup (½ stick) unsalted butter, at room temperature

¼ cup framboise or Chambord

4 cups fresh raspberries, blueberries, blackberries, strawberries, or a combination of some or all

Juice of ½ lemon

Vanilla Bean Ice Cream (recipe follows)

Place the syrup in a medium saucepan over medium-high heat. Bring to a boil and simmer for about 10 minutes or until reduced by half. Whisk in the butter and swirl the liquid to allow the butter to melt and thicken the mixture slightly. Remove the pan from the heat and stir in the liqueur.

Return the pan to medium heat, add the berries and lemon juice, and cook for about 1 minute, swirling the pan to keep the berries moving so that they don't overcook. You just want to heat them through. Remove from the heat.

Place a scoop of ice cream in each of 4 to 6 ice cream bowls. Spoon the warm fruit over the ice cream and serve immediately.

———

vanilla bean ice cream

Makes about 1 quart

1¼ cups milk

¾ cup heavy cream

1 vanilla bean

6 large egg yolks

¾ cup sugar

Combine the milk and cream in a medium saucepan. Using a small sharp knife, split the vanilla bean in half lengthwise and scrape the seeds from the pod into the milk mixture. Add the bean and place over medium heat. Cook just until bubbles begin to form around the edge of the pan. Immediately remove from the heat.

Combine the egg yolks with the sugar in the bowl of a standing electric mixer fitted with the paddle. Beat on medium speed until very light and airy. With the motor running, slowly add about ¾ cup of the hot milk mixture into the eggs to temper them.

Have ready a large bowl of ice water. Remove and discard the vanilla pod from the milk mixture. Slowly whisk the tempered eggs into the hot milk. Return the pan to medium heat and cook, whisking constantly, for about 3 minutes or until the mixture easily coats the back of a metal spoon. Remove from the heat and place in the ice bath to cool.

When cool, transfer to an ice cream machine and freeze according to manufacturer's directions.

"I always say music is a universal language. So is good food and good company. Michael seems to orchestrate everything, and there is a rhythm to the place. It's the right blend of ingredients: atmosphere, good food, and great people."

—NEIL SEDAKA, SONGWRITER, MUSICIAN, SINGER

mixed berries with crème anglaise and raspberry sauce

Serves 4

This dessert is so easy to put together. And it's perfectly delicious! You can make the Raspberry Sauce a couple of days in advance, cook the Crème Anglaise in the morning, and assemble the whole thing in a flash while your guests are discussing the wonderful meal they've just enjoyed.

And, by the way, Simple Syrup, used for the Raspberry Sauce, is good to have on hand for use as a sweetener in cold drinks and sauces. I always use the ratio of 1 cup sugar to 1 cup water. Using this formula, you can make it by the quart, as it will keep almost indefinitely.

Crème Anglaise (recipe follows)

4 heaping cups fresh mixed berries, such as raspberries, strawberries, blueberries, and blackberries, or even all of one

Raspberry Sauce (recipe follows)

4 sprigs fresh mint

Spoon about ¼ cup of the Crème Anglaise into the bottom of each of 4 compote dishes. Spoon an equal portion of the berries on top. Spoon some additional Crème Anglaise over the berries, drizzle with Raspberry Sauce, and garnish with a mint sprig. Serve immediately.

crème anglaise

1 vanilla bean

1 cup milk

1 cup heavy cream

6 large egg yolks, at room temperature

½ cup sugar

Pinch salt

Using a small sharp knife, split the vanilla bean in half lengthwise and scrape the seeds from the pod. Separately reserve the seeds and the pod.

Combine the milk and cream with the reserved vanilla pod in a medium-sized heavy saucepan over medium heat. Bring to a simmer. Immediately remove from the heat, cover, and set aside for 5 minutes.

Combine the egg yolks, sugar, and salt in a medium bowl. Using a handheld electric mixer, beat until the sugar has dissolved and the yolks are light yellow.

Return the milk-cream mixture to medium heat. Bring to a simmer. Remove from the heat and remove and discard the vanilla pod. Slowly whisk about ¼ cup of the hot liquid into the yolk mixture to temper it. When blended, whisk in the remaining liquid.

Pour the mixture back into the saucepan. Place over low heat and cook, stirring constantly, for about 3 minutes or until the mixture coats the back of a metal spoon.

Remove from the heat and pour through a fine-mesh sieve into a clean bowl. Place the bowl in a larger bowl of ice, add the vanilla seeds, and whisk constantly until cool.

raspberry sauce

2 cups fresh raspberries

Approximately ½ cup Simple Syrup (recipe follows)

Approximately 1 tablespoon fresh lemon juice

Place the raspberries in a blender and process to a smooth purée. Pour the purée through a fine-mesh sieve into a clean container. Add the syrup and lemon juice, stirring to combine. Taste and, if necessary, add more syrup if too tart or more lemon juice if too sweet.

simple syrup

1 cup water

1 cup sugar

Combine the water and sugar in a small saucepan over medium heat. Bring to a simmer, stirring frequently. As the sugar dissolves, raise the heat to high and bring to a boil. Remove from the heat and set aside to cool.

When cool, transfer to a clean container, cover, and refrigerate until ready to use.

NOTE: You can use any berry that is sweet and fresh in this combination. You can also add a scoop of Vanilla Bean Ice Cream (page 174) as well as replace the Raspberry Sauce with Chocolate Sauce (page 168).

grilled white peaches with crème fraîche

Serves 6

This dessert is one of the simplest I make. But, as simple as it is, there is nothing more delicious. You can use peaches that are a bit underripe, as the heat will bring out their sugars and caramelize them to an intense sweetness.

9 fresh white peaches, peeled

Fruity extra-virgin olive oil

Approximately ½ cup crème fraîche

18 fresh mint leaves

Cracked black pepper

Preheat the grill.

Cut the peaches in half lengthwise. Remove and discard the pits. Using a pastry brush, lightly coat the peaches with oil. Place cut side down on the preheated grill and cook for about 5 minutes or until nicely charred and softening.

Carefully transfer the peach halves from the grill, placing 3, cut side up, on each of 6 luncheon plates. Spoon a generous portion of crème fraîche in the center of each one and drizzle a light touch of olive oil over the plate. Garnish each peach half with a mint leaf and a sprinkle of cracked black pepper. Serve warm.

double fudge brownies

Makes about 3 dozen

Everyone loves brownies, with or without nuts. They make a great kid's treat as well as the base for a fancy dessert with a scoop of Vanilla Bean Ice Cream (page 174) and a drizzle of Chocolate Sauce (page 168).

12 ounces bittersweet chocolate, chopped

7 tablespoons unsalted butter, at room temperature

1½ cups granulated sugar

½ cup water

4 large eggs, at room temperature

3 cups chopped walnuts (optional)

1½ cups all-purpose flour

1½ teaspoons salt

12 ounces semisweet chocolate, chopped and chilled

Approximately 3 tablespoons confectioners' sugar

Preheat the oven to 325°F.

Lightly butter and flour a 13- by 9-inch glass baking dish. Set aside.

Combine the bittersweet chocolate and butter in a medium-sized heavy saucepan. Stir in the granulated sugar and water and place over medium heat. Cook, stirring constantly with a wooden spoon, for about 4 minutes or until the chocolate has melted and the mixture is blended. Remove from the heat.

Beating constantly, add the eggs to the chocolate. When blended, stir in the nuts, if using. Add the flour and salt and beat to incorporate. Stir in the cold semisweet chocolate until well combined.

Scrape the mixture into the prepared pan and place in the preheated oven. Bake for about 18 minutes or until the edges begin to pull away from the pan and a cake tester inserted in the center comes out clean of crumbs (it may have some melted chocolate clinging to it). Remove from the oven and place on a wire rack to rest for 10 minutes before cutting into squares. Dust with confectioners' sugar before serving warm or at room temperature.

lemon cookies

Makes about 3½ dozen

These are the perfect go-with cookies for fruit or ice cream. They are even delicious on their own with an espresso for an afternoon pick-me-up.

1 cup (2 sticks) unsalted butter, at room temperature

½ cup granulated sugar

1 large egg yolk

¼ cup fresh lemon juice

1½ teaspoons pure vanilla extract

⅛ teaspoon salt

2 cups all-purpose flour

1 teaspoon freshly grated lemon zest

Approximately ¼ cup confectioners' sugar

Place the butter in the bowl of a standing electric mixer fitted with the paddle. Beat on medium speed until light and creamy. Gradually add the granulated sugar and beat until light and fluffy. Add the egg yolk along with the lemon juice, vanilla, and salt, beating to combine. Stop the mixer and, using a rubber spatula, scrape down the sides of the bowl.

Place the mixer on low speed and gradually add the flour, blending until just incorporated. Again, stop the mixer and, using a rubber spatula, scrape down the sides of the bowl and work the zest into the dough.

Place the dough in the refrigerator for 1 hour or until well chilled.

Preheat the oven to 325°F.

Line 2 cookie sheets with parchment paper or a silicone baking sheet. Set aside.

Remove the dough from the refrigerator. Form the chilled dough into 1-inch balls and place the balls about 1½ inches apart on the prepared cookie sheets.

Place in the preheated oven and bake for about 12 minutes or until golden.

Remove from the oven and transfer the cookies to a wire rack to cool.

When cool, sprinkle with confectioners' sugar and serve.

"Michael teaches you that you don't have to have a sumptuous home to welcome people; it doesn't have to be the Taj Mahal, just a comfortable place. Michael's message to people is: Hey, you're welcome here. Come in and let's have a good time."

—HELEN GURLEY BROWN, AUTHOR AND LEGENDARY EDITOR IN CHIEF, *COSMOPOLITAN*

macaroons

Makes about 3 dozen

These cookies are terrific to keep on hand for serving with fruit or ice cream.

4½ cups (8½ ounces) shredded unsweetened coconut

1½ cups sugar

Pinch salt

1½ tablespoons unsalted butter

2 tablespoons honey

1½ tablespoons apricot jelly or jam, no fruit pieces included

½ cup (about 4 large) egg whites

Preheat the oven to 350°F.

Line a cookie sheet with parchment paper or a silicone baking sheet. Set aside.

Combine the coconut, sugar, and salt in a mixing bowl. Set aside.

Place the butter in a small saucepan over low heat and warm until just melted. Immediately remove from the heat and stir in the honey and jelly. Let rest for 1 minute.

Make a well in the center of the coconut. Pour in the egg whites, followed by the butter mixture. Stir with a wooden spoon until completely blended.

Using about 2 tablespoons of dough at a time, form the mixture into cone-shaped mounds on the prepared baking sheet, leaving about 1 inch between each cookie.

Place in the preheated oven and bake for about 18 minutes or just until the cookies are beginning to turn golden brown. Remove from the oven and transfer the cookies to a wire rack to cool.

"I have known Michael for a long time, since he opened Michael's in Santa Monica. My late former wife, Lenny Dunne, who had multiple sclerosis, was in a wheelchair, and in those days they didn't have ramps everywhere and a woman in a wheelchair was a pain in the ass in a crowded restaurant. And Michael was always so fantastic to Lenny, making room for her with his staff. He was so kind, and I think those feelings run through anything he's involved with. I go to Michael's New York three out of five days when I'm in the city, and there's always something warm and friendly about it, and Michael has a lot to do with that. It is the most fun place to go. If you're interested in media society, there it is—that's their place."

—DOMINICK DUNNE, AUTHOR

danish walnut cookies

Makes about 4 dozen

This recipe makes another very simple cookie that I like to serve on the side of a berry compote or with ice cream. You can replace the walnuts with pecans or almonds.

1 cup (2 sticks) unsalted butter, at room temperature

½ cup sugar

1 large egg yolk

1½ teaspoons pure vanilla extract

⅛ teaspoon salt

¾ cup chopped walnuts

2 cups all-purpose flour

Place the butter in the bowl of a standing electric mixer fitted with the paddle. Beat on medium speed until light and creamy. Gradually add the sugar and beat until light and fluffy. Add the egg yolk along with the vanilla and salt, beating to combine. Stop the mixer and, using a rubber spatula, scrape down the sides of the bowl.

Place the mixer on low speed and gradually add the walnuts, followed by the flour, mixing just to incorporate.

Place the dough in the refrigerator for 1 hour or until well chilled.

Remove the dough from the refrigerator and divide into 2 equal pieces.

Lightly flour a clean, flat work surface. Working with one piece at a time, roll the dough into 2 logs about 2 inches in diameter. Carefully wrap each log in plastic film and refrigerate for 1 hour or until well chilled.

Preheat the oven to 325°F.

Line 2 cookie sheets with parchment paper or a silicone baking sheet. Set aside.

Remove the logs from the refrigerator. Unwrap and cut each one crosswise into ¼-inch-thick slices. Place on the prepared cookie sheets, leaving about 1 inch between each cookie. Place in the preheated oven and bake for about 15 minutes or until golden brown.

Remove from the oven and transfer the cookies to a wire rack to cool.

"The food is light; the main room is open, with tables far enough apart to hold a private—okay, semiprivate—conversation; and there is a delicious buzz in the air, especially when Michael is in town."

—PAMELA FIORI,
TOWN & COUNTRY

almond tuiles

Makes about 28

Tuile means "tile" in French. These crisp cookies do resemble a roof tile when placed over a rounded shape such as a rolling pin or bottle. The classic French kitchen even has an implement called a tuile mold over which the cookie is shaped. Tuiles can also be left flat after baking. If you want to form them into curved circles, they must be placed over the molding object as soon as they come from the oven. They will be quite soft, but will firm up almost immediately and hold the curved shape permanently. Not only are tuiles tasty by themselves, they make wonderful garnishes for all kinds of desserts.

Humidity will kill tuiles, though, so if you make them in advance, be sure to store them in an absolutely airtight container.

¼ cup plus 1½ tablespoons all-purpose flour

¾ cup plus 2 tablespoons sugar

½ cup (about 4 large) egg whites

3 tablespoons warm, melted unsalted butter

1¾ cups sliced almonds

Combine the flour and sugar in a medium mixing bowl. Make a well in the center and pour in the egg whites, immediately followed by the warm butter. Using a wooden spoon, beat to incorporate fully. You do not want any lumps. When well blended, fold in the almonds.

Set aside for 30 minutes.

Preheat the oven to 325°F.

Line 3 cookie sheets with parchment paper or a silicone baking sheet. Set aside.

Place about a tablespoon of the batter on the prepared cookie sheet, spreading it out into a neat circle with a rubber spatula. Make sure that the almonds are in a single layer and completely covered by the batter. Continue making batter circles, leaving about 3 inches between each.

When the cookie sheets are filled, place in the preheated oven and bake for about 10 minutes or until golden brown.

Remove the tuiles from the oven and, working with one at a time, quickly and carefully transfer each one from the cookie sheet with a large metal spatula to a tuile mold, rolling pin, or small bottle so that it curves over the rounded shape to form a firm, curved cookie. Allow to cool on the mold. As the cookie firms up quickly, if it hardens before you have had a chance to mold it, return it to the oven to soften and then reshape it.

sandwiches

I'm a big sandwich fan. Not of a wide variety, just a few specials. Like every other American, I can't live without an occasional burger. For me, it is a cheese-burger made from a third of a pound of 20-percent-fat ground beef, grilled to medium-rare, topped with a couple of slices of Gruyère cheese, grilled onions, and pickles and served on a small, squishy, toasted sesame seed bun.

And after the holidays (and in between them, too) a turkey BLT hits the spot. I pile the turkey on a toasted Bays English muffin slathered with mayo and top it with a few slices of crisp thick-sliced bacon, some juicy tomato slices, and Bibb lettuce leaves.

My all-time favorite is a PB&J. Mine is a toasted Bays English muffin dripping with Land O'Lakes butter and then coated with Skippy super-chunky peanut butter and Smucker's strawberry preserves.

My famous croque mon-sieur is made with a toasted Bays English muffin covered with a hefty amount of Dijon mustard and filled with some *jambon de Paris*–style ham and a few slices of Gruyère. I grill it with butter on the flat side of my panini grill until the muffin is crusty and the cheese is oozing. I serve it with a bowl of cornichons and some more Dijon.

I make a mean pork sandwich, as well as a juicy steak sandwich. I use my barbecued Pork Tenderloins (page 142) and New York Strip Steak (page 129) for each of them, and I like to use a buttered toasted sourdough baguette with lots of watercress, grilled sweet onions, and Pommery mustard. A sandwich on lightly toasted Oroweat "winter wheat" bread, with ham, Swiss, sweet onions, Bibb lettuce, tomatoes, Hellmann's/Best Foods "bicoastal" mayo, and Dijon mustard rounds out my list of favorites.

"With Michael, there's always been a spirit of combining a sense of luxury, indulgence, and celebration with a great casual sense of life. He talks frequently about just pulling out a fabulous bottle of California Cabernet, pouring it into in a great glass, and drinking it with a hamburger off the grill. That's classic Michael."

—Greg Drescher, culinary institute of america,
greystone campus, napa valley

breads

In the restaurants and at home I most frequently use four breads: brioche, walnut, and walnut-raisin, all of which we make in-house, and great sourdough that is now available from artisanal bakeries all across the country. I serve the first three as accompaniments to hors d'oeuvres, appetizers, and cheese, and I serve the sourdough with main courses because it complements the food rather than overpowering it. It is wonderful that so many small bread baking companies have emerged over the past three decades. Americans now have a tremendous variety of hearth-baked breads as good as their European counterparts. So if you don't have the time or the inclination to bake, do what I do and buy great near-homemade bread from your neighborhood market or bakery.

"Sometime in the midnineties, I thought I'd make cinnamon rolls as a treat for the staff at Michael's Santa Monica, something to keep us going. They became a staple. Since they were made from brioche dough, they were already pure butter. But Michael would take a two-by-two-by-quarter-inch slab of butter and mash it down on a roll, saying it was missing something. Then, with his finger up in the air, he'd yell, 'Moisture is the key to life!' And he'd eat two or three rolls that way."

—DORTE LAMBERT, MICHAEL'S PASTRY CHEF, 1985–1990 AND 1993–1998

walnut bread

Makes one 11½-inch loaf

Toasted walnut bread with raisins added is an excellent partner for cheese. Without raisins, the bread is amazing when toasted and served with soft butter and oysters on the half shell. It makes a great base for hors d'oeuvres.

3⅓ cups (1 pound) all-purpose flour

2¼ cups (½ pound) rye flour

¾ ounce fresh yeast

¾ cup plus 2 tablespoons water

¼ cup milk

1 tablespoon plus ¼ teaspoon sugar

1 tablespoon plus ¼ teaspoon sea salt

1¾ cups coarsely broken walnuts

1 cup raisins (optional)

½ cup malt syrup (see Note)

4½ tablespoons melted salted butter

Combine the white and rye flours. Set aside.

Place the yeast in the bowl of a standing electric mixer fitted with the dough hook.

Combine the water and milk in a small saucepan over medium heat and bring to 115°F on an instant-read thermometer. Immediately remove from the heat. Add the hot liquid to the yeast, stirring to dissolve the yeast.

Turn the mixer to low speed and begin adding the flour mix along with the sugar and salt, processing until just blended. Add the walnuts and raisins (if using), mixing on low to incorporate. Add the malt syrup and mix just to incorporate.

Remove the bowl from the mixer and, using a spatula, scrape the dough down from the sides to make a neat round. Cover with a kitchen towel and place in a warm, dry spot to rest for about 1 hour or until doubled in volume.

Uncover, and, using your fingertips, punch down the dough. Re-cover and again set in a warm, dry spot to rest for about 45 minutes or until doubled in volume.

Preheat the oven to 350°F.

Lightly coat the inside of a 12- by 4½- by 3-inch loaf pan with about 2 tablespoons of the melted butter. Set aside.

Scrape the dough from the bowl and form it into a log shape that will fit into the prepared pan and transfer the dough to the pan. The bread should have a rustic, rough finish.

Place in the preheated oven and bake for about 30 minutes. Remove from the oven and, using a pastry brush, generously coat the top of the dough with the remaining melted butter. Return to the oven and bake for an additional 30 minutes or until the top is golden brown and a cake tester inserted into the center comes out clean.

Remove from the oven and invert onto a wire rack to cool before serving. When ready to serve, cut crosswise into slices about ⅜ of an inch thick.

NOTE: Malt syrup (also called malt extract) is a natural sweetener that is available from health food and baking supply stores as well as some specialty food stores. If you can't find it, use an equal mix of honey and molasses, though these are slightly sweeter so adjust the amount to about ⅓ cup.

brioche

Makes 1 loaf

This classic French bread is rich with butter and eggs. Its slightly sweet flavor is perfect to serve with a foie gras terrine, cured salmon, and other hors d'oeuvres. It is also a spectacular breakfast bread, as a side toast slathered with sweet butter and homemade raspberry jam. Or try it for French toast with butter, maple syrup, and breakfast party meats. I bake the dough in a standard loaf shape for ease of cutting and serving.

½ cup milk

½ ounce fresh yeast

3 cups (13 ½ ounces) all-purpose flour

4 large eggs plus 1 large egg yolk, at room temperature

¼ cup (1 ½ ounces) sugar

1 ½ teaspoons sea salt

1 cup (2 sticks) unsalted butter, cut into 1-inch pieces, at room temperature

2 tablespoons heavy cream

Place the milk in a small saucepan over medium heat and bring to 115°F on an instant-read thermometer. Immediately remove from the heat and pour into a large mixing bowl. Add the yeast, mixing just until it dissolves. Add ½ cup plus 3 tablespoons of the flour and, using a wooden spoon, beat it into the liquid. This is the "sponge."

When blended, pour the remaining flour on top of the sponge. Do not stir. Place the bowl in a warm, dry spot and leave undisturbed until you begin to see the sponge bubble up through the flour. This process can take anywhere from 45 to 75 minutes, depending on the temperature and humidity of the room.

Line a small baking pan with parchment paper. Set aside.

Place the whole eggs in the bowl of a standing electric mixer fitted with the dough hook. Mix just to blend. Scrape the flour-yeast mixture into the eggs along with the sugar and salt. Mix on low speed until just combined. Increase the speed to medium and mix until the dough begins to pull away from the sides of the bowl and form a ball. Add the butter and continue mixing until it is completely incorporated into the dough and the dough has again pulled away from the sides of the bowl and either formed a ball or begun to climb up the dough hook.

Scrape the dough into the prepared baking pan. Cover with

a sheet of parchment paper and place in the refrigerator for 8 hours or overnight.

Generously butter the interior of a 10- by 5- by 4-inch loaf pan (preferably glass). Set aside.

Remove the dough from the refrigerator and carefully pull off the top parchment. Gently roll the dough into a log shape that will comfortably fit into the prepared loaf pan. Do not handle too much or the dough will become too soft. Place in the prepared pan, seam side down. Cover and place in a warm, dry spot for about 1 hour or until the dough rises to the top of the pan.

Preheat the oven to 350°F.

Combine the egg yolk and cream in a small bowl, whisking to blend. Uncover the dough and, using a pastry brush, generously coat the top with the egg wash.

Place in the preheated oven and bake for about 1 hour or until a cake tester inserted into the center comes out clean and the top is golden brown.

Remove from the oven and invert onto a wire rack to cool before slicing.

"Michael's focus on simplicity and distilling all of its essences is his great contribution to food in America. His style of serving it in a comfortable dining environment took American food and dining from the fussy, contrived, so-called French dining of the fifties and sixties to a new modern era."

—KEN HOM, CHINESE CHEF, AUTHOR, TEACHER, AND TV PERSONALITY

grilled herb baguette

All you need to prepare this delicious bread is a fantastic crusty baguette (or a fat, round *boule*), some grassy extra-virgin olive oil, lots of fresh herbs, and a hot grill.

1 French or sourdough baguette, split in half lengthwise

Approximately ¼ cup extra-virgin olive oil

2 cloves garlic

3 tablespoons chopped fresh flat-leaf parsley, thyme, or rosemary, or a combination

Preheat and oil the grill.

Using a pastry brush, generously coat the cut sides of the bread with olive oil. Cut the garlic cloves in half and vigorously rub the oiled bread with garlic, allowing the garlic to mush into the bread. Sprinkle with herbs and use the pastry brush to push the herbs into the bread.

Place cut side down on the hot grill and cook for about 4 minutes or until nicely browned with some charring. Move the bread to a cooler part of the grill if necessary to keep it from burning.

Remove from the grill, cut crosswise into pieces, and serve.

NOTE: You can also coat the split bread with melted butter, minced fresh garlic, chopped flat-leaf parsley, and minced chives. Put it back together, wrap in aluminum foil, and bake in a preheated 450°F oven for about 20 minutes or until very hot.

cinnamon rolls

Makes 1 dozen

These rolls are a perfect morning treat when you have weekend guests. The brioche dough can be made a couple of days in advance and the rolls put together early in the morning. Pop them out of the oven just when the first pot of coffee is ready to pour. And if you make brioche for gravlax (page 112), you can use any extra dough to make these treats.

Brioche dough (see page 189)

¼ cup granulated sugar (or more)

¼ cup light brown sugar

2 teaspoons ground cinnamon

¼ cup (½ stick) melted unsalted butter

1 large egg yolk

¼ cup (or more) plus 2 tablespoons half-and-half

1½ cups confectioners' sugar, sifted

½ teaspoon pure vanilla extract

Pinch salt

Make the brioche dough, up to the point at which it has been refrigerated for at least 8 hours. Do not take it out of the refrigerator until ready to make the rolls.

Combine the ¼ cup granulated sugar, the brown sugar, and the cinnamon in a small bowl. Set aside.

Line a baking sheet with parchment paper. Set aside.

Lightly flour a clean, flat work surface. Remove the dough from the refrigerator and place it on the floured surface. Lightly sprinkle the top of the dough with additional flour. Using a rolling pin, gently roll the dough out to a ¼-inch-thick rectangle about 18 inches long and 13 inches wide. Work quickly, as the butter in the dough will soften, making the dough difficult to handle.

Using a pastry brush, gently coat the dough with the melted butter. Sprinkle the entire surface with the sugar-cinnamon mixture. Starting from the top, roll the dough toward you, creating a log that will be about 22 inches long when complete. Carefully transfer the log to the prepared baking sheet. Cover with parchment paper and refrigerate for 30 minutes.

Preheat the oven to 350°F.

Combine the egg yolk and the 2 tablespoons half-and-half in a small bowl, whisking to blend well. Set aside.

Lightly flour a clean, flat work surface. Remove the cinnamon roll from the refrigerator and transfer it to the floured surface. Using a serrated knife, carefully cut the log crosswise into 12 equal pieces.

Place a clean piece of parchment paper on the baking sheet. Carefully transfer the rolls to the baking sheet, leaving about 3 inches between each. Using a pastry brush, lightly coat the top of each roll with the reserved egg wash.

Place in the preheated oven and bake for about 18 minutes or until lightly browned. Remove from the oven and set aside to cool for 10 minutes.

While the rolls are cooling, whisk together the confectioners' sugar, remaining ¼ cup half-and-half, vanilla, and salt to make a thin glaze. (If too thick, add more half-and-half; if too thin, add more granulated sugar, a teaspoon at a time.)

Drizzle the glaze over the rolls and serve immediately. They are best when still warm.

a few words on cheese

Ce qu'il faut: "That which is necessary." To me, a cheese course is a necessity at all great meals. I always have a selection of cheeses on hand to serve after the main course, sometimes in lieu of a dessert and sometimes prior to one. I have my favorites and I often stick to them, but I am always game to try something new, particularly now with the explosion of artisanal cheese makers in the United States.

I usually present my cheese selection on wood or marble. I showcase the cheeses with dried fruits, perfect grapes, or sliced apples and pears—along with toasted Walnut Bread (page 188). If you don't have Walnut Bread on hand, toasted raisin English muffins make a good substitute.

My standard cheese platter is composed of one blue cheese, three hard cheeses, three goat cheeses, and a couple of creamy ones. For blue, I like Saint Agur, a medium-strong, cow's milk blue from Auvergne in France; English Stilton, a classic Roquefort, or a slightly pungent but creamy Italian Gorgonzola; a Spanish Cabrales; or one of America's offerings, such as Maytag blue from Iowa or Point Reyes blue from California.

For the creamy cheeses, I select the marvelous French masters, Epoisses; any number of Bries, such as Brie de Meaux and Brie de Coulommiers; Explorateur, Brillat-Savarin, or Pierre Robert; or one of the great American cheeses such as Red Hawk from Cowgirl Creamery in California.

Hard cheeses might be Comté, Gruyère, Emmenthaler, Cheddar, or a Tomme or even a really fresh Parmigiano.

There is now a huge variety of goat cheese available, and many, many American cheese makers specialize in them. Laura Chenel in Sonoma began the craze quite a few years ago, and several have joined the club. Coach Farm in New York State, which started as a hobby farm, now distributes its goat cheeses all across the country. There are now goat cheeses of every type—fresh and aged, hard and soft, creamy and firm. Some of my favorites are Humboldt Fog, Laura Chenel Taupinière, Redwood Farms Crottin and Camellia from California, and *chevrotin* or *chabicou* from France.

There are so many great cheeses produced all over the world, and today we have the opportunity to taste almost all of them at home. For me, it is difficult to recommend just one or two, as I think cooks should experiment with flavors to find those that they prefer; but serve only those that are at their ripe perfection. A good cheese store will always be happy to offer a taste as an enticement to buy. I suggest that you try a few at a time, make your selection, and then share a cheese platter and a nice wine with friends to help you choose your own favorites.

"Lunch at Michael's is a little like that Zen proverb. If you're having a business lunch and it wasn't at Michael's, it's like that tree that fell in the forest with nobody there to hear it. It didn't happen at all."

—GIL SCHWARTZ,
EXECUTIVE VICE PRESIDENT OF COMMUNICATIONS,
CBS TELEVISION

breakfast and brunch

At the New York restaurant, the "power" breakfast is *the* meal. We are often jammed from the moment we open, as CEOs and other hardworking executives begin their day with a breakfast meeting. We get a moment's lull when most people head back to their offices for a full day's work at about 9:30 or 10:00—before our "power" lunch hours begin. What a party!

At home, I love to pull together a great brunch for family and friends. It is such an easy way to entertain, and people are generally more relaxed and ready to unwind in those pre-lunch hours. I always have the makings of breakfast or brunch in the refrigerator, including fresh eggs and some kind of smoked party meat. I can quickly make an omelet with leftovers— crab or lobster meat, cooked asparagus, button mushrooms, zesty cheeses—almost anything that I have on hand will work.

"**Michael's may be the only restaurant in New York where the staff knows every single person who eats there. And I'll tell you, if they don't know, they Google!**"

—BOB SCHIEFFER, CBS NEWSMAN

blueberry pancakes

Serves 4

This recipe is for my famous mix: I start with a traditional Bisquick pancake batter, which has a great salty taste, but I leave out the eggs and double the milk to make these paper-thin pancakes, which remind me of buttery French crêpes. Rather than serve the butter and syrup on the side, I like to pour melted butter and warm syrup over the pancakes before I serve them with grilled breakfast sausages or crisp bacon.

2 cups Bisquick

2 cups milk (or more)

1 whole stick (½ cup) salted butter, chilled

2 cups fresh blueberries

1½ cups (3 sticks) melted salted butter

1½ cups grade-A pure maple syrup, warmed

Place the Bisquick in a mixing bowl. Pour in the 2 cups milk and whisk to blend. Set aside for 10 minutes at room temperature.

Preheat a griddle until extremely hot and preheat the oven to 200°F.

Peel the paper back from the chilled stick of butter. Quickly rub the end of the butter over the entire griddle. Using a 2-ounce (¼-cup) ladle, pour the batter onto the griddle to make 5- to 6-inch round, paper-thin pancakes. (The batter should be thin enough to spread out on its own. If not, add additional milk.) Scatter about 8 to 12 berries on top of each pancake.

When the edges of the pancakes are golden, using the spatula, very carefully flip each pancake. Cook for about 30 seconds or until cooked through and golden. Using the spatula, carefully transfer the pancakes to a large, warm serving platter. Keep warm in the oven while you continue making pancakes, until all the batter and berries have been used.

Serve at least 5 pancakes to each person. Pour about ¼ cup each of melted butter and maple syrup over each serving.

"All the years I've lived in New York, I don't remember a place lifting off and staying aloft as long as Michael's has."

—TOM BROKAW, NBC NEWSMAN

scrambled eggs with black or white truffles and chives

Serves 4

This classic Michael's brunch dish features creamy eggs accented with aromatic, earthy truffles. You need just a glass of good brut or rosé champagne, and your morning is set. I add a platter of "party meats" like chicken applewood sausage, pork sausage breakfast links, crisp, thickly sliced bacon, and a slab of ham. A basket of warm Walnut Bread toast (page 188) and Bays English muffins is a nice touch.

Another over-the-top mix is creamy scrambled eggs with smoked salmon and caviar, topped with chives!

12 large eggs

¼ cup heavy cream

2 ounces fresh black or white truffles

¼ cup clarified butter (see Note, page 48)

Sea salt and freshly ground white pepper

2 tablespoons chopped fresh chives

Combine the eggs and cream in a mixing bowl, whisking to blend well. Shave in the truffles and let rest for 15 minutes.

Heat the clarified butter in a large heavy skillet over medium heat. Add the eggs and let them rest, undisturbed, for 30 seconds. Using a heatproof spatula, begin gathering the eggs from the outer edge of the pan into the center in big, swooping ribbons until the eggs form soft, creamy curds. This process should take about 5 minutes. Season with salt and white pepper.

Spoon an equal portion of the eggs down the center of each of 4 large warm luncheon plates. Sprinkle each serving with chives and serve immediately; the heat from the eggs will perfume the table with truffle essence.

eggs benedict

Serves 4

A brunch menu would not be complete without eggs Benedict. This recipe is the classic, but you can replace the ham with smoked salmon or spinach (or both). Garnish the eggs with some shaved truffles or top with some caviar. Whatever you do, don't overcook the eggs—the yolks should still be runny when you cut into them.

1 tablespoon white vinegar

8 very fresh large eggs, at room temperature

4 Bays English muffins, split

Approximately 2 tablespoons salted butter or to taste

Eight ¼-inch-thick slices ham, cut into rounds to fit onto an English muffin

Hollandaise Sauce (recipe follows)

2 tablespoons chopped fresh chives

Have ready a large bowl of ice water. Set aside.

Place about 2½ inches of water in a large skillet. Add the vinegar and place over high heat. Bring to a gentle boil.

Working with one at a time, crack open an egg and carefully slide it into the simmering vinegar-water; repeat with the remaining eggs. Cook the eggs for about 2 minutes or until the whites are cooked but the yolks are still runny. If the edges of the eggs are ragged, trim them with kitchen shears. Using a slotted spoon, carefully transfer the eggs to the ice water bath.

Preheat the oven to low.

Toast the muffins and immediately cover them with butter. Place on a baking sheet in the preheated oven to keep warm.

Heat a nonstick grill pan over high heat. Add the ham and fry, turning occasionally, for about 4 minutes or until hot and nicely marked. Remove from the grill pan and transfer to the baking sheet in the oven to keep warm.

Bring a deep sauté pan of water to a simmer over high heat. Using a slotted spoon, carefully transfer the eggs from the ice water to the simmering water. Heat for exactly 2 minutes.

Place 2 English muffin halves on each of 4 luncheon plates. Place a piece of ham on top of each muffin half.

Working quickly so that everything remains hot, hold a clean kitchen towel in one hand and, with a slotted spoon, carefully lift an egg from the water. Lay the spoon on the towel to absorb excess water. Gently place 1 egg on top of each ham-topped muffin. Spoon an equal portion of Hollandaise Sauce over each egg, sprinkle with chives, and serve.

"Michael is a leader and a trendsetter and a great party animal. But there's also a deeper sense about Michael, his generosity and his sense of humanity, which makes him extremely human and likable. When you are with Michael, you are satisfied not only by the food you eat with him, but also by the feeling that you are his good friend and part of the family."

—Piero Selvaggio, restaurateur, Valentino

hollandaise sauce

3 very fresh large egg yolks

4 teaspoons cold water

½ cup warm clarified butter
(see Note, page 48)

2 teaspoons fresh lemon juice

Sea salt and freshly ground
white pepper

Combine the egg yolks and water in a small saucepan over medium-low heat. Using a whisk, beat the mixture for about 5 minutes or until the eggs are thick, pale yellow, and fluffy. Do not let the mixture get too hot or the eggs will curdle.

Remove from the heat and, whisking constantly, slowly add the butter. When incorporated, whisk in the lemon juice and salt and white pepper to taste. If the sauce seems too thick, whisk in a few droplets of warm water.

Serve immediately or keep warm in a bowl of warm water for no more than a half hour or so.

soft-boiled eggs with shallots, white truffles, and chives

Serves 4

This brunch dish is sensational in its simplicity. I can guarantee that everyone will want seconds, so be prepared. Of course, the truffles help make a statement!

Serve these eggs with Walnut Bread toast (page 188) or buttered Bays English muffins.

8 very fresh large eggs, at room temperature

Sea salt and freshly ground white pepper

2 shallots, minced

1 ounce white truffles

1 tablespoon chopped fresh chives

Bring a medium saucepan of water to a simmer over medium-high heat. Carefully lower the eggs into the water, which should cover them by 1 inch. Cook, at a bare simmer, for 5 minutes.

Using a slotted spoon, carefully lift the eggs from the water.

Working with one at a time, and using a small sharp knife, quickly and carefully tap the egg on the counter to break the shell and then carefully peel the egg. Place the peeled egg in a small warm bowl. Repeat the process with another egg, placing 2 eggs in each bowl. When all of the eggs are in bowls, season with salt and white pepper. Sprinkle an equal portion of the shallots on top of each one. Shave an equal number of truffle slices over each one and garnish with chives.

"The proof of the pudding is in the 'ka-ching!' Michael has managed to keep the most demanding clientele in the world. He's keeping current and is at the head of the pack of where American dining should be."

—Dorothy Cann Hamilton, founder and ceo, french culinary institute, new york

carbonara with green asparagus and pancetta

Serves 4

My mother gave me my first introduction to carbonara, and her version is still one of my favorite meals.

Although carbonara is usually made with spaghetti or penne, I use a dried pasta called *gnocci*. Its shell shape really holds the sauce, lardons, and asparagus. I often make this dish for a rich brunch, and it's great as a side along with grilled meats.

6 very fresh large egg yolks

¼ cup heavy cream

2 cups freshly grated Parmesan cheese

Freshly ground black pepper

1 tablespoon olive oil

8 ounces pancetta, cut into small dice

1 pound dried gnocci

½ pound asparagus, steamed and cut into 1½-inch pieces

Sea salt

Combine the egg yolks, cream, and 1 cup of the Parmesan cheese in a mixing bowl. Season with pepper and set aside.

Heat the oil in a large sauté pan over medium heat. Add the pancetta and fry, tossing and turning occasionally, for about 6 minutes or until very brown and crisp. Using a slotted spoon, remove the pancetta to a double layer of paper towel to drain. Keep the pan and oil warm.

Cook the pasta in boiling salted water according to package directions for al dente. Drain well, reserving about ½ cup of the cooking water.

Place the pasta in the warm sauté pan and begin tossing. Add the egg mixture, tossing constantly. If too thick, add some of the pasta cooking water, a bit at a time. Toss in the reserved pancetta and asparagus. Taste and, if necessary, season with salt and pepper.

Serve immediately in 4 warm pasta bowls, passing the remaining cheese on the side.

hors d'oeuvres and beverages of choice

As you know, the main reason that I became a restaurateur was because I love to host a party. You would think that working in the restaurants every day would satisfy my entertainment gene, but my wife, Kim, and I entertain at home a lot as well. Even in New York, where we live in a small penthouse, we've had many festive gatherings on our terrace. And in New York, especially, we might just get together a group of friends for cocktails before going to an art opening or trying one of the many new restaurants that pop up weekly. I always have a full bar, great champagne, and a tasty array of cocktail tidbits.

Most of the items that I serve as passed hors d'oeuvres can also be used as appetizers at a sit-down dinner—of course, in larger portions. You are most likely to find White Corn Blini with Caviar (page 48), fresh oysters (page 76), Sautéed Foie Gras (page 159), Shrimp Cocktail (page 102), and/or Gravlax (page 112) or Scottish smoked salmon on a passed hors d'oeuvre tray at my house. I don't serve massive amounts, just enough to whet the appetite while enjoying predinner cocktails. Four to five

"Very few restaurants have the taste to put up good art. That mix of art and food has a great appeal to me."

—DON BACHARDY, ARTIST-PORTRAITIST

pieces per person are more than enough if dinner is to follow; ten to twelve if you are doing cocktails only.

When entertaining casually, I almost always do a buffet service. I might put together a charcuterie platter (see page 143) accompanied by some fruit. My two favorite combinations are white Sharlyn melons with Serrano ham and black and green figs with prosciutto. I slice the melons lengthwise into thin strips, drape a few slices of ham over the top, and drizzle the plate with some spicy green extra-virgin olive oil. A final garnish of fresh mint chiffonade is the flourish that adds so much aroma and flavor to this simple presentation. For the fig platter, I cut a tiny sliver off the top and bottom of each fig and then cut down into the fig (without cutting completely through) so that each one can slightly open into quarters to form a flower shape. I drape thin slices of prosciutto on the plate, and, of course, finish with a drizzle of my favorite olive oil and some cracked black pepper.

here's a list of my favorite cocktails

tanqueray and tonic with five limes

Combine in a highball glass filled with ice 2 ounces Tanqueray gin and 4 ounces Schweppes tonic. Squeeze in 5 lime wedges, add the wedges to the glass, then stir.

bombay sapphire martini straight up with five olives

Into a cocktail shaker with ice, pour 6 ounces Bombay Sapphire gin; glance at a vermouth bottle; and then shake until almost frozen. Strain into a chilled martini glass and add 5 pitted picholine olives.

negroni

Into a cocktail shaker with ice, pour 2 ounces Tanqueray gin, 2 ounces Campari, and 2 ounces red vermouth; shake until ice-cold and strain into a chilled martini glass.

stoli gimlet

Into a cocktail shaker with ice, pour 5 ounces Stoli vodka and 1 ounce Rose's sweetened lime juice; shake until almost frozen and strain into a chilled martini glass.

robert del grande's margarita

Into a cocktail shaker with ice, pour 2 ounces Herradura Silver Tequila, 2 ounces Cointreau, and 2 ounces fresh lime juice; shake until almost frozen and strain into a martini glass that is salted on the inside only (moisten the rim, dip into coarse salt, and then use your finger to wipe off the salt from the outside).

mojito

Into a cocktail shaker without ice, pour 2 ounces Myers rum, 2 tablespoons Simple Syrup (page 176), and 4 torn fresh mint leaves, and mash together with a wooden spoon or pestle. Fill a tall glass with crushed ice and pour the rum mixture over it. Top up the glass with seltzer or club soda and serve with a squeeze of fresh lime.

new york bloody bull

Into a pint bar glass filled with ice, pour 2 ounces Stoli vodka, 2 ounces Campbell's canned beef bouillon, 1 tablespoon Worcestershire sauce, 1 tablespoon prepared horseradish, and 2 drops Tabasco sauce. Top up with good-quality canned tomato juice, squeeze in 2 lime quarters and add them as well, add a heavy sprinkle of celery salt and salt and pepper to taste, stir, and garnish with a stalk of celery.

california bloody bull

Into a pint bar glass filled with ice, pour 2 ounces Stoli vodka, 2 ounces Campbell's canned beef bouillon, 1 tablespoon Worcestershire sauce, 1 tablespoon chopped cilantro leaves, and ¼ teaspoon minced jalapeño. Top up with good-quality canned tomato juice, squeeze in 2 lime quarters and add them as well, stir, and garnish with a stalk of celery.

blood orange mimosa

Into a champagne glass, pour 2 ounces freshly squeezed blood orange juice. Top up the glass with chilled Prosecco.

AFTERWORD
the malibu vineyard

I love wine so much that the time came when I had to try making my own. And I'm not talking about some small-time home basement operation here—though you could definitely say I keep it close to home.

I created The Malibu Vineyard on the land that surrounds Kim's and my house in Southern California, a steep, terraced, southwest-facing hillside overlooking the coastal community of Malibu and the Santa Monica Bay. Though most people might not think of

that coastline as typical wine country, it's actually an ideal place to grow certain varietals.

The elevation ranges from 600 to 1,200 feet. The soil, referred to as both Malibu and Millsholm sandy loams, provides excellent drainage.

My goal from the start was to instill our wines with a sense of tradition. In 1985, under

the direction of my friend Dick Graff, who pioneered Burgundian-style winemaking at Chalone Vineyard in the Pinnacles near Monterey, we planted the original two acres with Cabernet Sauvignon, Merlot, Cabernet Franc, Pinot Noir, and Chardonnay. The wood for our vines was sourced from Mount Eden Vineyards in

OPPOSITE
Michael's Malibu Vineyard—the 1989 Cabernet Sauvignon, the first vintage produced by the vineyard; the 1991 Cabernet Sauvignon; the 1998 Cabernet Franc; and Pinot Noir—Ashley's 2002

RIGHT
Michael working on his Pinot Noir vines in Malibu

the Santa Cruz Mountains south of San Francisco and the Joseph Phelps Insignia Vineyards in Napa. We produced our first vintage with those grapes in 1989 and continued until 2000.

During the 1998 through 2000 growing seasons, we determined that weather conditions in Malibu had changed (global warming, Mr. Gore?), with winters becoming warmer and summers cooler. In response, we replanted the entire vineyard with three Dijon clones of Pinot Noir that better suited the climate. Those grapes were slated for their first appearance as The Malibu Vineyard Estate wines in the 2005 vintage.

Meanwhile, from 2002 through 2004, we bought two tons of grapes of the same clones annually from Ashley's Vineyard, one of Fess Parker's vineyards in the Santa Ynez Valley; and we asked Bruno D'Alfonso of Sanford Winery to make the wine, labeled The Malibu Vineyard "Ashley's" Santa Rita Hills.

I'm proud to offer my own wines in my restaurants on both coasts. They're a very important, highly personal expression of my commitment to the marriage of wine and food. It's Pinot time!

LEFT

Michael holding some of his favorite wines: Colgin Tychson Hill, 2002; Sine Qua Non, Pagan Poetry, 2001; Sancerre Chavignol les Comtesses Paul Thomas, 2005; La Tâche 2000; Krug champagne, 1995

ABOVE

Michael in the Malibu Village Wines shop with John Selman

michael's time line

1953–1969

Many wild parties courtesy of my parents: Briarcliff Manor, New York; Misquamicut Beach, Watch Hill, Rhode Island; Manchester, Vermont; "the 'cuse," New York; Rockford, Illinois; Lakeside, Michigan; and many more!! Saw the light at Restaurant Laurent, NYC, right before sailing to France with the wild Italian waiters for School Year Abroad, Rennes.

1970

P.M. sauté line cook at the Mayflower, Loves Park, Illinois. Proprietor Tony Salamone best first example of a man totally in charge of his restaurant. A.M. chocolate chip cookie teacher, Head Start Inner City, Rockford, Illinois. Four-year-old Clarence said, "Mike, cook! Cook!"

1971

Pots-and-pans dorm kitchen, Sewell Hall, University of Colorado, Boulder. Ex-Marine kitchen manager taught me the value of training the employee.

1972–1974

Certificat d'aptitude professionelle from L'Ecole Hôtelière de Paris; Grande Diplôme from Le Cordon Bleu, Paris; L'Académie du Vin. Lots of catering for American expats and their kids. The delicate balance of le Big Mac and food from three-star Lasserre, living with five student chefs and *plongeurs*, meals at almost all the 1-2-3-star Paris restaurants; best meal: Michel Guérard's Pot-Au-Feu. Chef at Restaurant Xavier, Ile St.-Louis, the beginning of "my food," the merging of classical Escoffier, *la nouvelle cuisine*, and the food of my parents. The revolution will be televised! Grad present to myself: great meals at La Pyramide (thank God for Fernand Point), Bocuse (met a maverick winemaker named Robert Mondavi and his trusty sidekick Margrit; how 'bout that '68 Cab Sauv Reserve?), Trois Gros, way too much fun and Sorrel. And then Mykonos: sea urchins and goat cheese salad. Summer program at Cornell Hotel School, discovered California and New York wines with Vance Christenson, wine expert and original big eater.

1974–1976

Taught French cooking in French at CU; relaunched the restaurant Le Fleur de Lis, Boulder; and launched My Friend's Restaurant and Bar, Evergreen, in Colorado, the next step in the evolution of "my food." Received University of Colorado, Boulder, bachelor of arts in the business and art of gastronomy; commuted to Malibu, California; fell in love with Kim; went to Switzerland to meet her dad; ate at Freddie Girardet's and did so for many years thereafter.

1975–1978

Los Angeles Times restaurant critic Lois Dwan introduced me to Jean Bertranou, chef-owner of L'Ermitage; partnered with him in Mad Ducks Inc. to breed the Mullard duck at our ranch in Acton and make foie gras in my garage in Malibu; Dennis Overstreet, The Wine Merchant, the beginning of teaching the marriage of food and wine and getting to know the handful of Angelinos who loved good eats and fabulous wine.

1978–Present

Founded Michael's Santa Monica. Whoa!! Packed!!!! Oh boy, did that work! Way too much fun—how 'bout those eighties? Let the good times roll! Still doin' it!

1983

Created and produced pivotal James Beard dinner at the Stanford Court, San Francisco, courtesy of Jim Nassikas, the best hotelier; filmed, written, and directed by the edgy filmmaker Paul Gurian for the American Institute of Wine and Food (AIWF), featuring chefs Alice Waters, Jeremiah Tower, Mark Miller, Bradley Ogden, Jimmy Schmidt, Paul Prudhomme, Larry Forgione, Barbara Kafka, Wolfgang Puck, and Jonathan Waxman—the launch of regional New American Cooking. Most of these chefs met one another for the first time! How 'bout those Lakers?

1984

Married young Kim Lieberman, Pire de Keem, Bengalese tiger, *artiste par excellence*, the best, for always . . .

1985

Created and produced the cutting edge of L.A. cuisine for the AIWF. Filmed by the Mystic Knights of the Oingo Boingo main man Rick Elfman, starring Mary Sue Milliken and Susan Feniger, Michael Roberts, Martin Garcia, Joachim Splichal, Piero Selvaggio, Roy Yamaguchi, John Sedlar, Evan Kleinman, and Kazuto Matsusaka. Big eats!

Planted The Malibu Vineyard (world famous) at our house in Malibu, released the first vintage Cabernet Sauvignon–Merlot–Cabernet Franc blend in 1989, replanted in 2000 to all Pinot Noir, first release 2005, good stuff! Homegrown!

1985–1992

Opened the Rattlesnake Club, Denver, with chef Jimmy Schmidt, in a fabulous 1890s brewery called the Tivoli; chefs Reed Heron, Jan Birnbaum; how 'bout that New Southwest Coousine?

1986

The Clancy G is born!! Baby soup, religion, and fashion world, look out!

1988–1992

Opened the Rattlesnake Club, Detroit, with Chef Jimmy Schmidt in a beautiful historic Art Deco building with a great view of the Canadian Club sign in Windsor. All furniture from Cranbrook Art Institute. New Midwest Coousine: how 'bout that mess o' perch? Rocking under Jimmy still to this day.

1989–1992

Opened Adirondacks, Washington, DC, with Chef Jimmy Schmidt in the Presidential Suite at Union Station, 18,000 square feet, totally restored by wild and crazy Greek and Italian artistes, Saarinen chairs and tables, unbelievable, with a single de Kooning in the main dining room, Ricardo's new Guatemalan eats in the bar.

1989

The Wylie Chas Man is born! Sit down and pull up an E-flat! Jack Kerouac, look out!!

Opened Michael's New York, finally: only took ten years, thanks Guido! The beginning of the bicoastal lifestyle and the power breakfast, lunch, and dinner. Thanks: William Morris, ICM,

CAA, UTA, Time Life, Condé Nast, Hachette, Hearst, CBS, NBC, ABC, FOX, CNN, Showtime, HBO, MTV, Bravo, Oxygen, *New York Times, Financial Times, Daily News, New York Post,* all the movie studios, fragrance and makeup central, MoMA, Whitney, Guggenheim, and all you finance and real-estate guys and girls!! OK, lawyers too! And last but not least, all the food and wine lovers!

Released *Michael's Cookbook.* Lots o' food, art, wine. For all your eighties cooking needs. See www .welcometomichaels.com.

1989–1995

Got my ass kicked attempting to build my dream Santa Monica beach hotel, 150 supersuites, spa, restaurant, unbelievable art collection, right on five beautiful beachfront acres at the old Marion Davies Estate. Bad, bad NIMBYs!!!! Recovered through the good graces of friends and family.

1995–Present

Got my life back and still doin' it! Absolutely love the Malibu-Manhattan bicoastal lifestyle. But don't forget London, Paris, the Lot, the Tarn, and best of all, Capri!!!!!!!!!!!!!

OPPOSITE FROM TOP:
Justin, Peter, Carol, Michael, Tombo, and, seated, J. T. McCarty, 1972, Rockford, Illinois; Madame Brandily and Michael, Chateau de la Voltais, La Bretagne, France, 1969; Michael, Paris, 1973; Michael McCarty (foreground), Jonathan Waxman, Mark Peel, and Ken Frank, 1979; The Bailli Délégué, Michael receiving Maître Grillardin, Chaîne des Rôtisseurs, 1980; Michael, Vincent Price, Coral Browne Price, D. Crosby Ross, 1982.

THIS PAGE FROM TOP:
Kim, Chas, Clancy, and Malibu (dog), first harvest, 1989; Adirondacks, Washington, DC, 1989; Rattlesnake Club, Denver, CO; Marion Davies at her estate on Santa Monica Beach, the future SMBH (in my dreams!); Julia Child, R. W. "Johnny" Apple, Michael, 1987.

michael's chefs

first generation
SALLY CLARKE, KEN FRANK, JONATHAN WAXMAN, MARK PEEL, BILLY PFLUG, JIMMY BRINKLEY

second generation
ROY YAMAGUCHI, KAZUTO MATSUSAKA, GORDON NACCARATO, NANCY SILVERTON, HIDEO YAMASHIRO, REBECCA BOLIN, ZACH BRUELL

third generation
DORTE LAMBERT, MARTIN GARCIA, ERIC TANAKA, DENNIS SCHARP, BUDDY TRINIDAD, MARK WILLIAMS, WENDY ROSKIN

fourth generation
SANG YOON, BROOKE WILLIAMSON

SALLY CLARKE ▶ Clarke's, & Clarke's, Clarke's Bread, *London, England*

KEN FRANK ▶ La Toque ▶ House of Blues ▶ Fenix at the Argyle ▶ La Toque, *Napa Valley*

JONATHAN WAXMAN ▶ Jams, Bud's, Hulot's ▶ Bryant Park Grill ▶ Washington Park ▶ Barbuto, *New York City*

MARK PEEL ▶ Chez Panisse ▶ Spago ▶ Chinois on Main ▶ Maxwell's Plum ▶ Spago ▶ Campanile, *Los Angeles*

BILLY PFLUG ▶ An American Bar and Grill ▶ The Nunnery, *Boston* ▶ The Lord's VIP Dining Room, *Heaven*

JIMMY BRINKLEY ▶ Sign of the Dove, Ecce Panis, Chequit Inn ▶ Acme Bread, Baker Extraordinaire, *Seattle*

ROY YAMAGUCHI ▶ 385 North ▶ Roy's *(33 of them at last count, coming soon to a location near you!)*

KAZUTO MATSUSAKA ▶ Spago ▶ Chinois on Main ▶ Zenzero ▶ Buddha Bar ▶ Barfly ▶ Beacon, *Culver City, CA*

GORDON NACCARATO ▶ Gordon and Grimsley's, Gordon's ▶ Campanile ▶ The Raleigh Hotel ▶ ZG Restaurant ▶ Monkey Bar ▶ The Shed ▶ Le Colonial ▶ Rix ▶ The Beach House at Purdy, Pacific Grill, Margarita Beach Cafe, *Tacoma*

NANCY SILVERTON ▶ Spago ▶ Campanile ▶ La Brea Bakery ▶ Osteria Mozza, *Hollywood, CA*

HIDEO YAMASHIRO ▶ Shiro, Orris, *Pasadena and Los Angeles*

REBECCA BOLIN ▶ Gordon and Grimsley's ▶ Dessert Works, *Seattle*

ZACH BRUELL ▶ Z's Contemporary Cuisine ▶ Ken Stewart's Grill ▶ Parallax, *Cleveland*

DORTE LAMBERT ▶ Tivoli, *Copenhagen,* Michael's ▶ Private Chef, *Los Angeles*

MARTIN GARCIA ▶ El Presidente, Polanco, *Mexico City* ▶ The Original Fish Company, *Los Angeles* ▶ Bishop's Lodge, *Santa Fe* ▶ La Huasteca, *Lynwood, CA*

ERIC TANAKA ▶ Adirondacks, *Washington, DC* ▶ Michael's New York ▶ Gotham Bar and Grill ▶ Dahlia Lounge, Palace Kitchen, Etta's Seafood, *Seattle*

DENNIS SCHARP ▶ Adirondacks ▶ Michael's New York

BUDDY TRINIDAD ▶ Noa Noa, Tryst ▶ Morton's ▶ Hard Rock Hotel ▶ Stars ▶ Stars Makati, *Philippines* ▶ Park Avenue Desserts, *Philippines*

MARK WILLIAMS ▶ Gordon's ▶ Syzygy ▶ Warner Brothers Studios Guest House, *Aspen*

WENDY ROSKIN ▶ Book Soup, *Hollywood* ▶ Professor, Cordon Bleu, Pasadena Culinary Institute, *Pasadena*

SANG YOON ▶ Father's Office, *Santa Monica*

BROOKE WILLIAMSON ▶ Zax ▶ Amuse ▶ Beechwood, *Venice, CA*

acknowledgments

I would like to offer a toast (of Krug Clos du Mesnil 1995) to the following people who have helped make this book possible:

Carol and Rhett Austell, my mother and stepfather, who continue to party on—splendidly, I may add.

Tombo, Peter, and Justin, my brothers; and their wives, Julie, Charlotte, and Tracy, who have always been in the program of good times.

Rhett, Lizzie, and Sara, my stepbrother and stepsisters, and their spouses, Barbara, Bill (R.I.P. with a Mac 18), and Ben the Rumster, who after the wedding of Carol and Rhett got right with the party program.

Irene Karney, the best mother-in-law, ever! And forever!! Generous, gracious, warm, you made it through,

we are proud of you, much, much love.

Ken and Rosemarie Lieberman, great father-in-law and *belle-mère* (she's a fab eating partner), see you in Gstaad, London, Geneva, Capri, Sardinia, St.-Tropez, and, of course, at the Peninsula, Beverly Hills. More tennis and golf!

Lori and Susan, the sisters-in-law (and Joe and Park), we've had some big times, they will continue, and thanks for being soooooo nice to your little sister.

Harry, Bette, and Sophie, worldwide eating partners.

Have we missed anything or anywhere? More Negronis.

Steve Millington, fabulous general manager of Michael's New York, who has completely embraced my ways (and then some!) in running the ship in NYC. Many people think he's my brother—or even me. That works!

Robert Ribant, the chef of Michael's New York, who's come a very long way (don't stop now!). His wonderful foie gras terrine; crispy roast chicken; the best (sorry, Mom) liver, bacon, yams, and sweet onions; and, of course, the 28 percent food cost. How 'bout that skate? Woo hoo! More chives!

Robyn Wolf, longtime private party directrix of Michael's New York, who rides roughshod big-time on

Millington and Ribant (I think they like it!). You can only imagine what she goes through dealing with the power players in NYC and all their party needs.

L. A. Perkel, sommelier, Michael's New York, wine expert. The best! Say, what haven't we tasted yet?

Loreal, gatekeeper, maitre d' extraordinaire, Michael's New York. Aaarrrggghhh!!!!! What a job!

Mike Nicol, general manager of Michael's Santa Monica. Lots of Texas charm, great wine guy. Used to be GM of Michael's New York, now rules the left coast: Hollywood 101, foodies, wine experts, great people!

Doug Silberberg, chef at Michael's Santa Monica, the new guy. He can do it! California coousine at its finest. Another Mr. 28-Percent Food Cost! I see a long and great future here. More green! No more dried fruits and nuts!

Heidi Ross, private party director, Michael's Santa Monica. Big momma! Spot on, she knows her stuff.

Andrew Turner, sommelier, Michael's Santa Monica. Good initiative, has learned the program. Keep doin' it!

Dorte Lambert, world-famous pastry chef, heir to the Banque Lambert fortune. One, two, three tours at Michael's Santa Monica. That's the charm, tanks!

Judith Choate, "MooMoo," great job, all I can say is thanks. This book would not have been possible without you. Chief cook, bottle washer, and of course, the author! Thank you, thank you!!

Steve Pool, whoa, "Coco." The *best* photographer. He did the job: West Coast, East Coast, food, wine, people, places. Unbelievable! There's always August!

Norman Kolpas, oh boy!! Yo da man, author of my first cookbook, *Michael's Cookbook* (1989), wrangler of luminary interviews and quotes for this one—and then some.

Joel Avirom, art director and designer. You got it!! Beautiful work!

Michael Sand, one great editor, you got it, too! Thanks for your invaluable input, patience, and support.

Bob Barnett, my attorney, The Attorney! Not the same bucks as Bill, Hillary, and Alan, but what the hell, a deal is a deal, I'll take it.

Larry Kirshbaum. No deal here without you. Thanks for pestering me every day at the power lunch at Michael's New York to do a book for you at Time Warner Books—now Hachette. *Merci!*

Maja Thomas, more red Burgundy! Great eating and drinking partner (along with Susan). Without your support, Kirshbaum might not have done it. *Mille fois mercis* and more foie gras and Vosne-Romanée!

Jesus Jaramillo. When people ask me who takes care of my vineyard, I say, "Jesus tends my vines." *Muchas gracias* since 1984. There is always next year!

All of my great general managers down through the years: Karl Miller, Michael Grimsley, Harvey Friend, David Rosoff, Mark Goldfarb, Peter Cocuzzo, and Abe Rubio. *Servis compris!* The Daane System! Hospitality 101!

To my first eating partner, Ricardo Salares, R.I.P., godfather of Clancy and Chas.

And to my fellow American chefs who continually strive to promote the evolution of New American Cooking, the revolution *will* be televised! We have succeeded! Great ingredients, great cooking, great growers, great wines—and, of course, great people!

sources

For updated sources and additional photographs and inspirations, visit www.welcometomichaels.com.

fish and shellfish

Browne Trading Company
800-944-7848
www.browne-trading.com

Farm 2 Market
800-663-4326
www.farm-2-market.com

International Marine Products
(IMP)
213-688-2577
www.intmarine.com

Ipswich Shellfish Group
800-IPSWICH (477-9424)
www.ipswichshellfish.com

Malibu Seafood Fresh Fish
Market
310-456-3430
www.malibuseafood.com

Santa Monica Seafood
Company
800-WOW-TUNA (969-8862)
www.santamonicaseafood.com

Taylor Shellfish Farms
360-426-6178
www.taylorshellfishfarms.com

Wild Edibles
212-687-4255
www.wildedibles.com

meat, poultry, game, and party meats

D'Artagnan
800-327-8246
www.dartagnan.com

Four Story Hill Farm
570-224-4137

Fra' Mani
510-526-7000
www.framani.com

Hudson Valley Foie Gras
845-292-2500
www.hudsonvalleyfoiegras.com

Jamison Farm Lamb
800-237-5262
www.jamisonfarm.com

La Española Meats
310-539-0455
www.laespanolameats.com

Niman Ranch
866-808-0340
www.nimanranch.com

Salumi Artisan Cured Meats
206-223-0817
www.salumicuredmeats.com

fruits and vegetables

Chef's Garden
800-289-4644
www.chefs-garden.com

Farmers' Markets Information
and Locations, Nationwide
www.ams.usda.gov/farmers-markets

Frieda's Finest
800-241-1771
www.friedas.com

specialty foods

Dean & Deluca
800-221-7714
www.deandeluca.com

Le Sanctuaire
310-581-8999
www.le-sanctuaire.com

Zingerman's
888-636-8162
www.zingermans.com

cheese

Artisanal Premium Cheese
877-797-1200
www.artisanalcheese.com

The Cheese Store of Beverly Hills
800-547-1515
www.cheesestorebh.com

Caseificio Gioia
626-444-6015
www.gioiacheese.com

Murray's Cheese Shop
888-MY-CHEEZ (692-4339)
www.murrayscheese.com

The Malibu Kitchen
310-456-7845

mushrooms, truffles, and caviar

Mikuni Wild Harvest
866-993-9927
www.mikuniwildharvest.com

Petrossian
800-828-9241
www.petrossian.com

Tsar Nicoulai
800-95-CAVIAR (952-2847)
www.tsarnicoulai.com

Urbani Truffles and Caviar
800-889-1928
www.urbanitruffles.com

index

Michael McCarty opened his first Michael's restaurant in Santa Monica, California, in 1979, and his second Michael's in New York City ten years later. Both restaurants continue to attract a wide assortment of luminaries from the worlds of entertainment, media, business, and politics—as well as lovers of great food and wine. Michael's first book, *Michael's Cookbook,* was published in 1989 to great acclaim.

Judith Choate is a writer, chef, and promoter of American foods. She has written and coauthored more than forty books, including *Homemade, Great American Food,* and *The Art of Aureole* with Charlie Palmer, and, with David Burke, *New American Classics.* She works as a consultant to the specialty food industry and lives in New York City with her husband, the food photographer Steve Pool.

Norman Kolpas is the author of more than forty nonfiction books, many of them about food. He worked with Michael McCarty on the original *Michael's Cookbook* and has also written hundreds of articles for magazines, including *Bon Appétit, Sunset, Home, Southwest Art,* and *Mountain Living*.

Steve Pool is a New York–based photographer with a special interest in documenting food in its natural setting.

Photo by Chas McCarty

Michael and Martin von Haselberg head off for the next meal.

OUPLE OF BIOUNES, THE WAY I READ IT ■ EAT THAT CHICKEN, THAD BE GIL SCOTT HERON ■ FREEWAY TRANSMISSION ■
RGGGHHH!!!!! ■ YOU CUR ■ YOU MANGY CUR ■ DON'T CALL ME SHIRLEY ■ GET THE POINT, POINT ■ MAY THE REVOLUTIO
ORTS ■ DISCO 9000 ■ WANKER ■ WANKSTER ■ THERE'S NO SUCH THING AS A FREE LUNCH ■ LIFE OF RILEY ■ IS EVER
ATE ■ FORMER EMPLOYEEEEEEEEEE ■ BAABAAABAAA CASHFLOW ■ IN THE REAR ■ HEIR TO THE BANQUE LAMBERT FO
VA Y QUAGA DESK QUA, GENGI DESH KOMBOWWA! ■ YOU GO, GIRL ■ I USED TO BE A NICE GUY ■ YOU'RE KILLING ME ■
AT IT'S THE QUALITY WE HAVE COME TO EXPECT ■ HIYA HIYA HIYA ■ YOU'VE GOT THE WHOLE TEAM HERE ■ VIPSSSSS
REEN, CRUNCHY, AND ACIDIC ■ BROWN, MUSHY, AND SWEET ■ FLED WITH MILLIONS ■ THE DUDEMEISTER ■ WE'RE ALL C
OU'RE WITH THE BIG MAN ■ YOU'RE WITH ONE OF MY BIG EATERS ■ MOISTURE IS THE KEY TO LIFE ■ RED FLAG ■ MORE
VAS THAT? ■ LEFT THE PROGRAM ■ UNNNBELIEVABLE ■ SWAB THE DECKS ■ SUBSTERS ■ I SEE YOU ARE WITH ONE OF M
VER FOR ANYTIME, IT'S MY HOUSE! ■ SAY MY NAME SAY MY NAME ■ EAT YOUR GREENS ■ THAT'S FOR SQUARES ■ IL ÉTA
ALEMENTE LES DONNACE PERQUE CE UNA COSA LA PIÙ IMPORTANTE DEL MUNDO ARTISTICO E CIENTÍFICO ■ DER IST EI
E, DEVIL WENCH ■ LET'S HOLD IT TOGETHER HERE ■ THE DARKSIDE ■ EVERYONE HAS A DARKSIDE ■ INCOMINGGGGGG
HE LIFE OF MIKE ■ YOU GOTTA BE KIDDING ME ■ YOUR MONEY'S NO GOOD HERE ■ YOU TALKIN' TO ME ■ IT'S DOG EAT D
O THE DISTANCE ■ THE TRUTH WILL SET YOU FREE ■ DEAD MEAT ■ TANKS ■ ARE WE BEATING A DEAD HORSE HERE? ■
OUSINE FRESH BASIL AND THYME SONOMA COUNTRY GOAT CHEESE ■ THAD'LL WORK ■ DON'T THROW THE BABY OUT W
XPERT BUSBOY UP THERE? (NYC) ■ ARE YOU THE GUY FROM THE AGENCY? ■ PLEASE STEP BACK FROM THE VEHICLE ■ KI
TO A PISSING MATCH HERE ■ LES PAUVRES MECS ■ UP THE WAZOO ■ OUT THE WAZOO ■ EN TOUT CAS ■ DE TOUT FAÇO
T BASTARDS ■ YOU DIRTY RATS ■ NEFARIOUS MISCREANT ■ SWINDLERS ■ FIVE!!!!!!!! ■ WHADDA YA TINK? ■ PARTY ON
VOULD YOU LIKE A FRESH ONE? ■ TUBETONNE ■ YOUR MONEY IS NO GOOD HERE ■ FLED WITH MILLIONS ■ THANK YOU,
ONC ■ ET ALORS ■ ZUT ALORS ■ THE DEATH MARCH (CAPRI) ■ CAR ■ G&T'S WITH 5 LIMES (ONLY MEMORIAL DAY TO LA
ROWD ■ WORKING THE ROOM ■ CAPITAL IDEA ■ SCREAMER ■ YOU GOTTA LOVE THAT! ■ GIVE YOURSELF TO THE MOUNT
E PARTY IN THE REAR? ■ IN THE REAR ■ EVERYTHING COME OUT ALL RIGHT?! ■ BIG TIME ■ HAVE A BIG TIME ■ ENTEND
E DOIT DES MILLIONS DES DOLLARS ■ GRACIAS POR TODO, CLARO QUE SÍ, PERO CON PERMISO ■ KANDAHAR WILL BE O
RGE LOAD ■ CERTAINLY ■ FOUL MOOD ■ PIPE DOWN ■ SHEET, MON ■ GOIN' DOWN THE PIKE ■ YULETIDE ■ CORNICHE

micha

AND UP, PLEASE STAND UP ■ MA MAN TUPAC, NOTORIOUS B.I.G., SHUG, AND THE SNOOP ■ BIG BIOUNE ■ A COUPLE OF B
AMS CASINO ■ WINE EXPERT ■ GREAT PARTY ■ CHEERS ■ CIAO ■ KEEP DOIN' IT ■ AAARRRGGGHHH!!!!! ■ YOU CUR ■ Y
EEDS ■ THE BEATINGS WILL CONTINUE UNTIL MORALE IMPROVES ■ BLOW IT OUT THE SHORTS ■ DISCO 9000 ■ WANKE
NE KLEINE FUFTEN HIER ■ MAUVAISE DE KEEM ■ PIER DE KEEM ■ SPEAK TO MY ASSOCIATE ■ FORMER EMPLOYEEEEEEEE
ORTUNE ■ QUALITY WE HAVE COME TO EXPECT ■ NEE HOW MAH WAK WOY, KO NICHE Y WA Y QUAGA DESK QUA, GENGI
ELLO???? ■ PERHAPS I SHOULD SAMPLE THAT TO SEE THAT IT'S THE QUALITY WE HAVE COME TO EXPECT ■ PAL, AS IN HI
OULTRY BARN ■ FULL METAL JACKET ■ GOOD EATS ■ BIG EATS ■ GREEN, CRUNCHY, AND ACIDIC ■ ONE OF MY BIG EATE
NE OF EACH ■ WE'LL HAVE ONE OF EVERYTHING ON THE MENU ■ BAYS ENGLISH MUFFINS ■ YOU'RE WITH THE BIG MAN
E ■ WHAT AM I, CHUMP CHANGE? ■ WIRED FOR SOUND ■ BABABABABAAAA . . . WHAT WAS THAT? ■ LEFT THE PROGRA
S CAVA TIME! ■ KEEP YOUR WITS ABOUT YOU ■ HORS TAXE ■ COME ON OVER FOR ANYTIME, IT'S MY HOUSE! ■ SAY MY N
NO QUI OGGI PER VENDERE QUAL COSA QUE TUTTI DEVE AVERE ESPECIALEMENTE LES DONNACE PERQUE CE UNA COSA
OLD IT TOGETHER HERE ■ THE DARKSIDE ■ EVERYONE HAS A DARKSIDE ■ INCOMINGGGGGG ■ GOTTA DO IT ■ MORE DUC
OTTA BE KIDDING ME ■ YOUR MONEY'S NO GOOD HERE ■ YOU TALKIN' TO ME ■ IT'S DOG EAT DOG OUT THERE ■ WHAT A
UTH WILL SET YOU FREE ■ DEAD MEAT ■ TANKS ■ ARE WE BEATING A DEAD HORSE HERE? ■ IS THIS HORSE DEAD YET?
ND THYME SONOMA COUNTRY GOAT CHEESE ■ THAD'LL WORK ■ DON'T THROW THE BABY OUT WITH THE BATHWATER.
ERE? (NYC) ■ ARE YOU THE GUY FROM THE AGENCY? ■ PLEASE STEP BACK FROM THE VEHICLE ■ THE GGGGGGGG ■ KN
ATCH HERE ■ LES PAUVRES MECS ■ UP THE WAZOO ■ OUT THE WAZOO ■ EN TOUT CAS ■ DE TOUT FAÇON ■ ENTONCES
U DIRTY RATS ■ NEFARIOUS MISCREANT ■ SWINDLERS ■ FIVE!!!!!!!! ■ WHADDA YA TINK? ■ PARTY ON DOWN THE PIKE ■
ESH ONE? ■ TUBETONNE ■ YOUR MONEY IS NO GOOD HERE ■ FLED WITH MILLIONS ■ THANK YOU, NO, THANK YOU, NO,
UT ALORS ■ CAR ■ THE DEATH MARCH (CAPRI) ■ G&T'S WITH 5 LIMES (ONLY MEMORIAL DAY TO LABOR DAY) ■ NOW OR
OM ■ CAPITAL IDEA ■ SCREAMER ■ YOU GOTTA LOVE THAT! ■ GIVE YOURSELF TO THE MOUNTAIN, ZARDOZ, GREAT MOVI
REAR ■ EVERYTHING COME OUT ALL RIGHT?! ■ BIG TIME ■ HAVE A BIG TIME ■ ENTENDU LES PIGEONS QUI RECUL . . . LE
LLIONS DES DOLLARS ■ GRACIAS POR TODO, CLARO QUE SÍ, PERO CON PERMISO ■ KANDAHAR WILL BE OURS BY MIDNIG
RTAINLY ■ FOUL MOOD ■ PIPE DOWN ■ SHEET, MON ■ GOIN' DOWN THE PIKE ■ YULETIDE ■ CORNICHE ■ TASTY ■ LAGO